New Democracies in Crisis?

This book considers whether the potential for democracy following the end of the Cold War was diminished by technocratic, judicial control of politics in the new democracies of Central and Eastern Europe. It explores the complexities and drawbacks of modern constitutionalism by offering a comprehensive theoretical and comparative-empirical assessment of the status and role of constitutionalism in five new EU Member States.

The democratization of countries in Central and Eastern Europe has been guarded by constitutions and constitutional courts. This book examines the implications of powerful courts and rigid constitutions for the democratic engagement of citizens and the political authority of politicians. Using an interdisciplinary and comparative approach, the book analyses the historical emergence of powerful constitutional institutions in the Czech Republic, Hungary, Poland, Romania and Slovakia. The author argues that the democratic promise of 1989 largely lost out to a technocratic and top-down view of judicial control of politics – a state of affairs reinforced by EU accession. The current backlash in countries such as Hungary and Romania indicates that the realization of democratization to the extent initially expected might be ever more remote in some new democracies.

New Democracies in Crisis? will be of interest to students and scholars of European Union politics, democratization studies, European constitutionalism, socio-legal studies, governance and comparative politics.

Paul Blokker is principal investigator in the research unit, Constitutional Politics in Post-Westphalian Europe (CoPolis), at the University of Trento, Italy.

Routledge advances in European politics

1 **Russian Messianism**
Third Rome, revolution, Communism and after
Peter J.S. Duncan

2 **European Integration and the Postmodern Condition**
Governance, democracy, identity
Peter van Ham

3 **Nationalism in Italian Politics**
The stories of the Northern League, 1980–2000
Damian Tambini

4 **International Intervention in the Balkans since 1995**
Edited by Peter Siani-Davies

5 **Widening the European Union**
The politics of institutional change and reform
Edited by Bernard Steunenberg

6 **Institutional Challenges in the European Union**
Edited by Madeleine Hosli, Adrian van Deemen and Mika Widgrén

7 **Europe Unbound**
Enlarging and reshaping the boundaries of the European Union
Edited by Jan Zielonka

8 **Ethnic Cleansing in the Balkans**
Nationalism and the destruction of tradition
Cathie Carmichael

9 **Democracy and Enlargement in Post-Communist Europe**
The democratisation of the general public in fifteen Central and Eastern European countries, 1991–1998
Christian W. Haerpfer

10 **Private Sector Involvement in the Euro**
The power of ideas
Stefan Collignon and Daniela Schwarzer

11 **Europe**
A Nietzschean perspective
Stefan Elbe

12 **European Union and E-Voting**
Addressing the European Parliament's internet voting challenge
Edited by Alexander H. Trechsel and Fernando Mendez

13 **European Union Council Presidencies**
A comparative perspective
Edited by Ole Elgström

14 **European Governance and Supranational Institutions**
Making states comply
Jonas Tallberg

15 **European Union, NATO and Russia**
Martin Smith and Graham Timmins

16 **Business, the State and Economic Policy**
The case of Italy
G. Grant Amyot

17 Europeanization and Transnational States
Comparing Nordic central governments
Bengt Jacobsson, Per Lægreid and Ove K. Pedersen

18 European Union Enlargement
A comparative history
Edited by Wolfram Kaiser and Jürgen Elvert

19 Gibraltar
British or Spanish?
Peter Gold

20 Gendering Spanish Democracy
Monica Threlfall, Christine Cousins and Celia Valiente

21 European Union Negotiations
Processes, networks and negotiations
Edited by Ole Elgström and Christer Jönsson

22 Evaluating Euro-Mediterranean Relations
Stephen C. Calleya

23 The Changing Face of European Identity
A seven-nation study of (supra) national attachments
Edited by Richard Robyn

24 Governing Europe
Discourse, governmentality and European integration
William Walters and Jens Henrik Haahr

25 Territory and Terror
Conflicting nationalisms in the Basque country
Jan Mansvelt Beck

26 Multilateralism, German Foreign Policy and Central Europe
Claus Hofhansel

27 Popular Protest in East Germany
Gareth Dale

28 Germany's Foreign Policy Towards Poland and the Czech Republic
Ostpolitik revisited
Karl Cordell and Stefan Wolff

29 Kosovo
The politics of identity and space
Denisa Kostovicova

30 The Politics of European Union Enlargement
Theoretical approaches
Edited by Frank Schimmelfennig and Ulrich Sedelmeier

31 Europeanizing Social Democracy?
The rise of the party of European socialists
Simon Lightfoot

32 Conflict and Change in EU Budgetary Politics
Johannes Lindner

33 Gibraltar, Identity and Empire
E.G. Archer

34 Governance Stories
Mark Bevir and R.A.W. Rhodes

35 Britain and the Balkans
1991 until the present
Carole Hodge

36 The Eastern Enlargement of the European Union
John O'Brennan

37 Values and Principles in European Union Foreign Policy
Edited by Sonia Lucarelli and Ian Manners

38 European Union and the Making of a Wider Northern Europe
Pami Aalto

39 Democracy in the European Union
Towards the emergence of a public sphere
Edited by Liana Giorgi, Ingmar Von Homeyer and Wayne Parsons

40 **European Union Peacebuilding and Policing**
Michael Merlingen with Rasa Ostrauskaite

41 **The Conservative Party and European Integration since 1945**
At the heart of Europe?
N.J. Crowson

42 **E-Government in Europe**
Re-booting the state
Edited by Paul G. Nixon and Vassiliki N. Koutrakou

43 **EU Foreign and Interior Policies**
Cross-pillar politics and the social construction of sovereignty
Stephan Stetter

44 **Policy Transfer in European Union Governance**
Regulating the utilities
Simon Bulmer, David Dolowitz, Peter Humphreys and Stephen Padgett

45 **The Europeanization of National Political Parties**
Power and organizational adaptation
Edited by Thomas Poguntke, Nicholas Aylott, Elisabeth Carter, Robert Ladrech and Kurt Richard Luther

46 **Citizenship in Nordic Welfare States**
Dynamics of choice, duties and participation in a changing Europe
Edited by Bjørn Hvinden and Håkan Johansson

47 **National Parliaments within the Enlarged European Union**
From victims of integration to competitive actors?
Edited by John O'Brennan and Tapio Raunio

48 **Britain, Ireland and Northern Ireland since 1980**
The totality of relationships
Eamonn O'Kane

49 **The EU and the European Security Strategy**
Forging a global Europe
Edited by Sven Biscop and Jan Joel Andersson

50 **European Security and Defence Policy**
An implementation perspective
Edited by Michael Merlingen and Rasa Ostrauskaitė

51 **Women and British Party Politics**
Descriptive, substantive and symbolic representation
Sarah Childs

52 **The Selection of Ministers in Europe**
Hiring and firing
Edited by Keith Dowding and Patrick Dumont

53 **Energy Security**
Europe's new foreign policy challenge
Richard Youngs

54 **Institutional Challenges in Post-Constitutional Europe**
Governing change
Edited by Catherine Moury and Luís de Sousa

55 **The Struggle for the European Constitution**
A past and future history
Michael O'Neill

56 **Transnational Labour Solidarity**
Mechanisms of commitment to cooperation within the European trade union movement
Katarzyna Gajewska

57 **The Illusion of Accountability in the European Union**
Edited by Sverker Gustavsson, Christer Karlsson, and Thomas Persson

58 **The European Union and Global Social Change**
A critical geopolitical-economic analysis
József Böröcz

59 Citizenship and Collective Identity in Europe
Ireneusz Pawel Karolewski

60 EU Enlargement and Socialization
Turkey and Cyprus
Stefan Engert

61 The politics of EU accession
Turkish challenges and Central European experiences
Edited by Lucie Tunkrová and Pavel Šaradín

62 The Political History of European Integration
The hypocrisy of democracy-through-market
Hagen Schulz-Forberg and Bo Stråth

63 The Spatialities of Europeanization
Power, governance and territory in Europe
Alun Jones and Julian Clark

64 European Union Sanctions and Foreign Policy
When and why do they work?
Clara Portela

65 The EU's Role in World Politics
A retreat from liberal internationalism
Richard Youngs

66 Social Democracy and European Integration
The politics of preference formation
Edited by Dionyssis Dimitrakopoulos

67 The EU Presence in International Organizations
Edited by Spyros Blavoukos and Dimitris Bourantonis

68 Sustainability in European Environmental Policy
Challenge of governance and knowledge
Edited by Rob Atkinson, Georgios Terizakis and Karsten Zimmermann

69 Fifty Years of EU–Turkey Relations
A Sisyphean story
Edited by Armagan Emre Çakir

70 Europeanization and Foreign Policy
State diversity in Finland and Britain
Juha Jokela

71 EU Foreign Policy and Post-Soviet Conflicts
Stealth intervention
Nicu Popescu

72 Switzerland in Europe
Continuity and change in the Swiss political economy
Edited by Christine Trampusch and André Mach

73 The Political Economy of Noncompliance
Adjusting to the single European market
Scott Nicholas Siegel

74 National and European Foreign Policy
Towards Europeanization
Edited by Reuben Wong and Christopher Hill

75 The European Union Diplomatic Service
Ideas, preferences and identities
Caterina Carta

76 Poland within the European Union
New awkward partner or new heart of Europe?
Aleks Szczerbiak

77 A Political Theory of Identity in European Integration
Memory and policies
Catherine Guisan

78 EU Foreign Policy and the Europeanization of Neutral States
Comparing Irish and Austrian foreign policy
Nicole Alecu de Flers

79 **Party System Change in Western Europe**
Gemma Loomes

80 **The Second Tier of Local Government in Europe**
Provinces, counties, *départements* and *Landkreise* in comparison
Hubert Heinelt and Xavier Bertrana Horta

81 **Learning from the EU Constitutional Treaty**
Democratic constitutionalism beyond the nation-state
Ben Crum

82 **Human Rights and Democracy in EU Foreign Policy**
The cases of Ukraine and Egypt
Rosa Balfour

83 **Europeanization, Integration and Identity**
A social constructivist fusion perspective on Norway
Gamze Tanil

84 **The Impact of European Integration on Political Parties**
Beyond the permissive consensus
Dimitri Almeida

85 **Civic Resources and the Future of the European Union**
Victoria Kaina and Ireneusz Pawel Karolewski

86 **The Europeanization of National Foreign Policies Towards Latin America**
Lorena Ruano

87 **The EU and Multilateral Security Governance**
Sonia Lucarelli, Luk Van Langenhove and Jan Wouters

88 **Security Challenges in the Euro-Med Area in the 21st Century**
Mare Nostrum
Stephen Calleya

89 **Society and Democracy in Europe**
Oscar W. Gabriel and Silke Keil

90 **European Union Public Health Policy**
Regional and global trends
Edited by Scott L. Greer and Paulette Kurzer

91 **The New Member States and the European Union**
Foreign policy and Europeanization
Edited by Michael Baun and Dan Marek

92 **The Politics of Ratification of EU Treaties**
Carlos Closa

93 **Europeanization and New Member States**
A comparative social network analysis
Flavia Jurje

94 **National Perspectives on Russia**
European foreign policy in the making
Maxine David, Jackie Gower and Hiski Haukkala

95 **Institutional Legacies of Communism**
Change and continuities in minority protection
Edited by Karl Cordell, Timofey Agarin and Alexander Osipov

96 **Sustainable Development and Governance in Europe**
The evolution of the discourse on sustainability
Edited by Pamela M. Barnes and Thomas C. Hoerber

97 **Social Networks and Public Support for the European Union**
Elizabeth Radziszewski

98 **The EU's Democracy Promotion and the Mediterranean Neighbours**
Orientation, ownership and dialogue in Jordan and Turkey
Ann-Kristin Jonasson

99 **New Democracies in Crisis?**
A comparative constitutional study of the Czech Republic, Hungary, Poland, Romania and Slovakia
Paul Blokker

New Democracies in Crisis?

A comparative constitutional study of the Czech Republic, Hungary, Poland, Romania and Slovakia

Paul Blokker

LONDON AND NEW YORK

First published 2014
by Routledge
Published 2014 by Routledge
2 Park Square, Milton Park, Abingdon, Oxfordshire OX14 4RN

and by Routledge
711 Third Avenue, New York, NY 10017

Routledge is an imprint of the Taylor and Francis Group, an informa business

First issued in paperback 2015

British Library Cataloguing in Publication Data
A catalogue record for this book is available from the British Library

Library of Congress Cataloging-in-Publication Data
Blokker, Paul.
New democracies in crisis? : a comparative constitutional study of the Czech Republic, Hungary, Poland, Romania and Slovakia / Paul Blokker.
pages cm.
Includes bibliographical references and index.
ISBN 978-0-415-69586-2 (hardback) – ISBN 978-0-203-79502-6 (ebook)
1. Constitutional law–Europe, Eastern, 2. Constitutional law–Europe, Central. 3. Post-communism–Europe, Eastern. 4. Post-communism–Europe, Central. 5. Europe, Eastern–Politics and government–1989– 6. Europe, Central–Politics and government–1989– I. Title.
KJC4445.B59 2013
342.43–dc23
2013007920

ISBN 978-0-415-69586-2 (hbk)
ISBN 978-1-138-95641-4 (pbk)
ISBN 978-0-203-79502-6 (ebk)

Typeset in Times New Roman
by Graphicraft Limited, Hong Kong

To Duccio

Contents

Preface and acknowledgements

This book is the result of ongoing research on the predicament of constitutional democracy in times of significant change. The objective is to reach a deeper understanding of the role of constitutions in enabling democratic practices in a context of increased disillusionment with democratic politics. In a preceding monograph – *Multiple Democracies in Europe: Political Culture in New Member States* (Routledge, 2010) – one of my objectives was to analyse the ways in which constitutions relate to different understandings of democracy, as expressed in a plurality of democratic political cultures available in the new democracies of Central and Eastern Europe. In this book, I criticize the widely accepted view of constitutions as autonomous, higher law constructs, guarded by specialist institutions, as detrimental to the view of democracy as grounded in the idea of self-rule. A democratically perceived constitutionalism – I employ the notion of civic constitutionalism in the book – emphasizes the need for interaction between the fundamental rules and values of a political community and its members. So, in contrast to the idea that essential aspects of politics need to be taken out of both the spheres of political and civil society in order to perform an external guarantee on democracy, civic constitutionalism is based on the assumption that democracy can only thrive if the members of a democratic community are effectively engaging with the primary rules and values of common existence. In this book, I concentrate on formal constitutional structures and their relation to civic constitutionalism in some of the new democracies in Central and Eastern Europe. In a research project I recently embarked on – Constitutional Politics in Post-Westphalian Europe (CoPolis) – I broaden the horizon to analyse not only formal structures and their transformations, but also the actual viewpoints and constitutional repertoires as articulated by crucial actors involved: juridical and political elites, as well as pro-democracy movements employing constitutionalist discourses.

I would like to acknowledge a generous post-doctoral fellowship (project CRISCON) of the *Provincia Autonoma di Trento*, Italy, without which I would not have been able to write this book. Parts of some chapters have been published in earlier versions in the following publications: (2011) 'Dissidence, Republicanism, and Democratic Change', in *East European Politics and Societies*, 25(2): 219–43; (2012) 'The Constitutional Premises of Subnational Self-Government in New Democracies', *Corvinus Journal of Sociology and Social Policy*, 3(1): 35–57; (2012) 'Dilemmas of Democratization: From Legal Revolutions to Democratic Constitutionalism?', Special Issue in honour of the centennial anniversary of Raoul Wallenberg, *Nordic Journal of International Law*, 81(4), 437–70; (2013) 'Constitutions and democracy in post-national times: a political-sociological approach', special issue on 'Engaging the Cosmopolitan: Contemporary Approaches', *Irish Journal of Sociology*, 20(2).

I would like to express my gratitude to the many colleagues and friends who enriched my views during the research and writing process (I am most certainly leaving out some, for which my apologies): Suzi Adams, Richard Bellamy, Vando Borghi, Andras Bozoki, Emanuela Bozzini, Robert Brier, Andrea Brighenti, Craig Browne, Patricia Chiantera-Stutte, Paolo Costa, Marco Dani, Endre Danyi, Gerard Delanty, Natalie Doyle, Barbara Falk, Alberto Febbrajo, Alessandro Ferrara, John Erik Fossum, Dariusz Gafijczuk, Denis Galligan, Martin van Gelderen, Dimitry Kochenov, Michal Kopecek, John Krummel, Laura Leonardi, Ulrike Liebert, Mel Marquis, John McGowan, Leonardo Morlino, Pat O'Mahony, Vittorio Olgiati, William Outhwaite, Cristina Parau, Pasquale Pasquino, Jiri Priban, Luigi Pellizzoni, Andrew Perrin, Andrea Petrella, Alan Renwick, Victor Roudometof, Wojciech Sadurski, Grazyna Skapska, Marek Skovajsa, Stijn Smismans, Jeremy Smith, Kacper Szulecki, Chris Thornhill, Roberto Toniatti, Jim Tully and Jens Woelk. My deepest gratitude cannot but go to my wonderful wife, Elena Maddalena, as well as to my two extraordinary sons, Elio and Duccio (the new arrival), who make me explore new horizons every day.

1 Introduction

New democracies in crisis?

> All these phenomena seem to demonstrate that, at the moment when we in the East are trying to accommodate ourselves to what are conceived of as the respectable norms of Western political life, the West is facing the problem of accommodating its traditional political institutions of democracy to some, not-yet clearly visible social undercurrents of change that are affecting the East as well. One thing that seems common to both situations, though I would not dare to take it as all-explanatory – the strain between representative and participative democracy has become too strong. It seems that both in the West and in the East, in the reunited North and in the South, there is a need for new political ideas that would allow the human normative potential to be realized better.
>
> (Jacek Kurczewski, *The Resurrection of Rights in Poland*, 1993)

Crisis rather than consolidation seems the best way to describe the current situation in some of the new democracies in Central and Eastern Europe. According to former dissident Janos Kis, 'Hungary is undergoing a genuine constitutional crisis', while the constitutional lawyer Kim Lane Scheppele feels that 'Romania unravels the rule of law' and Romanian constitutionalist Ioan Stanomir declares that the 'Romanian constitution has become an insignificant and irrelevant element' (Kis 2011; Scheppele 2012; Stanomir 2012). The political and constitutional crises can be related to the implications of the global financial and economic crisis, but the roots of democratic breakdown clearly lie elsewhere. The argument of this book is that one important dimension of the crisis is that democracy has been unevenly institutionalized in the new democracies. A one-sided emphasis on the formal institutions of the rule of law and the entrenchment of democracy has meant a neglect of substantive, participatory, and legitimatory dimensions. Part of the result is that now the 'strain between representative and participative democracy has become too strong' (Kurczewski 1993: xv). The democratic and constitutional transformations that the former communist countries go through have been unevenly defined and affected by visions and templates of constitutional democracy that prioritize a formalistic and elitist or technocratic understanding of democracy. Democratization trajectories have been strongly influenced by approaches that feel a 'discomfort with democracy'.[1] But while the transition 'mantra' prioritized formal institutions related to the rule of law, separation of powers, and rights regimes, a sociological-substantive dimension to the building of constitutional democracy was largely overlooked, that is, a dimension that involves democratic learning and deliberation, as well as engagement and participation. The current, and recent, crises in at least a number of the new democracies reveal the lack of dynamic interaction between society and politics as well as a persistent absence of a strong civil reservoir that is able to hold official politics and public institutions accountable (the case of Hungary is striking here). While the common explanation for weak civil societies has been cultural, historical, and even civilizational (cf. Sztompka 2004), the argument here will be that the main problem might lie elsewhere, that is, a problematic or at the very least uneven design and implementation of constitutional democracy.

The book will engage with the institutionalization of constitutional democracy from a specific angle. The emphasis is on the formal constitutions of five new democracies – the Czech Republic, Hungary, Poland, Romania, and Slovakia – but with a very specific question in mind. This question stems from a specific theoretical approach, which I coin 'civic constitutionalism', and asks to what extent the constitutionalization of the new democracy has involved a significant attention to civic engagement and participation. The idea is that constitutional democracy can only thrive if such attention in institutional design is there, and allows citizens and civil society movements to effectively interact with political and legal institutions, and, most importantly, to contribute to decisions and rule definitions that affect and constitute the political community.

The approach taken is interdisciplinary, and includes elements of political and legal theory, comparative constitutionalism, and historical and political sociology. In a sense, the approach in the book is provisional, in that it clears the way for further comparative studies on the societal role of constitutionalism in democracies. Even if the main focus in this book is on constitutionalist narratives (legal versus civic constitutionalism) and their translation into formal constitutional forms, the suggestion is that a fuller picture has to wait and can emerge only with the comparative analysis of juridical, civil and political society engagement with constitutions.[2] This does not mean that the book does not stand on its own, but rather that it paints a formal-constitutional picture from the point of view of democratic participation, and does not pretend to cover the dimensions of the implementation of constitutions and their interpretation by different actors 'on the ground'.

By focusing on the relation between democracy and constitutionalism, this book will engage with the point of view of three interrelated and topical (but often separately pursued) debates. The first debate focuses on the relation between constitutionalism and democracy, the second on constitutions in a global age, and the third on the predicament of representative, liberal democracy. All three debates are of great importance for understanding the challenges and tensions that the new democracies face.

The democracy–constitutionalism nexus

The first debate I will draw on, and contribute to, is the debate in constitutional and political theory on the relation between democracy and constitutionalism. This debate largely sees two views facing each other: legal and political constitutionalism, with the former emphasizing a rigid distinction between politics and law, and judicial supremacy, whereas the latter endorses interaction between laws and politics, and parliamentary supremacy (cf. Bellamy 2007). Constitutions and the institutionalization of formal legal frameworks have been a primary focus in the analysis of democratic transformation in Central and Eastern Europe, but there has been little reflection on the democratic implications of one-sided institutional formalism emphasizing legalism. The debate on the democracy–constitutionalism nexus is therefore highly relevant for the analysis of the 'democratic fatigue' in the new democracies, especially since these have often been seen as eager students in adopting a global standard of 'judicial democracy' or 'democracy by the judiciary' (Scheppele 2005). A key issue in the debate regards the role of constitutional courts and judicial review in constitutional-democratic systems, and whether democracy is stifled by too much 'juristocracy'. In other words, the question is whether legal constitutionalism might lead to perverse effects.[3]

The relevance of the idea of 'new constitutionalism' for understanding the constitutional changes in the post-communist region cannot be denied. At least two more or less shared, region-wide tendencies can be identified (Sadurski 2005). First, there is the emergence of a level of judicialization of democratic politics, in particular in terms of constitutional courts acting as the guardians of the constitution as well as protectors of pre-political rights. Second, an unusually strong emphasis on a legal language – if not always practice – of fundamental rights and a legalistic view of constitutionalism have emerged throughout the region. Both the politically substitutive role of constitutional courts and the strong attachment to legal constitutionalism and fundamental rights can be understood in the specific context of democratic transition (cf. Arjomand 2003; Sadurski 2005).

The first tendency, the prominence of the role of independent constitutional courts in the region, has been widely debated (see Prochazka 2002; Sadurski 2008; Schwartz 2000). In the specific context of transition, the idea of 'democracy by judiciary' finds two main forms of justification. First of all, the idea is that the post-communist societies are wanting in terms of both capable political and civil actors, and that independent, constitutional judges are the ones most capable of leading the new democracies into the direction of 'normal democracies'. Second, it is sometimes argued that judicial review by independent constitutional experts might actually enhance the substance of democratic politics, in terms of outcomes, and judicial supremacy can therefore be considered as endorsing a form of 'democratizing democracy' (cf. Sadurski 2005: 12–13; Scheppele 2005).

Regarding the second tendency, a widespread, if not dominant, interpretation of constitutionalism in the region is informed by what I have called elsewhere the 'ethic of rights' (Blokker 2010a), that is the idea that identifies democracy with the liberal model of constitutional democracy based on (natural) rights, legal procedures and the equality of citizens before the law. This monistic understanding of democracy often not only reduces democracy to liberal, representative democracy, but also understands a specific set of (predefined) rights and their protection as democracy's main aim. A general trend in the constitutionalization of the region has been the understanding of constitutions as vehicles of relatively unequivocal pre-political rights and values. But this legal-liberal emphasis has largely meant the absence of wider political and public debates on the foundations of the existing constitutions. In other words, constitutions have been mostly understood as foundational documents that merely need interpretation by judicial institutions, notably constitutional courts, and much less so as vehicles of continuing dialogue over foundational values and rights, and the overall nature of the political community.

In the context of the debate on constitutionalism and democracy, it can be argued that the region has been a laboratory for only one part of the contenders in the debate, that is those endorsing legal constitutionalism. But the legalist model they endorse is clearly not without problems and not beyond contestation. Indeed, depending on one's view, the new constitutionalism promoted in the region can be seen as both both enhancing and, alternatively, as compromising constitutional democracy. Regarding the latter, it seems hard to deny that a one-sided, legalistic emphasis in constructing constitutional democracy involves the potential danger of contributing to an overall depoliticized and essentialistic view of democratic politics that denies any role of the larger demos and civil society, in particular in terms of engaging in the definition of the foundational, ethical values that provide the constitutional context of the new democratic orders. One danger, as suggested by Wojciech Sadurski, is that a judicialized type of politics might become a self-perpetuating system rather than a temporary anomality (cf. Sadurski 2005). More in general, the depoliticization and juridification of democratic politics might have compromised democracy as a political form that is based on popular self-rule. If this is so, the legal-constitutionalist mode of democratization might fail in important ways to institutionalize a democratic regime as such (cf. Sadurski 2005).

Constitutionalism in a global age

A second debate that cannot be ignored in discussing the constitutional and democratic transformations in post-communist Europe is the debate on the predicament of modern, Westphalian constitutionalism, a debate variably referred to as 'constitutional pluralism', 'global constitutionalism', 'post-national constitutionalism' and so forth. It is by now largely accepted that constitutionalism is undergoing intensive and extensive transformation, not least due an internationalization and supranationalization of constitutional functions and templates. One implication of the changing and pluralized nature of constitutionalism is its relation to democracy and popular sovereignty. The debate directly relates to the situation of the new democracies for at least two reasons. First, the external dimension has been of primary importance in the constitutionalization of these democracies, if not immediately, than at least in a second step (Sadurski 2012). The accession to the European Union and the related conditionality-driven process are the most obvious examples, but the role of other highly important institutions such as the Council of Europe, and its Commission for Democracy through Law, is equally important (as recently has again become clear in the constitutional crises in Hungary and Romania). The external dimension to constitution-making does not only consist in the local adoption of external, European norms, but also involves a qualitative change in the building of constitutional democracies, that is away from the closed nature of national sovereignty towards a pluralistic regime based on 'divided sovereignty' (Přibáň 2010).

Second, in a somewhat paradoxical way, it can be equally argued that the constitutionalization process in the new democracies has largely followed a 'traditional' template of modern, Westphalian constitutionalism, with a closed and homogeneous conception of sovereignty, territory and people.[4] The importance of this template is, however, not only the result of desires to re-construct national self-government after decades of subjugation to the international Soviet 'empire' (cf. Albi 2005), but some of its dimensions have also been present and reproduced in a global drive to legal constitutionalism. The idea of legal constitutionalism, as at least partially endorsed by international and supranational institutions (cf. Parau 2012), could be described as an 'amplified' form of modern constitutionalism (cf. Arjomand 2003). In other words, legal constitutionalism can itself be seen as in some ways prioritizing a closed, sovereign and national system based on the idea of the constitution as the higher law or apex of the legal system, and a symmetry between jurisdiction, territory and people (cf. Tully 1995).[5] In some distinct ways, the legal-constitutionalist trend seems in this to discourage the emergence of more open, post-national and democratic constitutional structures.

Representative democracy in crisis

A third debate includes the strain between representative and participative democracy, and, in a slightly different and more structural sense, the challenges that liberal, representative democracy faces in current times of global change. Many scholars, even if not all (see, e.g., Ferrara 2011), accept the idea that liberal, representative democracy is in some sort of crisis, and that novel ways of engaging citizens with politics and the common good need to be found. The problematic state of representative, liberal democracy is well articulated by Fung and Olin Wright:

> As the tasks of the state have become more complex and the size of polities larger and more heterogeneous, the institutional forms of liberal democracy developed in the nineteenth century – representative democracy plus techno-bureaucratic administration – seem increasingly ill-suited to the novel problems we face in the twenty-first century. "Democracy" as a way of organizing the state has become to be narrowly identified with territorially based competitive elections of political leadership for legislative and executive

> offices. Yet, increasingly, this mechanism of political representation seems ineffective in accomplishing the central ideals of democratic politics: facilitating active involvement of the citizenry, forging political consensus through dialogue, devising and implementing public policies that ground a productive economy and healthy society, and, in more radical egalitarian versions of the democratic ideal, assuring that all citizens benefit from the nation's wealth.
>
> (2003: 3)

James Tully argues in this regard that modern constitutional democracies are subject to three 'illegitimate trends'. A first trend is the 'decline of democratic deliberation and decision-making within traditional institutions of representative nation-states' (2008a: 102). The decline of post-Second World War representative liberal democracy includes a complexity of dimensions, including the increased inability of political parties to represent societal pluralism, the growing distrust of citizens towards public institutions, the increasing depoliticization of politics by among others the increased technocratic behaviour of political elites, being more accountable to business interests and lobby groups than to the wider public (for a radical statement, see Wolin 2008), and the domination of democratic politics by 'media politics'. As Tully observes, '[c]itizen participation decreases and democratic apathy and malaise increases' (2008a: 103). A second trend, related to what has been described above as post-national constitutionalism, regards the marginalization of national democracies due to processes of global juridification, which involves global legal and regulatory regimes that are beyond the grasp of the legal jurisdiction of singular states, but do have a highly significant effect on their internal functioning. A third trend that Tully observes regards the 'devolution and dispersion of political power and forms of political association' (ibid.: 101). This trend involves an ambiguous moving away from the centralized political unit of the nation-state:

> On the one hand, this global trend towards legal and political pluralism, federalism and subsidiarity can be seen as the expansion of opportunities for the exercise of democratic freedoms. On the other, it is also a trend towards weaker political units. The new states, autonomous units within complex federations, and global political networks tend to be weak relative to the power of transnational corporations and their complementary regulatory regimes, such as the World Bank.
>
> (Ibid.: 102)

The debate on the predicament of representative, liberal democracy is of great relevance for the new democracies in Central and Eastern Europe. Their democratization trajectories were mapped out with the help of much of the allegedly now surpassed template of representative, liberal democracy (see Wydra 2007). Thus, even while important differences between the new democracies exist (see Blokker 2010a), it is at the same time true that relatively little experimentation with novel, deliberative or participatory dimensions of constitutional democracy has been going on in the region. It is from this perspective not a coincidence that some observers have argued that the new democracies suffer from an insufficiently institutionalized democratic-participatory dimension. Susan Rose-Ackerman argues that

> full democracy cannot be attained unless the policy-making process is accountable to citizens through transparent procedures that seek to incorporate public input. In a democracy, individuals and institutions must justify the exercise of power over others, and success in an election is, I argue, insufficient to make this claim.
>
> (2005: 1)

She further argues that '[c]reating institutions that channel and manage public participation by individuals and groups in policy making should be high on the reform agenda of the postsocialist states' (ibid.: 6).

The loss of legitimacy of modern representative democracy regarding its role as an 'effective vehicle for popular government' is directly relevant for the role of constitutions in modern democracies (Tierney 2012: 3). This is particularly evident in the case of the new democracies where it appears that historical legacies might discourage popular engagement with democratic politics. The call for democratic renewal directly affects constitutionalism, but the implications for democratizing democracy are not yet widely debated in constitutional terms (for exceptions, see Colon-Rios 2012; Tierney 2012). One of the exceptions is the 'empowerment approach' of Günter Frankenberg (2000: 20, 2003), which in my view has important affinities with the idea of democratic constitutionalism (see Chapter 2). Frankenberg's approach includes an emphasis on 'participation in the procedures of law-making and deliberative public processes' and the 'specific institutionalization of the formation of public opinion and public decision-making and their factual and not merely virtual openness to citizens willing to participate. Openness may therefore require measures to empower citizens for participation' (2000: 21). A related approach is a proposal by Peter Häberle of some decades ago. He argued in favour of a theory of constitutional interpretation based on the idea of an 'open society of constitutional interpreters'. In his view, constitutional interpretation includes 'potentially all state organs, all public authorities, all citizens and groups' (1975: 297). His argument was based on the idea that the person 'who "lives" the norm also (co-)interprets it'. While Häberle mostly calls for a theoretical opening up by means of the 'democratization of constitutional interpretation', the normative implications for constitutional democracy are clear: '[i]n a freedom-based democracy the citizen is a constitutional interpreter!' (ibid.: 302). And '[s]ociety is free and open to the extent that the circle of constitutional interpreters is opened up'. Equally relevant is Stephen Tierney's recent call for a civic-republican approach to constitutionalism. Tierney's suggestion is that such an approach might help to address the 'changing normative architecture in which older territorial, institutional and identificatory certainties which underpinned the unitary and hierarchical order of the constitutional state become ever more insecure and in which citizens increasingly look to new and often direct forms of political engagement to compensate for the perceived democratic failings of traditional constitutional models' (2012: 6).

In the case of the new democracies, what the empowerment approach, the open society of constitutional interpreters, and civic-republican constitutionalism point to is a crucial mode of integration of constitutionalized polities, which does not take recourse to external authorities (such as the state or law), but rather follows a republican-democratic model in placing 'trust in the unifying power of the self-civilizing tendency of the citizenry' (Frankenberg 2000: 19). In the context of the new democracies, this would mean the replacement of the 'heteronomy' of communist regimes with truly emancipatory democratic regimes grounded in collective autonomy. The question of whether some of such replacement has taken place in these societies, and what the main hurdles are for further extension, is at the heart of this book.

Overview of the book

The book starts with a theoretical excursion into the legal- and political-theoretical debate on constitutionalism and democracy, departing from the legal constitutionalist position to then traverse political, popular, societal and democratic constitutionalisms. The argument is that legal constitutionalism, in its emphasis on pre-commitments and strong judicial review, reveals a democratic deficit, in that it structurally disregards possibilities for political as well as civic engagement and participation. Political constitutionalism has strong reservations with regard to the undermining of popular sovereignty in legal constitutionalism due to its providing constitutional courts with the 'final word' on interpretation of constitutions and rights. Popular constitutionalism emphasizes the role of the (American) people and civil society in constitutional interpretation against an exclusively judicial interpretation of the constitution. Societal constitutionalism criticizes the mainstream views of constitutionalism as suffering from forms of state-centrism and 'methodological nationalism', thereby ignoring societal forms of constitution-making and increasingly also those beyond the nation-state arena. Finally, democratic constitutionalism criticizes mainstream approaches to constitutionalism for overlooking traditional forms of constitutionalism, for imposing exclusionary forms of modern constitutionalism, and for failing to promote civic, pluralistic participation 'all the way down'. The thrust that is present in all these critiques is that legal constitutionalism tends to ignore or underestimate the social and political dimensions to constitutions. I propose an alternative approach, civic constitutionalism, which emphasizes possibilities for the democratization of constitutional democracy. I suggest three potential areas, which indicate possible dimensions of more democratic forms of constitutionalism: constitutional politics, direct forms of democracy and decentralized forms of democracy.

Much of the debate on the constitutionalism–democracy nexus remains, however, on the theoretical level, while often taking recourse to anecdotal evidence rather than sustained comparison. In this book I attempt to add comparative-empirical substance to the debate by comparatively exploring constitutionalism and constitution-making in the context of the new democracies. Chapter 3 initiates a comparatively analysis of constitutionalization and constitutional politics in the Czech Republic, Hungary, Poland, Romania and Slovakia, by investigating the emergence of constitutional orders through the lens of legal constitutionalism. The chapter engages with the question of to what extent it can be argued that the democratization of former communist societies has in constitutional terms involved the predominance of legal constitutionalism as an idea and as an institutional template. Some core features of legal constitutionalism are comparatively analysed: the legal order as coinciding with the notion of national sovereignty; the constitution as independent higher law and the entrenchment of fundamental rights; and the constitutional court as guardian of the constitution. These core features are clearly evident in the constitutional structures of all the five countries, even if to different degrees (for instance, Romania could be understood in legal-constitutionalist terms only really from the early 2000s onwards).

In the following chapters, Chapters 4 and 5, I delineate an alternative constitutional dimension that has played an important, even if marginalized, role in the constitutionalization of the new democracies. This democratic-constitutionalist dimension is clearly informed by a conception of civil society, self-governance and openness. In Chapter 4, I discuss the intriguing question of the emergence of constitutionalist discourse and practice in the later days of communism, and comparatively discuss a dimension of republican democracy in dissident discourse in various national settings. The attempt is to explore possible 'rudiments' of an alternative constitutional tradition in the region, even if large differences between the cases exist (in particular Romania, even if not entirely without dissident references to legality, hardly developed a bottom-up critique of the communist regime). In most cases, dimensions of dissident discourse indicated a republican view of democracy, including ideas of civic engagement and the civic scrutiny of formal politics, notions of civic association, and endorsements of (local) self-rule and autonomy.

Chapter 5 follows up on the discussion of the republican-democratic tradition by comparatively analysing three dimensions of republican democracy in constitutional orders: (possibilities of civic participation in) constitutional revision, forms of direct democracy and decentralized forms of self-government, related to the notion of proximity. The argument is that a different constitutional tradition is available and has informed parts of the constitutional architecture, even if it is often rather latent and not well entrenched. In this, the constitutional revision procedures barely allow for civic engagement, either upfront or in the form of confirmatory referenda. But in terms of direct democracy and local self-government, many of the constitutions discussed are more robust in terms of their facilitatory role towards civic participation. And local and regional government are equally rather well entrenched in the new democracies, except for a number of peculiarities.

In Chapter 6, the constitutional trajectories of the new democracies are discussed in the light of external challenges and pressures, in particular those related to the European Union (EU) integration process. The argument is that legal constitutionalism has been strengthened, or at least reinforced, through EU accession and integration. From the perspective in the book, an important thrust in EU integration is then against civic constitutionalism. This becomes evident in an emphasis on independent constitutional courts in the EU accession processes, in particular in the cases of Romania and Slovakia. It also comes through in a generally technocratic-legalistic bias as well as a minimalistic understanding of democracy in enlargement policy. A significant counter-trend to (externally imposed) legal constitutionalism has emerged and tends to significantly undermine some of its key tenets (not least regarding the prominent role of courts and rigid, higher law constitutions). This trend is clearly worrisome from a legalistic point of view, but what is particularly cause for distress from a democratic point of view are the repercussions for civic constitutionalism. Admittedly, the narrative of the book, with legal and civic constitutionalism as its main protagonists, has been rendered more complex by the emergence and unfolding of these counter-constitutional projects, in particular the Fidesz constitutional 'revolution' in Hungary and the constitutional moves of the Romanian Social-Democratic government.

In the concluding chapter, I restate the problematic strain in the new democracies between legal and civic constitutionalism. The counter-constitutional projects in Hungary and Romania are clearly rendering a democratization of these constitutional democracies a distant project. It is, however, also possible to indicate some social resonance to the questions raised in this book, not least in the case of Romania. Actions and claims made by civil society actors provide in this not only some direly needed hope for the retrieval of the 'lost treasure' of civic constitutionalism, but also interesting and unexplored areas for the socio-legal analysis of constitutionalism, its current predicament and resulting democratic implications.

Notes

1 R. Unger (1996), *What should legal analysis become?*, London: Verso, p. 72, cited in: Bellamy (2007: 1).
2 I am currently developing comparative research along these lines in a project called Constitutional Politics in Post-Westphalian Europe (CoPolis) (see, for a preliminary statement, Blokker 2013).
3 As Albert Hirschman put it with regard to perversity: 'the attempt to push society in a certain direction will result in its moving alright, but in the opposite direction' (1991: 11).
4 Neil Walker has extensively elaborated on this in terms of what he calls 'a holistic method of constitutionalism' (2009: 15).
5 This is of course not to say that this entails a *necessary* relation. In some ways, the primacy of EU law and the role of the European Court of Justice replicate such a logic on a supranational level (even if in a very different context) (cf. Walker 2009: 3–4).

2 A critique of legal constitutionalism

The constitutional systems of the new democracies discussed in this book have been predominantly guided – or at least strongly informed – by a specific vision of constitutions. This vision could be referred to as legal or 'new' constitutionalism, and appears to be predominant both in theory and practice (and not only in the region discussed). This understanding of the role of constitutions in institutionalizing democratic regimes strongly emphasises what one could call a *negative* view of constitutions. A negative view prioritizes the imposition of limits on political powers (against the arbitrary use of power), the guarantee of adherence to standards of the rule of law and the guarantee of fundamental rights. It can be related to an instrumental rationality or function of constitutions, which can be understood in Weberian terms as permitting the purposive rationalization of politics and the political community (Přibáň 2007: 3). In this instrumental dimension, constitutions are portrayed as documents that ground legality as well as depoliticized sets of rights. And constitutions make a strong distinction between the public and the private, as well as between politics and the rule of law (see Blokker 2010b). A key concern is the protection of specific democratic *outcomes* that avoid, for instance, the tyranny of the majority (see Dworkin 1996; cf. Waldron 2006). The strong distinction between politics and law is allegedly best guarded by specialized institutions, such as constitutional courts, and through their safeguarding of fundamental rights and constitutional principles. The legal or new constitutionalism that has become dominant in recent decades emphasizes this instrumental dimension of constitutions strongly. This type of constitutionalism entails an important shift away from democratic politics and towards judicial supremacy. According to Michael Mandel '[r]epresentative institutions have been demoted from the sovereign entities with legally unlimited power of the nineteenth and much of the twentieth century to institutions hemmed in by legally enforceable constitutional limitations, most characteristically found in "rigid" Charters and Bills of Rights' (1997: 251). Also Ran Hirschl critically assesses the global trend towards legal constitutionalism:

> Over the past two decades the world has witnessed an astonishingly rapid transition to what may be called *juristocracy*. Around the globe, in numerous countries and in several supranational entities, fundamental constitutional reform has transferred an unprecedented amount of power from representative institutions to judiciaries. Most of these polities have a recently adopted constitution or constitutional revision that contains a bill of rights and establishes some form of active judicial review. National high courts and supranational tribunals meanwhile have become increasingly important, even crucial, policy-making bodies. To paraphrase Alexis de Tocqueville's observation regarding the United States, there is now hardly any moral, political, or public policy controversy in the new constitutionalism world that does not sooner or later become a judicial one. This global trend toward the expansion of the judicial domain is arguably one of the most significant developments in late twentieth and early twenty-first century government.
>
> (2004: 71)

The argument in the book is that the implications for democratization of what I will variably refer to as new or legal constitutionalism should be scrutinized more carefully than has been done so far.[1] In other words, while many proponents of legal constitutionalism argue for its indispensable nature in grounding democracy and democratic institutions (including fundamental rights),[2] not least in the context of post-authoritarian societies, the argument here is that there are important implications of the legalistic view of constitutionalism, which might not only 'precommit' democratic politics, but also more generally promote a sceptical view towards citizen engagement. In this, they might result in detrimental effects for the viability of constitutional democracy as well as the diffusion of the idea of constitutional democracy throughout wider political and civil society.

In this chapter, I will briefly discuss the main critiques of legal constitutionalism, to subsequently opt for a form of democratic constitutionalism as the most conducive for the emergence of robust constitutional democracies. The legalistic, liberal view of constitutionalism can theoretically be criticized from various theoretical angles. In my view, the most important and relevant ones for the discussion here are political constitutionalism (in particular Bellamy 2007; Waldron 1999,

2006), popular constitutionalism (Kramer 2004; Post and Siegel 2007; Tushnet 1999),[3] societal constitutionalism (Teubner 2012; Thornhill 2011; see also Skapska 2011) and democratic constitutionalism (Albert 2008; Colon-Rios 2012; Colon-Rios and Hutchinson 2011; Tully 1995, 2008a). Political constitutionalism has strong reservations with regard to the undermining of popular sovereignty in legal constitutionalism due to the latter's emphasis on constitutional courts as providing the 'final word' on the interpretation of constitutions and rights. In this, political constitutionalism promotes a republican view of non-domination, and emphasizes a rehabilitation of representative democracy and parliamentary sovereignty in the face of judicial supremacy. Popular constitutionalism, a largely American and rather variegated discussion, emphasizes the role of the American people and civil society in constitutional interpretation, against an exclusively judicial interpretation of the constitution. Societal constitutionalism criticizes the mainstream views of constitutionalism as suffering from forms of state-centrism and 'methodological nationalism'. The claim is that modern constitutionalism ignores societal forms of constitution-making (it builds here on the idea of legal pluralism), and increasingly also those beyond the nation-state arena. Finally, democratic constitutionalism relates the modern constitutionalist view to imperialism and a specific Enlightenment tradition of understanding constitutions. It criticizes mainstream approaches to constitutionalism for overlooking traditional forms of constitutionalism, for imposing exclusionary forms of modern constitutionalism (see Tully 1995, 2008), and for failing to promote civic, pluralistic participation 'all the way down' (Albert 2008; Colon-Rios 2012). The thrust that is present in all these critiques is that legal constitutionalism tends to ignore or underestimate the social and political dimensions to constitutions, and therefore to reiterate the distinction between law and politics, as well as law and society.

The objective in this chapter is, in a first step, to discuss the theoretical argument for, and the emergence in constitutional realities of, legal constitutionalism. In a second step, the four theoretical approaches to constitutionalism that are critical to an overly legalistic view of constitutionalism will be reviewed. Finally, in a third step, I will – inspired by the various forms of critique on legal constitutionalism – identify a number of constitutional areas where democratic participation could become more meaningful and made more upfront for a democratically understood constitutionalism. My aim is to contribute to the delineation of a more balanced understanding of democratic constitutionalism (cf. Tully 2008a). I point in this to a different understanding of constitutionalism, that of civic constitutionalism. This understanding has a bearing on the actual institutionalization of constitutionalism of the new democracies, but equally on some of the current constitutional problems these democracies are facing. But civic constitutionalism in the new democracies evidently needs reinforcement.

Legal constitutionalism: a multi-faceted critique

The abstract idea of a written constitution as the foundational basis of modern democratic societies is a relatively undisputed element in much of social, political, and legal theory (cf. Bellamy 2007: viii). In the two centuries of 'reign' of modern constitutionalism, a general, minimal consensus has emerged on the nature and functions of the constitution.[4] As Michel Rosenfeld argues, '[t]here appears to be no accepted definition of constitutionalism but, in the broadest terms, modern constitutionalism requires imposing limits on the powers of government, adherence to the rule of law, and the protection of fundamental rights' (1993: 497). Modern constitutionalism corresponds largely with the Westphalian idea of a state system of separate and homogeneous nation-states. In this, it comprises a tendency to 'presuppose the uniformity of a nation state with a centralised and unitary system of legal and political institutions' (Tully 1995: 9). In a slightly different formulation, the 'understanding of a constitution and its assigned role as the guardian of the political process is commonly associated with modern constitutionalism and builds on institutionalised and mythical links with statehood that had been forged over centuries' (Wiener 2008: 23).

In this, modern constitutions tend to share a number of generic features (the following list is not meant to be exhaustive). First, a modern constitution is regarded a 'structure of law' that is in important ways separate from its subjects. Whereas the modern constitution is ultimately dependent on the people for its legitimation, once constituted, it becomes a relatively autonomous set of meta-norms and rules that constitutes social and political interaction. James Tully (2008a) calls this relative autonomy or externality the 'formality' of modern constitutions. Second, one of the essential ideas behind the constitution is to channel and express popular sovereignty. In this, popular sovereignty has been widely understood in a monist way, that is as the expression of a singular, mythical people. At any rate, the idea is that the 'raw' constituent power of the people is relevant only in constitutional foundation, in that the act of the constitution transfers popular sovereignty from the *pouvoir constituant* to the *pouvoir constituée*. Third, the singular understanding of the people presupposes a shared civic or ethnocultural identity, which is symbolically reflected in the constitution, either implicitly or explicitly so (cf. Weiler 2003). Fourth, modern constitutions are understood as coherent and non-contradictory, contractual structures, in which 'constitutional essentials are unambiguously settled and made binding into the future' (Chambers 1998: 149). Fifth, while most of the dimensions noted above invoke a pre-political, restrictive and foundational perception of constitutions, constitutions also provide for a positive or enabling democratic dimension. This includes positive civil and political rights, which enable citizens and political actors to act set their own rules, even if within the limits set by the very same constitution.

At the risk of simplifying our understanding of modern constitutionalism, it is possible to condense the five generic features described above and focus on two imperatives or meta-political principles of modern constitutionalism. The two imperatives are the *limitation of sovereignty* (constitutionalism) and *popular sovereignty* (democracy) (Cohen and Arato 1992; Loughlin and Walker 2007: 1; Tully 2008a: 91–2). The first principle, that of constitutionalism or the rule of law, understands a constitutional order as legitimate when

> the exercise of political power in the whole and in every part of any constitutionally legitimate system of political, social and economic cooperation [is] exercised in accordance with and through the general system of principles, rules and procedures, including procedures for amending any principle, rule or procedure.
>
> (Tully 2008a: 92)

The emphasis is on order and the provision of an orderly process of politics. The second principle, that of democracy, which

> requires that, although the people or peoples who constitute a political association are subject to the constitutional system, they, or their entrusted representatives, must also impose the general system on themselves in order to be sovereign and free, and thus for the association to be democratically legitimate.
>
> (Ibid.: 93)

The second principle is about (collective) autonomy or self-rule, in which people give themselves their own laws, rather than being subject to some form of 'heteronomy'. Today, the balance between the two tilts towards constitutional order. As Joel Colon-Rios and Alan Hutchinson observe: 'today, the prevailing view is decidedly more constitutionalist than democratist' (2011: 3).

The rest of the chapter will engage with the emergence of new constitutionalism as a particular form of modern constitutionalism, and the forms of critique such a legalistic view of constitutionalism has attracted by various scholars.[5] The main divide can be said to be between an emphasis on the imperative of limiting sovereignty and an emphasis on popular sovereignty. Many forms of critique on legal constitutionalism regard the 'colonization' of the democratic dimension by the constitutional one, or the depoliticization of democratic politics.

Legal constitutionalism

The legal-constitutionalist view in principle endorses liberal constitutionalism, that is 'as a normative framework that sets limits on and goals for the exercise of state power' (Bellamy and Castiglione 2000: 172). In this view, the constitution is largely seen as providing the preconditions for democracy. Democracy can only function as such if democratic politics abides to the constitutional limitations set to it. The constitution, and increasingly the idea of an included set of entrenched fundamental rights, provides, then, an independent and superior law that secures the working and outcomes of democracy. One of the key assumptions of legal constitutionalism is that it is in principle possible to reach a reasonable consensus on what such preconditions of democracy ought to be, and how to translate them into a language of rights and fundamental law (Bellamy 2007: 3). Before democratic politics is possible, essential framework conditions need to be entrenched. In this, it is in principle possible to arrive at a pre-political set of 'essential preconditions for democracy', the 'right' abstract principles (Dworkin 1995) or 'best answers' (Bellamy 2007) that all can rationally agree to, and which identify what democracy ultimately is about.[6] Indeed, Ronald Dworkin's concern is with 'what democracy, accurately understood, really is' (1996: 15). For Dworkin, constitutionalism means a 'system that establishes individual legal rights that the dominant legislature does not have the power to override or compromise' (1995: 2). In this, the 'constitutional conception presupposes democratic conditions. These are the conditions that must be met before majoritarian decision-making can claim any automatic moral advantage over other procedures of collective action' (1996: 23). Since, in a well-designed constitutional democratic system, a consensus on the right norms can be presupposed, there is no need to change such norms in the future, only to ensure their correct implementation. In other words, it is possible to depoliticize principled, constitutional questions and take these out of the democratic political process altogether, because a rational consensus has been reached or can be presumed on those questions once a constitution is in place.

A second key assumption is that it should be ultimately legal actors that identify and interpret key constitutional principles, as the judicial branch is more reliable than political majorities in doing so (Bellamy 2007: 3). In other words, democratic politics is 'regarded not only as something apart from law, but as inferior to law. Law aims at justice, while politics only looks to expediency. The former is neutral and objective, the latter the uncontrolled child of competing interests and ideologies'.[7] According to Dworkin,

> In some circumstances . . . individual citizens may be able to exercise their moral responsibilities of citizenship better when final decisions are removed from ordinary politics and assigned to courts, whose decisions are meant to turn on principle, not on the weight of numbers or the balance of political influence.
>
> (1996: 30)

The emerging view of the constitution is a static, permanent framework, which is only to a very limited extent open to political and civic influence, in the form of amendment, revision or otherwise. The legal-constitutionalist view in essence understands the constitution as a 'meta-norm', which is not implicated in, as it transcends, substantive views on the common good, and in this provides a 'neutral framework that rests on a separation of the right from the good' (Bellamy and Castiglione 2000: 174–5).

It is a conception and template influenced by this view of constitutionalism that has emerged in the last decades as the predominant way of institutionalizing constitutional democracy. By the early twenty-first century, new constitutionalism (Arjomand 2003; Stone Sweet 2008, 2009) has allegedly become predominant, even if not uncontested. The emphasis is on written constitutions with an entrenched 'catalogue of rights', and a 'system of constitutional justice to defend those rights' (Stone Sweet 2008: 219). The novelty is that the constitutional court as an independent institution is not only the ultimate guardian and interpreter of the constitution, but equally so of fundamental rights.

In terms of the generic features of modern constitutionalism mentioned above, new constitutionalism prioritizes the higher law status of the constitution and of the bill of rights, as well as normative coherence and legal certainty, and takes an amplified understanding of the rule of law. The latter is part of post-authoritarian and post-totalitarian transitions to new democracies, such as those in Central and Eastern Europe. It includes a constitutional politics that comprises both the 'judicialization of politics' – which encompasses the reconstruction of the normative basis of the state – and the political activism of judicial actors as the guardians of the process of democratization (Arjomand 2003). The emphasis in democratic transitions has thus been on legal formalism and coherence, and constitutionally entrenched democratic preconditions, while democratic participation has been largely confined to 'normal politics'. In a more general sense, the shift is towards legal constitutionalism, while, '[w]ith very few exceptions, legislative sovereignty has formally disappeared. The new constitutionalism killed it, paradoxically perhaps, in the name of democracy' (Stone Sweet 2008: 218).

If new constitutionalism amplifies some of modern constitutionalism's main dimensions, it at the same time seems difficult to deny that a number of the key features of modern constitutionalism have become increasingly untenable (in a normative, democratic sense), and unrealistic or anachronistic (in terms of correspondence with political, social, cultural, and economic realities) (cf. Krisch 2010).[8] Here, I will focus in particular on a democratic critique, that is, the idea that new constitutionalism one-sidedly promotes constitutional order, while ignoring dimensions of civic enablement and societal participation. The latter dimension builds on the idea of *isegoria*, or the idea that all members of a political community should have an equal chance to have their voice heard in legislative and foundational matters. Below, I will discuss different critiques of legal constitutionalism from this distinct viewpoint,[9] that is, legal constitutionalism's problematic relation to the ideas of democratic participation and (societal) self-government or self-determination.

Political constitutionalism

The most visible contender of a legalistic theory of constitutionalism, which as we have seen endorses *inter alia* judicial supremacy and the strong entrenchment of rights, is the theory of political constitutionalism (see, most prominently, Bellamy 2007; Waldron 1999). The political-constitutionalist conception takes a wholly different view of the role and substance of the constitution, and its relation to democratic politics. Its dispute with legal constitutionalism starts from the observation that the

> need for [an] alternative and more political approach arises from the *contested* nature of rights. Despite widespread support for both constitutional rights and rights-based judicial review, theorists,

> politicians, lawyers and ordinary citizens frequently disagree over which rights merit or require such entrenchment, the legal form they should take, the best way of implementing them, their relationship to each other, and the manner in which courts should understand and uphold them.
>
> (Bellamy 2007: 16; emphasis added)

Rather than understanding the constitution as a 'right basic norm', political constitutionalists understand the constitution as providing a basic framework for resolving disagreements over the right and the good. This also means that foundational norms should always be subject to reconsideration and reformulation. In other words, the constitution is not seen as in need of an entrenched set of fundamental principles, but rather as the framework for the articulation of and deliberation over conceptions of self-government and the common good. As Bellamy aptly expresses it: 'we could see constitutions not as constraints imposed upon democracy but as the *limits that a mature democracy places upon itself*' (2007: 91; emphasis added).

The relation between democracy and constitutionalism in political constitutionalism is not based on the need for 'pre-commitments' or extra-political guarantees, nor on the idea of superior judgemental capacity (of judicial experts). Rather, the emphasis is on the idea of political equality and a thrust towards the inclusion of a wide range of people's judgements (see Goldoni 2012). Political constitutionalism starts from the idea that reasonable disagreement is part and parcel of democracy. The critique of legal constitutionalism is that a 'failure to acknowledge the disagreements that surround constitutional values, and the resulting need for political mechanisms to resolve them, can itself be a source of domination and arbitrary rule that impacts negatively on rights and the rule of law' (Bellamy 2007: 145; cf. Waldron 1999).

The attempt is, then, not to transcend the plurality of political views with regard to different understandings of constitutional values and rights, but to include the widest range of substantive views possible. Political constitutionalism points to a continuously evolving process of politics, including constitutional politics, in terms of political debate grounded in the principles of mutual recognition and *audi alteram partem*. The political view of the constitution opens a door for the influence of politics on the law, in that it emphasizes the negotiation of differences and a continuous quest for mutually agreeable conditions. Political constitutionalism does not attempt to sever democratic politics from questions of justice and right, but, in full acknowledgement of the impossibility of settling constitutional questions and rights issues once and for all, it makes the relation between politics, and rights and legality visible by means of a continuous political engagement with acceptable interpretations.

It can, however, be argued that political constitutionalism ultimately attempts to defend a *status quo ante*, that is the system of parliamentary supremacy. As indeed Bellamy argues in his *Political Constitutionalism*, 'the democratic arrangements found in the world's established working democracies are sufficient to satisfy the requirements of republican non-domination' (2007: 260). Indeed, Bellamy holds that

> the workings of actually existing democracies promote the constitutional goods of rights and the rule of law. Party competition and majority rule on the basis of one person one vote uphold political equality and institutionalise mechanisms of political balance and accountability that provide incentives for politicians to attend to the judgments and interests of those they govern and to recruit a wide range of minorities into any ruling coalition.
>
> (2007: viii)

Also in Waldron's work, his theoretical views start from an assumption that '[i]n general, . . . the democratic institutions are in reasonably good order' (2006: 1361), and therefore, that legal constitutionalism is mostly a threat to what otherwise would be reasonably well-functioning constitutional democracies. But there is also a sense that times are changing and that representative, liberal democracies might be facing important challenges. Bellamy acknowledges as much when he argues that '[i]t will be objected that I have praised a version of actually existing democracy that is currently passing out of existence' (2007: 260). Ultimately, however, the main argument in political constitutionalism remains that only parliamentary legislative politics can provide an inclusive and legitimate form of politics. In this, it is indirect, representative democracy that is seen as the only legitimate basis of constitutional democracy. As the same Bellamy argues '[d]eliberation, consensus, direct citizen participation through social movements, consultative juries and other mechanisms besides the ballot box – these all have their place, but a secondary one' (ibid.: 210).

Popular constitutionalism

Different theoretical conceptions of democracy have, in contrast, emphasized the importance of wider societal engagement in constitutionalism, in this going beyond a conception of constitutionalism as confined to the judicial and political societies. An example of a more societal understanding of constitutionalism is popular constitutionalism. Popular constitutionalism[10] consists of a view of constitutionalism and constitutional interpretation that is primarily formulated against a conservative view which endorses an 'originalist' view of the American constitution. Some of originalism's understandings have a distinctively legalistic flavour, in that the constitution is understood as a closed legal order that should be only open to judicial interpretation, which in itself should stay as closely as possible to an original meaning. Originalism[11] thus argues in favour of a very distinct understanding of the American constitution, that is one that remains as close as possible to the text and the 'original' understandings (for instance, that of the constitution-framers at the end of the eighteenth century and that regarding later, crucial moments of change such as the 14th Amendment; see Post and Siegel 2009: 29). In this, it strongly emphasizes a rigid separation of law from politics. In the originalist view, the 'primary purpose of the Constitution [is] to bind judicial decision making to meanings created in discrete and limited moments of constitutional lawmaking, like the 1789 founding or the 1868 ratification of the Fourteenth Amendment' (Post and Siegel 2009: 29).

Popular constitutionalism, in contrast, sees the constitution as in need of change so as to respond to changing societal views and constitutional culture. Rather than advancing a view of the constitution as ultimately grounded in a singular, true and knowable original meaning, popular constitutionalism emphasizes 'interpretive disagreement as a normal condition for the development of constitutional law' and thus the possibility of constitutional change over time as understandings of the role and substance of constitutions change (Post and Siegel 2007: 374). This also implies the questioning of the role of (constitutional and higher) courts as ultimate guardians of the constitution, and points to the role of legislators, as well as the people (in the form of citizens and civil society movements) in the interpretation of constitutional values and rights (Tushnet 1999: 11).

As argued by Mark Tushnet, if one rejects judicial supremacy in interpreting the constitution, one

> does not thereby defend an anarchic system in which the law is whatever anyone thinks it ought to be. The Declaration's principles define our fundamental law. Vigorous disagreement over what those principles mean for any specific problem of public policy does not mean that we as a society have no fundamental law in common.

> I argue throughout this book that disagreements over the thin Constitution's meaning are best conducted *by the people*, in the ordinary venues for political discussion. Discussions *among* the people are not discussions by the people *alone*, however. Politics does not occur without politicians, and political leaders play an important role in the account of populist constitutional law I develop here. Most generally, the politicians we ought to admire most are those who help us conduct our discussions with reference to the Declaration's principles, and not simply as political contests over what different groups of people happen to want.
>
> (1999: 14)

The legalistic view of constitutionalism in which the final arbiter is the judicial court is rejected, because 'the authority of the Constitution depends on its democratic legitimacy, upon the Constitution's ability to inspire the Americans to recognize it as *their* Constitution' (Post and Siegel 2007: 374). In the view of Robert Post and Reva Siegel, courts play a 'special role' in the process of a 'complex pattern of exchange' between citizens and governments over the meaning of the constitution (ibid.). However, when the courts' opinions diverge too far from the 'deeply held convictions of the American people', the latter will display resistance and make objections against court interpretations. Such popular resistance has often been interpreted as a threat to the constitution as such, but is better understood as a lively engagement of citizens with the constitution and therefore enhancing in a way its democratic legitimacy (ibid.: 375). It could even be argued that 'citizen engagement in constitutional conflict may contribute to social cohesion in a normatively heterogeneous polity' (ibid.: 377).

Societal constitutionalism

Another relevant and highly interesting debate concerns the context of a sociological approach to constitutionalism. A particularly rich and astute theory regards that of societal constitutionalism, grounded in Luhmannian theoretical concerns. The object of critique is here not just that of legal or liberal constitutionalism, but rather the 'obstinate state-and-politics centricity' of various, more established legalistic and political understandings of constitutionalism (Teubner 2012: 3). The theory is relevant to the discussion because legal constitutionalism can be understood as an amplified form of modern, state-centric constitutionalism, which renders the critique of societal constitutionalism particularly pertinent.

Much of the thrust of societal constitutionalism is towards (in particular transnational) private forms of self-steering and governance, but many of its critical insights are directly relevant for the discussion of democracy and constitutionalism here. Indeed, societal constitutionalists claim that the *problématiques* that the nation-state faces today (a variety of forms of constitutionalization beyond the state, a loss of democratic control over relevant norms) have to do with a 'basic deficiency of modern constitutionalism' (Teubner 2012: 5). Modern constitutionalism has wrongly portrayed the modern constitutional state as omni-present and as covering the whole of constitutional politics within the context of a polity: 'we should relieve politics of its delusions of omnipotence. The political constitution of the state cannot bundle the collective energies of the whole society, founding the nation's unity' (ibid.: 63). According to societal constitutionalists, the political constitution is a misrepresentation of the constitutional state of affairs, in that modern constitutionalism has always been in tension with tendencies of societal differentiation and the emergence of self-governing regimes (as, for instance, in the economy, science and the medical sphere). The current prominence of alternative constitutional regimes to the constitutional state has to do with globalizing tendencies, but these in themselves merely intensify the differentiation, fragmentation and autonomization of the social. An important emphasis, if not the *raison d'être*, of societal constitutionalism is the establishment of distinct constitutional regimes by societal actors, somewhat ambiguously called 'civil constitutions', in the absence or in direct defiance of political constitution-making.

Some of the key insights of societal constitutionalism are particularly relevant for the discussion on the democracy–constitutionalism nexus here. It provides the insights that state constitutionalism never fully integrated and controlled society, that constitutionalism can be related to non-state forms of constitutional norm production and interaction on its basis, as well as that political or legal constitutionalism potentially diminishes societal autonomy. At the same time, it seems to me that many societal constitutionalists ultimately underestimate or avoid important dimensions of the question of democratic politics by largely avoiding the questions of constituent power and collective autonomy. Teubner indeed suggests that 'we should maybe avoid the term "self-determination" when discussing other social sub-orders or we should use a purely "functional" definition of the term constitution. Or maybe we should abandon self-determination as "emphatic republicanism" and see it as only one of several possibilities for constitutional foundation' (2012: 61). Jiri Přibáň (2012), in discussing Teubner's *Constitutional*

Fragments, hints at an intrinsic 'fear of the political' in societal constitutionalism. The question of collective autonomy becomes particularly problematic when, after having suggested its potential irrelevance, Teubner actually relegates forms of autonomy to the societal sphere, while relating formal politics to potential authoritarian tendencies. It seems, then, that democratic politics, or at least forms of collective autonomy or self-government, emerge in the global civil society, whereas political constitutionalism appears as threat to civil autonomy and self-government (cf. Anderson 2012: 371). In this, Teubner makes a strong distinction between the state, the political and power, on the one hand, and society and self-governance, on the other. As observed by Jiří Přibáň:

> The paradox of the political self-denial and external expansion of the concept of constitution is a hall-mark of societal constitutionalism which both completely depoliticizes the concept of constitution and gives it the most prominent political role by relocating it to a higher level of theoretical abstraction and identifying it with both functional differentiation and societal alternatives to institutionalized politics.
>
> (2012: 457)

The problematic status of politics and the political comes further through in Teubner's take on the distinction between '*le politique*' and '*la politique*'. He narrows the distinction down – in contrast for instance to Claude Lefort's definition of this distinction – to formal politics and politics in society (Teubner 2012: 114; cf. Lindahl 2011). What is ignored here is what Lefort indicated with 'the political' or '*le politique*', that is, the foundational and ontological definition of the political in the genesis of historical societies, or the meta-political definition of what forms of social interaction are understood as political in terms of providing collectively binding decisions. In the case of the modern, democratic nation-states this entails a distinction (which Teubner in a way reproduces) between formal politics (grounded in a constitution) and social interaction (enabled by rights).

What remains obscure in such an approach regards the meta-political dimensions of autonomy, that is who are the actors that can legitimately set the rules that are binding on a wider political community and what are the foundational norms for identifying such actors (cf. Lindahl 2011: 236). Such questions are strongly related to issues of constituent power. Chris Thornhill has suggested that classical constituent power is now increasingly replaced by (transnational) rights regimes:

> the contemporary constitution establishes a deeply internalistic political system, in which the original external reference of the political system, expressed in the idea of constituent power, is superseded. Rights, recursively entered and re-entered into the political system, construct a matrix for the ongoing reproduction of society's political structure, against a societal background of extreme acentricity and external contingency.
>
> (Thornhill forthcoming: 12)

Much of the (implicit) thrust seems to be that the modern idea of collective autonomy, in which the ruled have some say over the making of the rules to which they obey, is hopelessly outdated, but it is not clear what democracy still means in a global order of civil constitutions, in which collective self-determination is understood in largely functional ways.

Democratic constitutionalism

In a final theoretical interpretation of constitutionalism I want to discuss, a critical, radical-democratic or agonistic dimension is at the forefront. The argument in 'democratic constitutionalism' is that contemporary or modern constitutionalism is deficient in terms of its democratic nature. In Joel Colon-Rios' view, democratic constitutionalism 'rests on the idea that ordinary citizens should be allowed, to the extent to which it is practically possible, to propose, deliberate, and decide on important constitutional transformations through the most participatory methods possible' (2011a: 3).

The thrust of democratic constitutionalism is against a one-sided understanding of constitutional democracy in which constitutional order and stability take the overhand over the possibility for the ruled to interfere into the setting of the rules. Main problems in contemporary constitutionalism involve exactly its depoliticizing/juridifying tendencies. In particular James Tully's historical exploration of modern constitutionalism becomes important here.[12] Contemporary state as well as global legal forms can, according to Tully, be understood on grounds of their common basis in the logics and biases of 'modern constitutionalism' (and despite the latter's fragmentary and pluralistic nature). Rather than an erosion of the significance of modern constitutionalism in a novel and fragmented post-state order, Tully observes its continuation in a form of 'informal imperialism'. The latter refers to the diffusion and imposition of modern constitutional forms – including state-based 'constitutional democracy' and 'systems of law beyond the state' – over the globe (2008a: 199). Tully's view is relevant here in that he takes the critique on legal constitutionalism to its roots, that is to the key features of modern constitutionalism as such (there is some affinity with Gunther Teubner's views here). In other words, whereas the critique of political constitutionalism, and to some extent that of popular constitutionalism, tends to remain confined to a 'test of reality'[13] of the existing constitutional order, largely reproducing its ontology, democratic constitutionalism's critique addresses the foundations of the existing constitutional paradigm.

In Tully's view, some of the key features of modern constitutionalism, and relevant for us here, include: the formality of modern constitutional forms, in that constitutional orders are 'disembedded' or separated from wider society; a constituent political power that is at the basis of constitutions; the intermediary role of a constitutive sovereign, in the modern world most commonly the state; and a meta-narrative of constitutional democracy which portrays itself as representative and universal (ibid.: 197–209). Democratic constitutionalism understands modern constitutional orders as having significant problems with democratic legitimacy, in that the constitutional meta-dimension overshadows the democratic meta-dimension. This is particularly evident on the post-national level, where global juridification reproduces some of the features of modern constitutionalism, but at the same time leaves out the democratic dimension of 'democratic deliberation of the humans who are subject to [global constitutional regimes]' (ibid.: 2008a: 101), while confining the constituent dimension to a restricted group.

A democratic constitutional approach attempts then to critically analyse the unbalanced constitutional forms and orders as well as to indicate ways of rebalancing them. What is significant is that Tully points to practices *beyond* existing institutions and sees as relevant a 'multiplicity of sites' where citizens can engage in democratic practice (ibid.: 98). Democratic constitutionalism consists of a critical, normative suggestion of how to radically rebalance the legal and democratic dimensions in the contemporary situation in favour of the democratic-participatory dimension. In this, the approach builds on a rehabilitation of non-modern, alternative experiences of 'customary constitutionalism'[14] and grass-roots struggles 'in the most effective forums' against inequalities and heteronomy that are continued through informal imperialism (ibid.: 103).

In its emphasis on a multiplicity of relevant sites of democratic practice, democratic constitutionalism has a more outspoken agonistic ring, and in this goes beyond the idea of parliamentary supremacy in political constitutionalism. What is significant is that democratic constitutionalism invokes both practices of 'democratic governance' or day-to-day democratic politics and the level of 'fundamental law' or the foundations of existing constitutional orders (in the terms of Colon-Rios 2009). In this view, the shift towards a re-evaluation of democratic politics in political constitutionalism goes quite some way, but it falls short of obtaining its own, self-set ultimate aim. As observed above, it can be argued that political constitutionalism supports the *status quo ante* of liberal representative democracy. A radical democratic view of constitutional democracy, in contrast, claims that democracy would need to entail a more direct and substantive participation of citizens in the democratic process, including constitutional or meta-politics that aims at transforming existing institutions (cf. Colon-Rios 2009).

Democratic constitutionalism shares with political constitutionalism an emphasis on the open-endedness of the democratic process, on a difference in public points of view that 'goes all the way down', and includes an ultimately open-ended view of rights. For democratic constitutionalism this means that the nature of the constitution itself is understood in a radically different way from modern constitutionalism's foundationalism. That is, whereas modern constitutionalism understands 'constitution making as an 'act of completion', the constitution as a final settlement or social contract in which basic political definitions, principles, and processes are agreed, as is a commitment to abide by them', democratic constitutionalism entails a 'conversation, conducted by all concerned, open to new entrants and new issues, seeking a workable formula that will be sustainable rather than assuredly stable' (Hart 2003: 2–3; cf. Chambers 1998). While the foundational nature of modern constitutionalism is not dissolved completely, the idea of a 'final act of closure' is replaced by one of flexibility and a 'permanently open process' (Hart 2003: 3). This derives from an unwillingness to tie down democracy to choices made by previous generations, the recognition of the continuously changing nature of society and identity, as well as the realization of the ultimate impossibility of grounding foundational principles once and for all.

Democratic constitutionalism departs significantly from political or republican constitutionalism in that it judges representative constitutional politics as insufficient. Instead, democratic constitutionalism endorses a more open democratic settlement which aims at the 'extension of democratic process to include, free, open, and responsive discussion of the constitutional settlement'. The latter provides the framework under which 'diverse and disagreeing groups can live, while continuing to engage in a freely accessible debate about that settlement itself' (Hart 2003: 5, 3). If, then, both political and democratic constitutionalism understand the constitution not as fully entrenched and pre-political, but as an outcome of the continuous political process itself, it is only in the latter that democratic politics is understood in its radical sense as the 'rule of people extended to all matters . . . , including the creation and re-creation of the fundamental laws' (Colon-Rios 2011b: 17). In democratic constitutionalism, the democratic dimension of constitutional legitimation clearly has the upper hand, even if the constitutional ordering type of legitimacy is not abandoned.

Civic constitutionalism or democratizing constitutionalism

The approach to constitutionalism taken in this book accepts much of the overlapping critique of legal constitutionalism as emerges in the various critical strands identified above. Civic constitutionalism takes inspiration from Tully's suggestions regarding an 'open-ended or non-restricted approach' to democratization. Tully suggests four dimensions that are of importance in such an approach. First, the 'democratic negotiation of norms of integration takes place not only in the official fora of the traditional public sphere, but also *wherever* individuals, groups, nations or civilizations in the EU come up against a norm of integration they find unjust and a site of disputation emerges'. In a related way, 'it is not only the official representatives of constituencies who have a right to enter into the multiplicity of public spheres, but, in principle, every member represented by an official spokesperson who is affected by the norm in question'. Second, the fundamental norms and 'procedures of negotiation' are themselves open to different interpretations, and cannot, therefore, be 'placed beyond question by some dubious argument or another about their meta-democratic status'. Third, the general norms cannot 'be imposed before-hand by an appeal to allegedly universal, necessary, or self-evident processes of modernization, democratization, juridicalization or Europeanization'. And, fourth, democratic politics is based on 'multilogues' that consist of 'on-going, open-ended and non-final constituents of a democratic way of life' (2007: 74–5).

In the analysis presented in this book, I will only focus on a few small but significant steps towards such an inclusive, participatory, post-foundationalist and open-ended approach. I will suggest a number of areas where the democratization of democracy can already be observed (even if sometimes tendencies in reverse are visible), and which could be the basis of future processes of deepening democracy. These constitutional areas include the area of constitutional change, building on the idea of constitutions as changing, open-ended structures (as in a Jeffersonian view, cf. Closa 2012); the area of democratic renewal, grounded in the idea of the importance of a multiplicity of forms of civic access and voice; and the area of constitutions as participatory vehicles, based on the idea of possibilities for self-government (the principle of self-determination).

One common thrust is the argument that legal constitutionalism tends to narrow down the space for democratic politics. Such a view becomes particularly important in the context of societal transformation. It could be argued that the constitutionalization of emerging democracies involves a paradoxical and simultaneous experience in which legalization both helps to build constitutional democracy and undermines some of its dimensions. This is not least because of a tension between a universalistic model and local capacities, in which the former takes the guise of a 'top-down transitional justice model', in which

> modernizing authoritarian rule, with external military, financial, legal, and governmental support and advisors, and subordinate local participation in institution building and processes of reconciliation, are said to be necessary stages in the development of the standard Western model of constitutionally limited representative government, elections, an official public sphere, a military tied to the West, and capitalist market open to free trade, constitutionally shielded from democratic control, and subordinated to the global economy, international trade law and institutions of global finance.
> (Tully 2012: 3)

The combined argument, undoubtedly relevant for the experiences in Central and Eastern Europe, is that the adoption of a 'new constitutionalist' model and its reinforcement by external forces has informed the marginalization of other (local) models of constitutionalism and related democratic rules and practices.

At the same time, in this book the critique of some approaches to modern constitutionalism (i.e. societal constitutionalism and Tully's democratic constitutionalism) will not be taken all the way, that is in terms of their call for 'paradigmatic' change.[15] In other words, here it will be accepted that the adoption of modern constitutionalism – at least in an incomplete way – has contributed to the democratization of the post-communist societies and could possibly be open (or have been opened) to more democratic forms of constitutionalism, based on a multiplicity of democratic channels and forms of civic participation (cf. Arato 2000, 2009). In other words, the democratization of democracy is deemed a possibility. The assumption is that constitution-making and constitutional politics are importantly about competition and conflict between social forces (including external ones) endorsing different understandings of constitutionalism, including legal or new constitutionalism, communitarian constitutionalism, and political and democratic understandings of constitutionalism.

The suggestion is – without being exhaustive – that there are at least three ways in which the institutionalization of constitutional orders has (or could have) resulted less in the construction of forms of closed constitutionalism, grounded in an emphasis on judicial review and entrenchment, and more in the construction of forms of open, democratic constitutionalism, in which there are more extensive possibilities for civic engagement.[16] Here, I suggest three significant areas, which indicate possible dimensions of more democratic forms of constitutionalism: constitutional politics, direct forms of democracy and decentralized forms of democracy.

Constitutional politics

From the point of view of democratic constitutionalism, the legal view of constitutionalism provides only limited scope for democratic self-rule. As argued by Colon-Rios and Hutchinson, '[u]nder liberal constitutionalism, democracy is exhausted by a constitution that establishes representative government, protects liberal rights and enables all citizens to "participate" in government by the episodic election of legislative representatives or through the judgements of their judicial officials' (2011: 52). As we have seen, from the point of view of various forms of critique on legal constitutionalism, such a view might be detrimental to democracy. As again Colon-Rios and Hutchinson put it:

> from a democratic standpoint, the challenge for the citizenry is not so much about defining the values of constitutions, but constitutions whose change is outside the scope of popular decision making, supposed to take place exclusively through judicial interpretation or through an amendment formula designed to make change difficult and unlikely. Too often, constitutions place checks and limits on democratic participation in the name of some other set of vaunted truths or elite-favouring values.
>
> (Ibid.: 44)

From a political-constitutionalist view, a balance between democracy and constitutionalism could be restored by shifting constitutional politics towards the legislative. In more radical accounts, in particular that of democratic constitutionalism, the citizens as such are seen as the ultimate subjects of constituent power. Such a view seems more relevant in an age in which traditional, legislative-centred representative democracy seems in great troubles invoking societal legitimacy (cf. Rosanvallon 2011). In other words, the in-built distrust towards citizen participation in legal (and to a lesser extent in political) might not provide the right answers to the decline of representative democracy, related to its elitist, technocratic, and altogether distant nature. Democratic constitutionalism takes a view of 'strong democracy', which holds that it is 'formal constitutions and their institutional paraphernalia that do more to inhibit and dull democracy's emancipatory potential than to nurture and fulfill it' (Colon-Rios and Hutchinson 2011: 44).

In this, a democratic-constitutionalist view points to possibilities of democratic self-government, not only on the level of 'politics', but also on that of the 'political'. In constitutional terms, democratic constitutionalists see possibilities for constitutional politics in which ordinary citizens play a significant role. The idea is that a 'vital dimension in the assessment of any legal norm as just is the fact that it originated in an exercise of self-legislation by the governed, not simply imposed on their behalf' (Colon-Rios and Hutchinson 2011: 48). The idea is thus that 'input-oriented legitimacy' is of crucial importance if constitutional democracy is to be revived. Such input should also relate to matters of constitutional fundamentals, meaning the 'amenability of constitutional arrangements and fundamental laws to periodic reconsideration and revision seems an indispensable part of any democratic compact' (ibid.: 49).

As Colon-Rios has argued, one can distinguish between two dimensions of democracy, one related to daily governance and the adoption of ordinary laws (democratic governance) and the other to fundamental laws (2009: 3). The first dimension of democratic governance is of great significance with regard to possibilities for civic participation and forms of civic engagement (e.g. by means of legislative initiative, various forms of electoral influence, recall procedures, and deliberative practices). However, from a radical-democratic point of view, this dimension can only play a limited role in fully realizing an ideal of popular self-rule. In other words, it is only when citizens are able to participate in the formulation of fundamental rules and laws that they are able to engage in democratic self-government. While many liberal, legal constitutions are not at all conducive to civic participation in the second, fundamental dimension, there are different mechanisms that can facilitate such involvement, and that can be found in some new constitutions as adopted in Latin America and Africa, predominantly.

Relevant mechanisms include the ideas of civic constitutional assemblies, popular constitutional initiatives and civic constitution-drafting (cf. Colon-Rios 2009: 24–6). It remains to be seen, and I will discuss this in Chapter 5, to what extent such views have also had some influence in the post-communist societies.

Various dimensions of constitutional politics or possibilities for civic influence on revision and amendment are important for a discussion of democratic constitutionalism. There is the question of whether a constitution is relatively rigid or not, that is whether it includes parts that are safeguarded from amendment, and whether the procedure to change the constitution puts up large hurdles for amendment, for instance by requiring supermajorities for constitutional changes, affirmative popular referenda, or the adoption of constitutional changes by two successive parliamentary sessions. There is also the salient question of the right to initiative, that is which actors are able to engage in the initiation of a process of constitutional change (this role can be bestowed on the executive (the president), the legislative, as well as on the wider citizenry).

Direct forms of democracy

As argued above, a major concern with liberal, legal forms of constitutionalism is its limited take on forms of civic participation and political engagement. This becomes visible in a liberal-constitutional emphasis on representative democracy, the entrenchment of fundamental rights and the endorsement of the interpretation of the constitution by a specialized body. In a political-constitutional view, the emphasis shifts towards representative politics through legislatives, also concerning fundamental norms and laws. Both constitutional perceptions have in this relatively little to offer in terms of a revival of or stimulus for civic-democratic participation and engagement as a mode of reinvigorating democratic institutions.

There is, however, increasing attention for how more participatory, deliberative and direct forms of democracy might play important roles in redirecting modern democratic regimes towards more legitimated and reciprocal forms of modern rule. This is not least visible in the context of the EU, where rights-based understandings of citizenship are understood as insufficient, and in need of complementation by republican understandings of participation.[17] One institution that has also enjoyed renewed attention from constitutionalist scholars is that of the referendum (see in particular Tierney 2012). Stephen Tierney argues it is best to see direct democracy not in contrast to representative democracy, but rather as a supplement or sometimes as a 'supplant' of representative democracy (Tierney 2012: 1; cf. Frey 2004). Obviously, for the promoters of direct democracy and referenda, the role of referenda goes further: 'referendums encapsulate the democratic ideal of government by the people' (Tierney 2012: 2). From this more radical, civic-republican perspective, representative democracy is unable to respond to demands for self-rule, and remains a form of democracy that is one step away from democratic autonomy. Be that as it may, it can in general be argued – despite critical views that understand referenda *tout court* as plebiscitarian and therefore dangerous devices – that

> [t]he referendum is fully entwined with the changing dynamics of contemporary representative government as some of the established certainties both of constitutional supremacy and of citizen trust and efficacy erode in the face of normative, political, and economic pressures which today affect the established contours of statal constitutionalism.
>
> (Ibid.: 6)

Thus, in our larger picture of the changing contours and substance of modern constitutionalism, it can be argued that forms of direct democracy, including that of referenda, play an important role in the reconfiguration of modern democracies. As Tierney goes on:

> The referendum in this sense becomes in fact a fascinating case study with which to address a changing normative architecture in which older territorial, institutional, and identificatory certainties which underpinned the unitary and hierarchical order of the constitutional state become ever more insecure and in which citizens increasingly look to new and often direct forms of political engagement to compensate for the perceived democratic failings of traditional constitutional models.
>
> (Ibid.: 6)

Relating back to the discussion of constitutional politics above, instruments of direct democracy have relevance regarding both ordinary and constitutional politics. One can, in this, make a three-fold distinction: first, direct democratic instruments that have to do with constitutional amendment (for instance, in the form of confirmatory referenda or citizens' initiative for constitutional change); second, direct democratic instruments that have to do with the wholesale adoption of new constitutions (cf. Tierney 2012: 11)[18]; and third, direct democratic instruments that have to do with civic participation in ordinary democratic governance (also this last form, even if not directly engaging with constitutional matters, has an important constitutional dimension in terms of its entrenchment as constitutional principle).

While the most common direct democratic, constitutional instrument is probably the popular referendum (in the cases of constitutional amendment or wholesale renewal) (cf. Frey 2004: 3–4), it could be argued that in its standard execution (that is, an often political elite-initiated form of change or renewal which is subsequently to be approved or confirmed through a referendum) a popular referendum is only rather marginally about civic participation. As Colon-Rios (2011b) has argued, popular referenda are not infrequently lacking in widespread public deliberation and contain questions on pre-designed alternatives. In this regard, other, more innovative and novel instruments should be considered as part of a direct-democratic repertoire. Such instruments include constituent assemblies which combine civic participation with deliberative methods[19] and could include mechanisms by means of which such assemblies can be triggered by citizens themselves (while more traditionally such assemblies are invoked by legislatures).[20]

Decentralization of democracy

A further dimension of democratic innovation is that of the (radical) decentralization of, and enhancement of (local) participatory mechanisms in, national democratic systems. Decentralization offers some potential for the reinvigoration of democracy and citizen participation, in the sense of providing opportunities for citizens to engage in the creation of common rules for living together, for instance in the form of direct participation through referenda or legislative initiative. Even though one should be aware of the pitfalls involved, decentralized forms of democracy might offer an effective and viable antidote to a closed and elitist democratic-constitutional order. The constitutional dimension is relevant here, even if not widely discussed in this sense, in that the enshrinement of the right to self-government and the constitutionalization of dimensions of local democratic self-government can importantly help to entrench possibilities for local civic engagement. As, for instance, argued by Martin Loughlin, '[the role of law] is an aspect of central-local government relations which is neglected in many contemporary studies and yet is of vital importance in identifying the character of that relationship' (1996: 1).

One set of examples of a radical-democratic constitutionalism specifically promoting popular participation and decentralization relates to Latin America in a recent, 'fourth wave' of constitutional reform (Colon-Rios 2011c). Among the aims in this novel constitutional model are the promotion of civil society participation in government and the political inclusion of disempowered parts of society, stemming from a critical approach towards representative democracy. What is significant here is that the monistic and centralistic approach of liberal and legal constitutionalism (cf. Tierney 2004: 9) is rejected in favour of a constitutional order that promotes diversified political access to various groups and communities. One reason why such a model might be relevant in the Central and Eastern European context is that a similar tradition of civil society thinking and activity exists, and that a similar question in post-authoritarian constitution-making relates to how to meaningfully institutionalize forms of civil society while keeping bottom-up politics open to renewal and innovative practices (Olvera 2013). It should at the same time be acknowledged, as forcefully argued by James Tully (2008a), that decentralization of constitutional democratic systems carries with it the risk of a weakening of political decision-making powers. In the neo-liberal ideology that became dominant in the 1980s, local democracy was not endorsed on the basis of the principle of self-government, but rather to diminish the influence of the centralized state and enhancing the role of society, notably in the form of economic agents. This is a dimension that is clearly significant also for the new democracies in Central and Eastern European dimensions (see Ost 2011).

While this dimension cannot be denied, and should be carefully taken into account, it can equally be argued that local democracy, if institutionalized in a robust way, might contribute to democratic autonomy and enhance relevant influence of society on democratic politics. In an understanding different from the neo-liberal view, a civic-republican view has emerged – in particular from the 1990s onwards and not unrelated to the notion of civil society that emerged in the 1980s in Central Europe – that purports 'that political decentralization and local autonomy were important elements of democracy itself' (Loughlin *et al.* 2011: 5). Strengthening local government and democracy could then for a number of reasons be seen as potentially enhancing the quality of a democratic state. Such democratization of democracy might result from the proximity of local politics to the citizens, the higher accessibility of local politics to participation, in particular if in the form of direct and deliberative forms of democracy (Schiller 2011), and the shorter reaction time of local government to policy issues (Bailey and Elliott 2009: 436). As Rosanvallon has argued, the relevant notion of 'proximity' has increasingly gained foothold since the 1990s (he mostly discusses the French context), and does 'not so much designate a precise object as suggest a preoccupation'. As he continues,

> [proximity] indicated that the usual language and concepts of politics no longer seemed adequate to express the expectations of citizens . . . it expressed in a general way the sense that distant, aloof government would no longer do – distance and aloofness being proximity's opposites. Proximity was not only an expression of value but also the core of a justificatory ideology. Leaders appropriated the term in the hope of regaining lost legitimacy, while citizens seized on it to express their disillusionment and their hopes for change.
>
> (2011: 4282–90)

In political-theoretical terms, the local democratic narrative that emphasizes the democratic surplus value of local democracy can be understood as a kind of amalgam of republican political thought (emphasizing civic virtue, public autonomy and civic engagement), communitarianism (politics close to the citizens), as well as ideas of deliberative democracy (politics as based on inclusion, deliberation and consensus-building). It seems undeniable that at least in superficial terms this narrative has become increasingly important in addressing problems of policy-making in European democracies. One clear sign of this is the emphasis on regionalization in European integration and the adoption of the European Charter of Local Self-Government (1985).

The increased attention for forms of decentralization, public participation and forms of participatory and direct democracy has emerged, interestingly, exactly in a period in which constitutional democracy is increasingly subject to great tensions and transformations. First, in Europe there is the evident shift in political and constitutional weight towards the European level. In other words, the overlap and concentration of jurisdiction, territory, and people is increasingly less evident as important decisions and politics regarding a variety of political communities are taken outside of those communities. Second, in a related way, there is the increasing complexity and arcane streak that matters of governance and democratic politics display, not least through forms of technocratization and juridification. Third, there is the increasing civic disattachment – in both East and West – vis-à-vis representative democratic politics. National political elites and institutions are profoundly lacking in civic trust and legitimacy.

In normative terms, it can be argued that local self-government might – at least in some circumstances – provide a partial antidote to these democratic deficits and disengagement. This is so in a number of ways. First, the strengthening of local democracy potentially makes constitutional democracies more pluralistic, in that political power becomes divided and diffused on the vertical level, which helps to avoid, on the one hand, the political hegemony of central governmental institutions (a salient objective in former totalitarian societies) and, on the other, might help recover some of the lost grasp of democratic sovereignty on politics. Second, local self-government makes it easier for citizens to participate in democratic politics and governance in a meaningful way than it would be when politics is completely centralized. Third, and as is probably most famously argued by J.S. Mill, local possibilities for democratic participation might help to foster sentiments of public autonomy among the citizenry:

> It is necessary, then, that, in addition to the national representation, there should be municipal and provisional representations; and the two questions which remain to be resolved are, how the local representative bodies should be constituted, and what should be the extent of their functions. In considering these questions, two points require an equal degree of our attention: how the local business itself can be best done, and how its transaction can be made most instrumental to *the nourishment of public spirit and the development of intelligence*.
>
> (2004: 512; emphasis added)

Fourth, local self-government might in some instances also be a more effective type of government, in that it is more likely to have a capacity of responsiveness, in terms of responding to local problems according to local views.

Local government and democracy are, however, no obvious panacea to democratic and governance problems. Stephen Bailey and Mark Elliott have recently argued that local government is only likely to deliver the goods when a 'virtuous circle' is created, that is a situation in which 'the obvious importance and responsiveness of local government incentivizes the participation of individuals in local politics and elections' (2009: 436). In other words, '[a]ttempts to strengthen local democracy must, on this view, go hand-in-hand with attempts to strengthen local government'. In reality, however, many central governments have failed to induce such a virtuous circle 'within which strong local democracy and powerful institutions of local government enjoy a symbiotic, mutually constructive relationship'. Rather, governments have tended to contribute to a 'vicious circle' in which 'extensive central control, the consequent limitations to local power and autonomy and the disengagement of individuals and communities are factors that are mutually reinforcing' (ibid.: 437).

In this, local democracy has obvious constitutional dimensions. This brings us to the process of the constitutionalization of subnational democracy. In the case of the post-communist societies, an important question to ask is whether the transformation process has significantly contributed to the consolidation of vital constitutional democracies, which involve robust dimensions of pluralized and decentralized politics and the promotion of active citizenship, or whether constitutional democracy has largely remained a fiction (cf. Skapska 2011: 9). Any attempt at answering this question will need to take into account the foundations of these new democracies, and will have to enquire into whether the new democratic regimes are conducive or not to civic democracy. Indeed, with regard to subnational self-government, the assessment of a 'virtuous circle' of local government and democracy as identified by Bailey and Elliott above needs a holistic view of the place of local government and democracy in the wider democratic-constitutional order. This means that the problems related to stimulating a virtuous form of local democracy 'can be fully faced up to only if important questions about the legal and constitutional role of local government are squarely addressed' (ibid.: 437). In other words, the foundations of decentralization and devolution are significant and need to be explicit and clear-cut if a virtuous type of local government and democracy is to be expected to emerge.

In the context of democratic constitutionalism, various instruments of local self-government are relevant. In general, what is important is that the 'state is granting local self-government with meaningful jurisdictions and not only administrative tasks under central control' (Schiller 2011: 9). In the more distinctive sense of local democracy as a context for civic engagement and participation, many forms of democratic channels and instruments can be pointed to, not least because this is an area that throughout Europe is subject to experimentation and reform. In this book, a number of instruments beyond representative politics will be emphasized, even if it is acknowledged that a robust form of representative politics on the local level is significant in its own right. But civic participation is more at the core of reforms related to direct democracy, in particular in the form of (different types of) referenda, legislative initiatives and recall procedures (see Schiller 2011: 15–17). But these instruments could evidently be just the forefront of possibly more experimental mechanisms, such as local deliberative fora or participatory budgeting.

Concluding remarks

Much of the theoretical critique on legal constitutionalism appears convincing and warrants further – including comparative-empirical – analysis. The thrust in political constitutionalism against strong judicial review and in favour of a hold of representative politics on constitutional values is shared here, as it emphasizes a view of democracy as an open-ended process, rather than as a closed political form grounded in pre-political essentials or pre-commitments (which in themselves are identified by enlightened theorists). The understanding that constitutional politics should be open to a plurality of points of view is in agreement with such a democratic imaginary. The arrest of political constitutionalism before democratic politics beyond parliamentary, representative forms is, however, not shared here. Rather, the observation that current representative democracies experience forms of fatigue and crisis is accepted, and the assumption that new (or forgotten, old) forms of democratic participation should be explored forms the basis of the understanding of constitutional democracy in this book. In constitutional theory, some resonance regarding these concerns can be found in a number of approaches that contest a view of constitutionalism that presupposes a strong distinction between the constitution and society. In popular constitutionalism, this is visible in an understanding of constitutions as needing to reflecting societal views and change, and the acceptance of the role of political and societal actors in constitutional politics. In a very different manner, societal constitutionalism strongly criticizes the formal-political emphasis in constitutional theory, and attempts to detach the idea of constitutionalism from formal, and in particular state, politics altogether. Societal constitutionalism in general might be affected by a 'fear of the political', and in this suggests an a-political form of societal self-governance, avoiding, however, crucial questions of collective autonomy and political access for the many. It is, then, above all in democratic constitutionalism that the challenge of democratizing constitutionalism is taken up most explicitly. Here, the idea that constitutional politics should be explicitly opened up to citizens' proposals, deliberations and decisions is endorsed. I have argued above that in democratic constitutionalism, we see an important, alternative conceptualization of the constitution emerging, that is not so much as a negative frame for democratic politics, but rather as a vehicle for inclusive, democratic political interaction and as a continuous deliberative process on the fundamental values of a political community.

My argument – and subsequent comparative empirical analysis (see Chapters 3 to 6) – is sympathetic to much of what is claimed in the critical approaches to legal constitutionalism. On the basis of these critiques, I have outlined a variety of democratic constitutionalism, which I have called *civic constitutionalism*. The thrust of this approach is that it is possible the democratize the democratic-constitutional state, and that a number of dimensions are of immediate importance, including the dimensions of constitutional politics and change, the dimensions of alternative, direct forms of democracy, and the dimension of decentralized democracy. Much of the inspiration for the civic-constitutional approach is provided by an 'activist' view of constitutions in which citizens potentially play an active role (cf. Frankenberg 1997), the ideas of weak constitutionalism (cf. Albert 2008; Colon-Rios 2012) and democratic constitutionalism (Tully 2008a). These critical approaches suggest that viable constitutional democracy needs the active inclusion and participation of civil society. In this view, constitutions are understood as vehicles of democracy and as co-constituting civil society and the public sphere.

In the rest of the book, I will explore the constitutionalization of democracy in five new democracies (the Czech Republic, Hungary, Poland, Romania and Slovakia) from this perspective. In Chapter 3, I will analyse the emergence of legal constitutionalism and analyse to what extent some of the negative, disabling dimensions of a legalistic constitutionalism are evident in the new democracies. In Chapter 4, I will explore an alternative, historical narrative of constitutionalism that can be identified in some of the dissident ideas that emerged in the later decades of communism. In Chapter 5, I will comparatively analyse to what extent we can equally identify positive, enabling dimensions in the constitutions of the new democracies, exploring constitutional dimensions that provide possible counterweights to legal constitutionalism. In Chapter 6, I will place the constitutionalization process of the new democracies in the context of European integration, and indicate significant problems and tensions that have emerged in the integration process regarding the balance between democracy and constitutionalism in the region.

Notes

1 A significant exception can be found in the work of Wojciech Sadurski; see, e.g., Sadurski (2008). See also Puchalska (2011); Skapska (2011).
2 A classical statement is Dworkin (1995).
3 For discussions, see Colon-Rios (2011a); Goldoni (2010).
4 At the same time, it can be argued that the nature, form and distinct functions of the constitution in – and increasingly also beyond – modern democratic realities is an ever more frequent object of dispute. This is

not least because of the profound changes that affect constitutional democracies and constitutionalism as a result of processes of globalization and sub-state empowerment, as well as internal transformations of the modern polity and democratic politics, and related diversification of democratic imaginaries.

5 A concise version of this discussion can be found in Blokker (forthcoming, 2013).

6 One of the best-known formulations of such an idea is that of an 'overlapping consensus' (Rawls 1993; cf. Bellamy 2007: 101–2).

7 Judith Shklar, cited in Goldoni (2012: 929).

8 Relevant trends include the emergence of alternative (transnational, international, non-state) authorities that claim constitutional capacity and some hold on sovereignty, beyond or parallel to the traditional sovereign nation-state. The European Union is the most significant and evolved example of this (other such phenomena include the World Trade Organization and human rights charters). But constitutionalization beyond the state equally includes private, economic actors that engage in the production of 'self-validating contracts' and 'closed circuits' that differ from state legal orders not only in terms of geographical site but also in terms of the novel, self-referential quality of the norms themselves (cf. Teubner 1997). A concomitant, but not altogether overlapping, trend is that of a devolution and differentiation of democratic sovereignty towards sub-state levels. This trend is related to processes of post-state constitutionalization, but is much more importantly inspired by political resistance to imposed, Western forms of majoritarian constitutionalism and by political projects for cultural recognition, regional autonomy and self-government.

9 Here, I will not be able to extensively address the highly salient question of post-national constitutionalism and its relation to new constitutionalism.

10 I refer here to a wider debate which also includes the 'democratic constitutionalism' of Post and Siegel (see Post and Siegel 2007, 2009) as well as Tushnet's 'populist constitutionalism' (Tushnet 1999), but here I will use 'popular constitutionalism' so as to be able to distinguish between the American, populist approach and James Tully's (and others') project of democratic constitutionalism. Further, I realize that I am side-stepping some differences between various contributors to the progressivist debate (e.g. between Post and Siegel and Kramer), but I hope that the main thrust I present here is indeed one that is shared by the various contributors. Many contributors discussed here are now contributing to the debate on the 'Constitution 2020'. For a subtle and historically grounded discussion of popular constitutionalism, see Colon-Rios (2011a).

11 For a discussion of various strands within originalism, see Colon-Rios (2011a).

12 Other relevant and related approaches are 'weak constitutionalism' (Albert 2008; Colon-Rios 2011b) and 'participatory constitutionalism' (Hart 2003). Anderson mentions Tully's approach in a discussion of 'paradigmatic readings of globalization', as opposed to 'sub-paradigmatic approaches' (these are de Sousa Santos' terms) (Anderson 2012: 381). Using the language of Cornelius Castoriadis, one could refer to Tully's work, and democratic constitutionalism more in general, as having an 'instituting' thrust, as opposed to an 'instituted' one.

13 Reality tests can be related to a reformist type of critique. The latter attempts to close an observed gap between the order of symbolic propositions and the order of the state of affairs (for instance, when a president is said to have acted unconstitutionally). As such, though, the reality test does not threaten instituted reality, but ultimately corrects it (Boltanski 2009).

14 As argued by Tully, a customary approach to constitutionalism is radically different from the modern one, in that it entails a 'different idea of constituent power', in that 'the constituent powers of humans (and non-humans) are always already immanent in the specific forms of transposable *habitus* they take in the countless normative relationships of interaction (non-formal customary laws) that humans and non-humans both bear and transform *en passant*' (2008b: 469 emphasis in the original). In other words, constituent power is not something prior to or outside of (democratic) interaction, but intermingled with the latter.

15 Although an underlying view of understanding constitutions (as in particular endorsed by Tully) as flexible structures that ought to be re-created *en passant* and in a participatory way forms clearly an inspiration for civic constitutionalism.

16 Up to a certain, even if rather limited, extent, distinct dimensions of a more democratic constitutionalism have been institutionalized in the five new democracies under discussion; see Chapter 5.

17 Even if the institution of a European Citizens' Initiative 2012 can be understood as the institutionalization of a republican view of civic participation, instruments of this type are in general not robust, neither on the supranational, nor on national and subnational levels. A related discussion is the critical reading of in particular 'new governance' approaches (Smismans 2007).

18 Tierney refers to these two types as 'constitution-changing' and 'constitution-framing' instruments, referring to referenda (2012: 11).

19 An experiment along these lines was recently undertaken in, for instance, Iceland. A recent, less citizen-driven experiment was that of the European constitutional convention; see, e.g., Frey (2004).

20 Other instruments that should perhaps be discussed more extensively here are less related to influencing representative democratic institutions, but rather to influencing judicial review (such as in the Hungarian institution of *actio popularis*) or the protection of rights (for instance, by means of the institution of ombudsman). I will briefly allude to the former in the concluding chapter, but not extensively discuss these in the rest of the book (but see, e.g., Kurczewski and Sullivan 2002).

3 The prominence of legal constitutionalism in the new democracies

The centrality of legalism, constitution-making and human rights in the radical changes in 1989 in Central and Eastern Europe has been widely noticed and analysed. One can notice, however, a certain tendency in prioritizing the external and modernizing (or catching-up) dimensions in democratization and constitutionalization (e.g. Magen and Morlino 2009; Morlino and Sadurski 2010). These include, for instance, the adherence to an apparent European standard (as displayed by the constitutional traditions in Western Europe, in particular those of Germany and France) as well as the adaptation process to the European integration project (in terms of EU accession, conditionality and the *acquis*). Comparative attention for local constitutional and democratic traditions and experiences tends to be less upfront. In this, there is a risk of downplaying some of the complexities related to local factors and tensions in the process of democratization, and exaggerating the positive effects of the adoption of 'tested' institutions and structures. Legality, the rule of law, and constitutionalism as available in longstanding democratic societies are often seen as the extreme opposite of the reality of the communist regimes, and hence are logically taken as the core of the post-communist transformation process. But potential risks and dilemmas in the building of democracy are not always sufficiently appreciated.

In this chapter, I will discuss the emergence of legal constitutionalism from a historical and political-sociological perspective, emphasizing local dimensions to this process. I will start with a brief discussion of some of the intricacies of the constitutional dimensions of the communist regimes, and provide a concise account of the understandings of legalism and rights that were involved in the dissident struggle against the communist regimes, and the (modest) constitutional reforms initiated by some of the latter.[1] The significance of this lies not least in the way these phenomena interacted with the emergence in the region of legal constitutionalism in the post-1989 period. In the second part of the chapter, I will comparatively explore to what extent the constitutional orders of the new democracies can be said to adhere to a legal-constitutionalist paradigm in a meaningful sense.

Socialist legality

The 'socialist legality' that underpinned the political structure of communist regimes was based upon 'paper constitutions' that had very little to do with the Western understanding of the rule-of-law (in either a procedural or substantive sense). In a superficial way, these constitutions were rather a fiction or form of symbolism (in a pejorative sense) that displayed a huge discrepancy with the arbitrary nature of political-legal reality (cf. Skapska 2011). But it can be argued that the communist constitutions and legal orders were more complex, in that they had a dual nature; that is, on one the hand, the law could be used to exercise terror and to persecute enemies of the communist project, but, on the other hand, the law could equally be used 'as an engineering tool in the pursuit of social welfare'. As argued by Inga Markovits, '[t]he fact that the Party could choose whether to use the law for benign or repressive purposes made the normative state vulnerable to attacks from its prerogative counterpart' (2007: 238). It could be argued that while the 'paper' communist constitutions helped to enhance existing traditions of 'us and them', or, in other words, a deep distrust of society against the ruling elites, there was at the same time some attempt at creating order and social integration around a positive constitutional dimension in the form of aspirations and social rights. In other words, the law was like two laws: 'the law of political repression and that of ordinary daily life' (ibid.: 237). One result of the latter might have been a certain emphasis on social rights and welfare in constitutionalism (and political cultural expectations) after 1989 (Sajó 1996, 2004).

Communist constitutions followed the original Stalinist model of 1936 in a fairly uniform way. The constitutions of the Central and Eastern European countries all clearly reflected the dominant ideology of communism, which served as a justification for the entire political and economic order of the communist regimes, and the dominant role of the communist party as the ultimate authority in these systems. In external terms, the constitutions also conveyed close relations (usually termed 'friendship') with the Soviet Union (Skapska 2011: 81). The Stalinist constitutions had a logic largely diverse from modern constitutionalism in at least two senses. First of all, Stalinist constitutions were of a declaratory as well as aspirational kind. These constitutions declared the scientific superiority of the socialist project as well as invoked specific state goals that were to be met. Stalinist constitutions thus included most importantly references to the Marxist ideology, the vanguard role of the party and the international community of communist states. Arjomand in fact includes Stalinist constitutions in the type which he calls 'ideological constitutions', which indicates that these 'constitutions [were] instruments of social transformation according to total ideologies [and] marked by the subservience of narrowly conceived rule of law and legality to the dominant ideology of the regime' (2003: 9). And in Günter Frankenberg's terms, the communist constitutions were 'plan or program constitutions': 'Program constitutions translate the "laws of scientific socialism" and historical materialism into ideological blueprints for socio-economic and political-cultural development. From a higher-law viewpoint they are dismissed as "façade constitutions"' (ibid.).

The declaratory nature also regarded the extensive catalogues of rights that were included in all these constitutions, not least social rights, such as the right to work or the right to housing. Despite these extensive references to rights, these constitutions were not juridical constitutions, and rights were not understood as entitlements of citizens against the state, but mostly as granted by the party–state, and therefore subject to the arbitrariness of interpretation by the communist party apparatus. Also, rights were interpreted within the context of communist ideology, and could therefore not be invoked against the communist goals of the regime.[2] But even such limited socialist legality was anyhow not guaranteed in that the actual constitutional text did not provide the basis for court rulings or any other form of legal certainty, but was rather open to the interpretation of the communist party elites, who provided the ultimate reading of the constitutional principles. What is more, the invocation of one's constitutionally enshrined civil rights was always risky in that one could be classified as 'enemy of socialism' (Frankenberg 2003: 85–6).

Second, the main function of Stalinist constitutions included that of social guidance. Communist constitutions were supposed to lead the way through the various stages of development towards the ultimate communist goal. As again Frankenberg argues:

> They offer a frame of reference for political unity and collective identity, and they mirror and project stages of progress along the guidelines provided by Karl Marx, V. I. Lenin, Mao Tse-tung, and other such authorities. Moreover, program constitutions tend to become obsolete and need revision, once the ruling cadres decide, on the basis of their superior insight into the laws of development

> and the authoritative scriptures, that a certain developmental stage has been reached.
>
> (2006: 453–4)

In the ultimate instance, the communist constitutions should contribute to the creation of 'Soviet man', a member of communist society 'liberated' from ethnic, religious, or other social ties and fully in service of the communist state (Skapska 2011: 82).

Rights and legal revolutions

The changes that accelerated in 1989 (but had been maturing since at least a decade) were in part the outcome of claims for taking seriously existing constitutional arrangements. In other words, an important part of the struggle against communism had been based on a legal language of rights and the invocation of the existence of such rights in a formal sense against the abuses of the political regime. It was in particular Charter 77 in Czechoslovakia that had started to use the language of rights in order to contest the illegitimate nature of political practices of the communist regime. In the original declaration of Charter 77, the adherence to the Helsinki Act of 1975 by the incumbent regime was welcomed, but at the same the validity only on paper denounced (Charter 77: 1977). Also in Poland the rights language played a crucial role in the discourse of what can be regarded the most important and visible dissident movement in the region, Solidarnosc. In the Thesis 23 of its 1980 declaration, a document which is generally referred to as the 'Self-Governing Republic', Solidarnosc stated: '[The] legal system must guarantee basic civic freedoms, [and] respect principles of equality of all citizens and all institutions of public life before the law.'[3]

Admittedly, already in the 1960s protesters in the Soviet Union had called for a 'respect for the constitution' (Cătănuş 2011: 187). The rights language proved an important means of dissent, and was invoked not only in the more rebellious societies (Czechoslovakia, Hungary, Poland), but also in an extremely closed society such as the post-1971 Romania of Nicolae Ceauşescu. Here it was, among others, the writer Paul Goma as well as the historian Vlad Georgescu who invoked human rights in a protest against the regime. Goma argued against 'this lack of fundamental rights, this derision of man, this shamelessness of lies – everywhere. Everywhere: poverty, economic chaos, demagogy, insecurity, terror' (Goma 1979; cf. Stănescu 2004). And Georgescu directly invoked the Romanian Constitution in his writings, and argued that the 'Romanian dissent recognizes the Constitution of the country and asks for nothing but its firm keeping, in its spirit and letter' (Cătănuş 2011a: 189–90).

As Jiří Přibáň has argued, the rights dimension to the dissident discourse, in Czechoslovakia, but to different extents also in Poland and Hungary, and as we have seen, in more isolated forms also in Romania and other societies, was a crucial dimension in the struggle against totalitarianism and paper constitutions. Indeed, '[t]he basic strategy of the Czechoslovak dissidents was to exploit the distance between the concept of socialist legality and political reality' (Přibáň 2002: 166). Přibáň speaks about a dual language of dissidents that comprised a legalist strategy, emphasizing that the communist regime should live up to its superficial claim to legality and the rule of law. This strategy was, however, closely related to a second one, a moral strategy, in which a particular, substantive idea of the rule of law was invoked. In other words, the rule of law was inextricably related to distinct values, according to the dissidents, in particular those enshrined in human rights. This emphasis on human rights as sacred and inviolable was, then, the starting point for a possibility for people to experience autonomy and authenticity, what Havel called to 'live in truth'.

The deep changes at the end of the 1980s could be seen in terms of a rights revolution, or, in slightly different terms, as the culmination of a spun-out process in which the notion of human rights gained an ever more normative foothold in the communist societies. This was reflected in both the language of the dissident movements, as seen above, and in the declarations and actions of the communist regimes. As put by Irina Grudzinska-Gross, the legal and constitutional changes from above in the 1970s ultimately brought about the 'gradual change that permitted the peaceful and orderly transitions of 1989' (Grudzinska-Gross 1997: 65). The changes of 1989 displayed, in this, another legal dimension which equally referred to the rule of law, but rather than a substantive view emphasising the protection of individual rights, it followed the legal-positivistic doctrine of legal continuity. In other words, the notion of legal revolutions reflects the idea that the comprehensive and in many ways systematic changes in 1989 were to be somehow managed with the limits of the existing constitutional and legal rules. The most clear-cut case of this was probably that of Hungary. As argued by Petr Paczolay, '[t]he consciously chosen Hungarian way was through so-called "constitutional revolution", which means the choice of law instead of power, not only for the future political system, but also as the basis for the mode of transition' (Paczolay 1993: 560). It is in this light not surprising that the Hungarian constitutional trajectory was until very recently (1 January 2012) defined by legal and constitutional continuity with the communist constitution of 1949 (Law XX/1949).

The transformative moment of 1989 then frequently followed the idea of legal continuity, and attempts to revolutionize the political orders from within by preserving and using the rules of revision of the constitutions of the old communist order (Arato 2000: 172). This is, as Andrew Arato has pointed out, an original choice in a context in which past institutions had little to offer for political forces that wanted to install some kind of liberal-democratic constitutional order. The emphasis on legal continuity was then above all an attempt to create an orderly transition, or a 'self-limiting revolution', that would result in a complete, revolutionary revision of the existing institutions without legal rupture or vacuum. Legal continuity as a guiding principle was particularly visible in the Polish and Hungarian transformations, and to an extent also in the cases of Czechoslovakia and Bulgaria. Indeed, in the case of Hungary the constitution of the old order remained the basis of the new constitution (until 2012). In this, the Constitutional Court was the main actor in promoting legal continuity as the creation of the rule of law by means of the rule of law (Arato 2000: 174). As stated by the then President of the Hungarian Constitutional Court:

> The Constitutional Court has played a major role in 'harmonizing' preconstitutional norms with the Constitution through a process of abstract judicial review. The new Constitution did not automatically suspend pre-existing laws. Instead, it required Parliament to review all pre-constitutional laws and regulations to insure that they would be consistent with the newly established Constitution. In the process, such old laws acquired validity in the new system.
> (Solyom 1994: 224)

It should be said, however, that this logic was much less prominent in other cases, notably that of Romania, where no negotiated transformation took place, but rather a second layer of the communist party took over political power, which in the form of the newly erected National Salvation Front dominated the constitution-making process. And even if subsequent events invoked some of the symbols of negotiation, and the constitutional assembly pretended a negotiatory nature, much of the transformation was predominated by the post-communist National Salvation Front (Carp and Stanomir 2008).[4]

The negotiated transformation was then predominantly a feature of the Hungarian and Polish transformations, even if constitution-making and the idea of the rule of law played a crucial role in all post-communist societies. On the level of ideas, it can be argued that an innovative mode of transition, as found in particular in Central and Eastern European countries, was grounded in an anti-foundationalist understanding of the changes. In other words, the revolutionary past, which had been based on the idea of a violent, *ex nihilo* creation of a new societal order from above, was denied in favour of a gradual and bottom-up approach – inspired by what Michnik had called 'new evolutionism'[5] – that is, the non-violent, peaceful negotiation of a new order with the involvement of new and old political forces.

New constitutionalism

A region-wide emphasis on legal constitutionalism is in the light of the dimensions discussed above – the dissident emphasis on human rights and the language of legalism shared by communist reformers and opposition forces – not surprising. A further significant reason for the emphasis on legalism, legal continuity and the rule of law can be found in the fact that legalism was perceived as an antidote to the 'ideological' (Arjomand 2003) or 'contradictory' (Přibáň and Sadurski 2006) socialist legality of the communist regimes. As has been argued by Kim Lane Scheppele, the constitutions emerging in the region after 1989 were predominantly 'not-like-that constitutions'.[6] In this, the dominant discourse in the region had affinity with legal constitutionalism. The latter could be related to a constitutional-ontological position, to which Wojciech Sadurski has referred as a 'moral realist position', that is the idea that 'the correct meaning of rights is objectively discernible by human reason, with the correct institutional incentives optimising the circumstances in which the ascertainment of the right meaning is likely' (2008: 28). Such a position can, among others, be derived from the views of those that have argued for a strong position of constitutional courts and a related status of the constitution as higher law.

The post-1989 'return' to constitutionalism and the rule of law or, at the very least, the complete rejection of the instrumentalization of the law for political purposes reconnected with a trend of globally emerging constitutionalism. As discussed in Chapter 2, in recent times a distinct understanding of the modern constitutional form has emerged. By the early twenty-first century, new constitutionalism (Arjomand 2003; Stone Sweet 2008, 2009) has allegedly become predominant, even if not uncontested. In the new democracies, the role of new constitutionalism has not least been seen as one of securing the transition to robust constitutional democratic orders. What makes new constitutionalism relevant in the East-Central European situation includes, among others, the following dimensions: the (re-)establishment of sovereign, democratic orders grounded in the rule of law, the idea of constitutional law as a higher law (and thus particularly entrenched against the influence from politics), the idea of fundamental rights and the idea of a guardian of the constitution in the form of a constitutional court. In other words, new constitutionalism provides one possible way of protecting societies from succumbing to totalitarianism and dictatorship. The emphasis, in this, is on written constitutions with an entrenched 'catalogue of rights', and a 'system of constitutional justice to defend those rights' (Stone Sweet 2008: 219). The constitutional court plays a primary role in the protection of society in that it is an independent institution, which is not only regarded as the ultimate guardian and interpreter of the constitution, but equally so of fundamental rights. Much emphasis in democratic transition has then been on legal formalism and coherence, and constitutionally entrenched democratic preconditions, while democratic participation was largely confined to 'normal politics'.

The first feature that characterizes new constitutionalism is an understanding of constitutionalism as closely related to the ideas of politico-legal autonomy and state sovereignty (cf. Preuss 2010; Tully 2008; Wiener 2008). My contention here is that new constitutionalism reproduces, and in some ways even strengthens, the 'classical' modern understanding of sovereignty. A classical view of sovereignty is explained in a particularly apt way by Martin Loughlin: '[s]overeignty is to be understood as a representation of the autonomy of the political, and as providing the foundational concept of the discipline of public law' (2003: 56). And,

> sovereignty has been devised for the purpose of giving expression to the distinctively political bond between a group of people and its mode of governance. Sovereignty comes into existence through a process in which a group of people within a defined territory is moulded into an orderly cohesion through the establishment of *a governing authority that can be differentiated from society and which is able to exercise an absolute political power*. This concept of sovereignty is bound up with the emergence of the modern state and the establishment of an institutionalised form of government which is able to impose itself on society as an instrument of power.
>
> (Ibid.; emphasis added)

New constitutionalism follows a traditional understanding of state sovereignty,[7] that is sovereignty as indicating the relative autonomy of the state from both the external world (external sovereignty) and the internal citizenry (internal sovereignty). But it does so with a twist, in that 'absolute political power' is now juridically circumscribed and (partially) taken over by specialized legal institutions. The affinity also means that part of the ontology of new constitutionalism corresponds to 'constitutional nationalism', that is the idea that sovereignty is grounded in a national state, which has the 'final word' (cf. Frankenberg 2003: 48).[8] In this regard, it could be argued that new constitutionalism corresponds to, or amplifies, conventional modern constitutionalism (cf. Wiener 2008), in which the constitutional form or order, popular sovereignty as constituent power, and the state as sovereign actor (in a Hobbesian sense) form a whole in a contentious set of relations (cf. Tully 2008a: 202). In this, state sovereignty reflects a form of relatively autonomy of the state, also vis-à-vis its own subjects: a 'modern constitution, Kant famously argued, does not arise from the spontaneous interaction of the pre-civil people but requires some kind of master or legislator to impose law on the crooked timber of the people and to act without their consent and independent of law in exceptional circumstances until they are "civilised" by centuries of subjection to civil law' (Tully 2008a: 203). New constitutionalism tends to reproduce the modern constitutional tradition in its division of legal and political power from society (by means of embedding such powers in a constitutional order grounded in stability and what Tully has called formality), and further separating a legal guardianship over the ground rules from democratic politics and popular sovereignty. One might argue that in new constitutionalism, there is a tendency to resolve the tension inherent in modern constitutionalism between state sovereignty and popular sovereignty in favour of the former. In other words, a constitutional order which safeguards the state and its people constrains the execution of popular sovereignty on the nature of the constitutional order itself.

This dimension of new constitutionalism seems relevant in the new democracies in that at least one scholar has argued that the new constitutions adopted in the region display a disproportionate 'souverainist' character. Albi argues that a 'characteristic feature of the post-Communist constitutions of Central and Eastern Europe is that they are distinctively more protective of sovereignty than most constitutions in Western Europe' (2005: 24; cf. Albi 2003). According to Albi, '[a]utonomous control or even statehood having been (re-)established merely a decade ago, Central and Eastern European countries (CCEEs) operate firmly in the traditional language of sovereignty, independence, the ethnically defined nation-state and national self-determination'

(2003: 401). Regarding the latter point, 'Eastern European academic discourse as well as citizenship and language legislation tend to approach the nation through the ethnocultural concept of the homogeneous nation-state' (ibid.: 419). Albi identifies the souverainist tendency through four features: a distinction between independence and sovereignty in constitutions[9]; the protection of sovereignty provisions by safeguards; the initial absence of references to the transfer of powers to international organizations; and the prohibition of the amendment of sovereignty in some cases (2005: 25). In my comparative discussion below, I will mainly focus on the dimension of external and internal sovereignty, and definitions of nationhood.

The second feature – that of the constitution as the apex of the legal system – is a primary dimension in all of the post-1989 constitutions. New constitutionalism tends to endorse the constitution in the form of a higher law, that is as a law that is situated 'above' ordinary laws and is more difficult to change by political means. In other words, such a law is entrenched. The level of entrenchment of the constitution, however, differs importantly between constitutions, and equally within the region. Entrenchment further also relates to judicial review in that constitutional court decisions are more difficult to override the more entrenched a constitution is. As Sadurski has argued,

> [t]he degree of 'finality' of decisions of constitutional courts may then be measured by the degree of entrenchment of the constitution: the easier it is to amend the constitution, the less final are the court's decisions. On the one side of spectrum, there will be cases of an 'absolute' entrenchment: when the constitution itself precludes a possibility of amending certain provisions . . . On the other side of the spectrum, there will be constitutions that are weakly entrenched, that is, those that envisage a reasonably easy amendment process.
>
> (2008: 80–1)

As also Ludwikowski has argued, in the processes of democratization in East-Central Europe the 'constitution, recognized as the apex of hierarchically structured laws, was to provide a clear background for the assessment of legality of governmental and individual activities' (2000: 157). The higher law status has constitutionally been enshrined in the form of limitations of revision ranging from simple supermajorities (as in the case of Hungary a two-third parliamentary majority) to complex provisions regarding initiators of revision, parliamentary approval and ratification by means of a popular referendum.

The third feature, the idea of a set of essential individual rights, became an equally widely endorsed element of the constitutions in the new democracies. As discussed above, the communist constitutions had included ample catalogues of rights, without, however, granting these rights the status of individual entitlements. Rather, individual rights were benefits granted by the state to citizens who were supposed to fulfil a range of duties, and were anyway interpreted arbitrarily and always within the context of the socialist ideal (Kurczewski and Sullivan 2002: 254–5). A main aim in all constitutions in the region was to entrench rights so as to protect these from political interference and arbitrariness. Basically, there are two constitutional dimensions relevant for the entrenchment of rights. One is the stipulation of when rights can be restricted by statute (the fewer opportunities for such restriction, the less rights are open to political interference and the more they will be guarded by independent judicial review). Another is the general revision rules of constitutions. Particular parts of the constitution, including rights, can be made more difficult to amend, and thus, again, less susceptible to political interference.

A fourth dimension is that of the role of constitutional courts. The East-Central European countries adopted a more or less similar model of concentrated or centralized review, in which one singular institution has the responsibility and independent status to 'authoritatively scrutinise laws in terms of their constitutionality' (Sadurski 2008: 5). In this respect, the most important of the judicial review powers is that of review *in abstracto*, that is the power to review the constitutionality of laws without reference to a specific case. While on the one hand we could speak of a region-wide phenomenon, on the other it is necessary to recognize relatively different trajectories and institutional make-ups in the various countries. Generally, there is no tradition of constitutional courts in the region (except for the Czechoslovak case, where such a court was established by the 1920 Constitution and operated from 1921 onwards). Many countries looked to Western Europe for inspiration. In one case, some form of legal constitutionalism emerged already before 1989, as Poland set up a Constitutional Tribunal in 1985, in an attempt to enhance legitimacy of the regime and reflecting a growing acceptance of a constitutionalist idea.[10] The role and importance of constitutional courts differ throughout the region, as will be seen below. While Hungary could boast one of the strongest courts in the world under Chief Justice Solyom in the 1990s, in Poland it took until the 1997 Constitution for a legal constitutionalist argument to prevail, while in Romania it was only with the 2003 amendments that the Constitutional Court gained a final say in matters of constitutionality.[11]

In the rest of the chapter, I will briefly explore the constitutional dimensions I attribute to legal constitutionalism, that is, modern sovereignty as a conspicuous part of the constitutional order, the idea of constitutional law as a higher law and the idea of entrenched fundamental rights, and, finally, the role of specialized constitutional courts.

Country Cases

Czech Republic

Sovereignty

The split of the Czechoslovak federation in 1992 heralded in a new era of independent statehood for the newly formed Czech Republic. A new Constitution was adopted in December 1992 and clearly reflects the idea of an autonomous constitutional order. This is for instance reflected in the preamble, which refers to the Constitution's adoption 'at the time of the renewal of an *independent* Czech state' as well as in article 1: 'The Czech Republic is a *sovereign*, *unified*, and democratic law-observing state . . .' (emphasis added). According to Anneli Albi, the Czech Constitution involves in this a dimension of 'classical' souverainism, in that it invokes both independence and sovereignty (as articulated in the preamble and articles 1, 2(1), and 9(2)).

In terms of internal sovereignty and definitions of statehood, the understanding is less grounded in a homogeneous notion of the Czech people, in contrast to the new-born Slovak state (and other states in the region), and rather refers to a 'sovereign community as the entire citizenry' (Nedelsky 2009: 231). The Czech Constitution was in this much less than its Slovak counterpart 'symbolic of [the] desire to secede' (Kopecky 2001: 331; cf. Přibáň 2007: 90). Instead, the predominant emphasis is a civic definition of sovereignty, that is, as expressed by Vaclav Klaus, the 'foundation of the state is the free citizen' (Nedelsky 2009: 235). This 'civic' principle is also reflected in the preamble and appears to indicate less of a legalistic, closed and more of a participatory, civic conception:

> We, the *citizens* of the Czech Republic in Bohemia, Moravia, and Silesia, at the time of the renewal of an independent Czech state, being loyal to all good traditions of the ancient statehood of Czech Crown's Lands and the Czechoslovak State, resolved to build, protect and develop the Czech Republic in the *spirit of the inviolable*

> *values of human dignity and freedom*, as the *home of equal and free citizens* who are conscious of their duties towards others and their responsibility towards the whole, as a free and democratic state based on the *respect for human rights* and the *principles of civic society* . . .
>
> (Emphasis added)

Higher law and fundamental rights

The new Czech Constitution clearly displays a perception of the Constitution as higher law. Such perception was recently reiterated in a ruling by the Czech Constitutional Court: 'the Constitution is a fundamental document that provides binding and uncrossable rules' (2009/09/10 – Pl. ÚS 27/09). At the same time, however, the Czech Constitution is relatively weakly entrenched, in that it foresees a relatively simple procedure for revision of the constitution (the Venice Commission has classified the Czech Republic system in terms its amendability as 'relatively easy' to amend, see CoE 2010: 15). The revision procedure foresees amendment only by means of constitutional acts (art. 9(1)) and does in this not allow for a plurality of actors to initiate amendment. For the adoption of constitutional acts, a qualified majority in both houses of parliament is necessary; that is the Constitution stipulates that for such adoption the 'concurrence of three-fifths of all Deputies and three-fifths of all Senators present is required' (art. 39(4)).

The Czech Constitution further includes a dimension of unamendability, in that article 9(2) states that '[a]ny changes in the essential requirements for a democratic state governed by the rule of law are impermissible'. According to the Council of Europe's Venice Commission, '[t]his does not mean that the provisions on the form of government are unamendable, but merely that reforms should not be so radical as to change the core republican form of government' (CoE 2010: 41).[12] The Czech Bill of Rights – the Charter of Fundamental Rights and Freedoms – further restricts possibilities for limiting fundamental rights. Its first article states that '[a]ll people are free and equal in their dignity and rights. Their fundamental rights and freedoms are inherent, inalienable, non-prescriptible, and irrepealable.' A general clause stipulates the modalities for the restrictions of rights, which, as in other similar cases, 'operates in a blanket fashion on all constitutional rights and liberties' (Sadurski 2002: 244). At the same time, the clause also includes a limitation of possible restrictions themselves. In article 4(4), it is stated that '[w]hen employing the provisions concerning limitations upon the fundamental rights and freedoms, the essence and significance of these rights and freedoms must be preserved. Such limitations shall not be misused for purposes other than those for which they were enacted.' This reference to an 'essence' or 'core' of rights is also present in the above-mentioned article 9(2) of the constitutional text, and provides some leeway for constitutional courts to restrict the limitations of rights (Sadurski 2002: 245).

Constitutional Court

The Czech Republic (with Slovakia) is the only country in the region with prior experience of a Constitutional Court. A Constitutional Court, modelled along the lines of Hans Kelsen's ideas of a 'negative legislator', was instituted in the interwar period. The Court's powers were relatively limited, and the experience lasted for 20 years (until 1941), but the experience did play a role in later periods, in particular after 1989 (Přibáň 2002: 373–4). During the Prague Spring of 1968, the idea of a constitutional authority was re-proposed and found reflection in the constitutional act on the Czechoslovak Federation (143/1968), but remained unimplemented until the changes of 1989 (Přibáň 2002: 374). The Constitutional Court that was established in 1993 (after the brief experience of a Czechoslovak Constitutional Court) followed the model of a distinct institution that protects the separation of constitutional powers, human rights and freedom, and an overall constitutional system based on the rule of law. One observer has judged the court as not one of the 'most visible institutions' (Kopecky 2001: 342), but it seems without doubt that the Constitutional Court has played a prominent role in the emergence of a Czech democratic regime, even if being contested throughout transition and struggling for a distinct position (Přibáň 2002).

Without doubt, the Czech Constitutional Court is the most important institution that protects the constitutionality of norms in the Czech system. It 'conforms' to the more general pattern in Central and Eastern Europe in that the Court's powers include both abstract and concrete review of norms. Abstract review regards the power to annul laws and other regulations that are found to be in contradiction with the constitutional order or international agreements (art. 87(1) a and b). Abstract review can be commenced, in the case of statutes, on the basis of a proposal of the President, a group of at least 41 Deputies or a group of at least 17 Senators, or a panel of the Court in connection with deciding a constitutional complaint; the government, and anyone who submits a constitutional complaint or who submits a petition for rehearing (182/1993 Sb, par. 61(1)). In the case of regulations other than statutory laws, paragraph 61(2) of the constitutional act indicates initiation on the proposal of the government, a group of at least 25 Deputies or a group of at least ten Senators, a panel of the Court in connection with deciding a constitutional complaint, anyone who submits a constitutional complaint or who submits a petition for rehearing, the representative body of a region, the Public Protector of Rights or Ombudsman, and, in relevant cases, the Interior Minister, the competent ministry or other central administrative office, the director of a regional office, and representative bodies of a municipality. Concrete review includes adjudication of constitutional complaints as filed by natural or legal persons against a final decision or other encroachment on constitutionally guaranteed rights and freedoms by public authorities (art. 87(1) c and d). The Constitutional Court further has powers regarding mandates of deputies and senators, decisions of international courts, competences of public authorities. The position of the court is strengthened by means of article 89(2) which declares that the Court's enforceable decisions are 'binding on all authorities and persons' (cf. Přibáň 2002: 377).

Hungary

Sovereignty

The amended Hungarian constitution of 1989/90 constituted a break with the communist regime's incorporation into the Soviet Union's sphere of influence by articulating Hungary's *independence* (article 2(1)). It also provided the basis for the grounding of constitutional democracy in *popular sovereignty*, in the form of both representative and direct democracy (article 2(2)).[13] Also in the Hungarian case, Albi identifies a certain 'souverainist' character, even if the Hungarian Constitution is 'amongst the constitutions with less numerous safeguards' (2005: 30). The sovereign dimensions come through in various invocations of the notions of sovereignty and independence (ibid.: 27). In the new Basic Law, the new constitution that was adopted in 2011 and implemented in 2012, such a souverainist dimension is probably more upfront, in particular if one focuses on the long preamble. The preamble explicitly mentions independence as well as a re-won national sovereignty. A specific indication to an attachment to modern sovereignty and national independence can be found in references to historical continuity and to the 'Holy Crown': 'We honour the achievements of our historical constitution and we honour the Holy Crown, which embodies the constitutional continuity of Hungary's statehood and the unity of the nation.' These references indicate visions of a larger Hungarian state, as existed until 1919, as also becomes evident in references to Hungarians that reside beyond the borders of the current state. In the actual text of the Basic Law, independence is invoked right at the start, as in the old Constitution: 'Hungary is an independent, democratic state under the rule of law' (article B1), while independence is further mentioned in articles 29(1), 44(1) and 45(3). What is peculiar is that no mention of the notion of sovereignty can be found in the Basic Law.[14]

Regarding internal sovereignty and understandings of nationhood, the 1989 Hungarian constitution largely invoked a civic understanding of the Hungarian political community, indicating a more open relation between the state and civil society. This came also through in its inclusion of national minorities as constituent minorities (Přibáň 2007). As articulated in article 68(1), '[t]he national and ethnic minorities living in the Republic of Hungary participate in the sovereign power of the people: they represent a *constituent part* of the State' (emphasis added). Also its preamble was 'entirely prospective and surprisingly makes no references to history, culture, tradition and religion' (Přibáň 2007: 87). In the new Basic Law, this civic outlook has been largely substituted for a strong, communitarian and homogeneous understanding of the Hungarian nation (I will discuss this further in Chapter 6). The Basic Law changed in this the 'characteristics of Hungarian constitutionalism, from one grounded in the idea of a 'secular state based upon a pluralist society' to one having its foundations in souverainist, 'historical and religious considerations' and placing emphasis on the 'family, nation, loyalty, faith and love' (Kovács and Tóth 2011: 198). The category 'We the People' is reinterpreted in that in the 1989 Constitution the people referred to 'those citizens who reside in the country and who are the subjects of the legal rights and obligations', while in the Basic Law the reference is to 'one single Hungarian nation that belongs together' (ibid.: 199).

Higher law and fundamental rights

Until the rupture in 2012, the Hungarian constitutional transition had the most gradual nature in the region. It could thus be argued that a 'higher law', in the sense of a constitutional text that is hierarchically prior to ordinary law, was created in a piecemeal fashion in the Hungarian context, beginning with the Roundtable Talks in 1989 (cf. Arato and Miklosi 2005; Drinoczi 2007).[15] As argued by the chief justice of the Constitutional Court in the 1990s, László Sólyom:

> The Constitutional Court has played a major role in 'harmonizing' preconstitutional norms with the Constitution through a process of abstract judicial review. The new Constitution did not automatically suspend pre-existing laws. Instead, it required Parliament to review all pre-constitutional laws and regulations to insure that they would be consistent with the newly established Constitution. In the process, such old laws acquired validity in the new system. (1994: 224)

In terms of amendability, and thus the entrenchment of constitutional norms, the Hungarian constitution (until 2012), could be understood as weakly entrenched in that the constitution could be easily amended by a two-thirds majority in Parliament, as stipulated in article 24(3): 'A majority of two-thirds of the votes of the Members of Parliament is required to amend the Constitution and for certain decisions specified therein.' The two-thirds rule means that a majority in parliament is sufficient for changing the constitution, with, for instance, no obligations of dissolving the parliament and/or holding a referendum on the new text. In terms of the absoluteness of fundamental rights, however, the Hungarian Constitution (until 2012) could be seen as strongly entrenched in that it did contain something akin to an *Ewigkeitsklausel*, that is stipulations regarding the essential and irrevocable nature of specific rights.[16] Sajó has argued that '[a]s a reaction to communism's abuse of human rights and also because of the drafting techniques used, the Hungarian Constitution offers an extremely wide-ranging and rigid protection of fundamental rights and freedoms' (1995: 261). Article 8 invokes 'inviolable and inalienable fundamental human rights' (1), while law may limit rights but not 'the basic meaning and contents of fundamental rights' (2).[17] Furthermore, 8(4) allows for the restriction of rights in the case of a national crisis or state of emergency, but not in the case of a number of specifically identified fundamental rights, such as the right to life and human dignity (art. 54). The court used the right to life and human dignity for instance in its well-known ruling on the death penalty (23/90), in which it used article 8(2) referring to the essential meaning of fundamental rights (Sadurski 2008: 101). As observed by Sajó, the Constitutional Court used the concept of inalienable human dignity in various cases to extend the protection of rights, in some cases 'creating' rights not explicitly mentioned in the constitution, such as the right of a individual to know his/her origins (1995: 259–60).

In the new Basic Law adopted in 2012, the amendment rule has remained the same (article R). In this respect, the constitution is thus weakly entrenched and fairly easy to amend. What has changed is the essential nature of fundamental rights. As in the old document, the essential nature of fundamental rights is protected, while fundamental rights have been 'delocalized' from Chapter XII to part I of the new constitution (Balogh and Hajas 2012). At first sight, then, also in the Basic Law, a number of fundamental rights are made 'absolute' and very difficult to restrict. In the chapter significantly entitled 'Freedom and Responsibility', article I invokes the 'inviolable and inalienable' nature of such rights. On closer scrutiny, though, fundamental rights protection can be said to have diminished in status in the Basic Law, not least because of a strong emphasis on the relation between rights and duties (hence the title of the chapter); that is the enjoyment of rights seems to have been made dependent on the fulfilment of duties to the political community (Arato *et al.* 2011: 13–16). Furthermore, the entrenched rights reflect a particular conservative ideology, such as with regard to the right to life and the protection of unborn life. But not only substantively, but also procedurally, fundamental rights protection has declined, in terms of a weakening of the prerogatives of the Constitutional Court as well as in terms of its composition (ibid.: 25–6).[18]

Constitutional Court

The Hungarian Constitutional Court was established in 1989 by means of the Act on the Constitutional Court (Act XXXII). The Court was both endorsed by the anti-communist opposition that wanted an independent institution and by the governing communist party that wanted to institutionalize its influence beyond the imminent elections (cf. Halmai 2003: 191). The Constitutional Court played a major role in the democratic transition in that it was the main actor in promoting legal continuity as the creation of the rule of law by means of the rule of law. In terms of its prerogatives, it has been argued that the Hungarian Court is the strongest of its kind in a global perspective (at least with regard to the 1990s). As Scheppele has argued, '[f]or close to a decade, the Hungarian Constitutional Court has been perhaps the most powerful court of its kind in the world' (1999: 81). Under the 1989 constitution, it 'has an exceptionally wide jurisdiction even in international comparison since it initially had to oversee the activity also of the . . . Parliament' (Halmai 2003: 192). Two dimensions of the early Hungarian Court stand out: its activism and its recourse to a so-called 'invisible constitution'. Its activism relates to its active part in shaping the institutions and form of constitutional democracy throughout the 1990s (as for instance in its famous decision on the death penalty).[19] The idea of the invisible constitution meant that the Court perceived its role also in terms of filling out gaps in the existing constitution (which was based on the work-in-progress of the amended communist constitution), by taking recourse to its own ideas of constitutionalism, apparently grounded in a wider, European constitutional tradition. The president of the Court, Sólyom argued later that '[b]y receiving international and eminently European standards, the constitutional court became the representative in Hungary of an important ideological trend, which was non-nationalist and which emphasized the return to Europe, and the same time an equality with older democracies' (2003: 152).

The Constitutional Court's role is to protect the Constitution by means of the review of the constitutionality of legal norms. The Constitutional Court Act specifies Court powers, which include the power to examine the unconstitutionality of statutory law which has not yet been promulgated (1a) (*ex ante* review). The right to initiation is confined to the president (and previously also 50 members of parliament). In terms of *ex post* examination, the court can examine the unconstitutionality of legal provisions and other legal instruments of the state (1b). *Ex post* examination could (until the 2012 Basic Law) be initiated by practically anyone by means of the *actio popularis* procedure.

Important changes with regard to the status of the Hungarian Constitutional Court have taken place since 2010, when the centre-right Fidesz government started a veritable constitutional counter-revolution (see for a more elaborated account, Chapter 6). Some of the implications of the Fidesz constitutional programme include a drastic curtailment of the independence of the Hungarian constitutional court as well as of its powers of constitutional review, including a curtailment of powers to review financial legislation. The Constitutional Court's functionality has been importantly reduced because of a radical restriction in terms of the actors that are able to initiate constitutional review. Other amendments involved changes in the nomination of judges and the extension of the judges' mandate, as well as the number of judges and the nomination of the chief judge.

Poland

Sovereignty

Polish constitution-making only resulted in a new constitution by 1997, after protracted debate and political strife. In one respect, the 1997

Constitution could be understood as relatively open, that is, in its understanding of (external) sovereignty and its explicit reference to international cooperation (see Albi 2005: 31). But in other respects, a souverainist dimension can be detected also in the Polish document. In particular the preamble contains indications of perceptions of sovereignty that correspond more to a traditional, centralistic view of sovereignty embedded in a homogeneous Polish nation, referring for instance to the 'struggle for *independence* achieved at great sacrifice'. In addition, one could refer to, among others, article 3 in the main text, 'The Republic of Poland shall be a *unitary* State', article 4(1), 'Supreme power in the Republic of Poland shall be vested in the Nation', and article 5 that starts with 'The Republic of Poland shall safeguard the *independence* and integrity of its territory . . .' (emphasis added).

In terms of internal sovereignty and definitions of statehood, the way sovereignty is defined in the Polish 1997 Constitution could be understood as a mixed or hybrid one: it refers both to a communitarian understanding of the pre-political Polish nation which grounds (centralized) state sovereignty and to a more civic-legalistic view where it is individual citizens and plural power centres that are relevant. The latter comes also through in a more open-ended, pluralistic understanding of (internal) sovereignty in the preamble, when it mentions 'the principle of subsidiarity in the strengthening the powers of citizens and their communities'. The latter – subsidiarity – can be taken as an important reflection of a civic-constitutionalist approach (cf. Albert 2008; Popławska 2002).

Higher law and fundamental rights

The constitutional 'revolution' in the Polish case was more a form of 'creeping constitutionalization'; that is main steps towards enhancing a constitutional dimension to the Polish political regime were already taken from the 1970s onwards. This included the establishment of a Constitutional Tribunal and a Commissioner for Citizens' Rights. The gradual nature of the emergence of the idea of constitutionalism – understood in legal-constitutionalist terms as comprising a higher law which is protected from political influence – becomes even more clear if one considers the fact that a new Constitution was adopted only in 1997. The nature of constitutionalism itself was object of debate as well as that of the status of the framers. The suspicion that ordinary politics based on particular party interests was defining the contents of the constitution was a constant fear (cf. Cholewinski 1998: 248).

Such political influence could compromise the perception of the impartiality and 'higher' nature of the constitution in the making. At the same time, many observers have argued that a consensus existed throughout about the necessity and obvious nature of the protection of human rights (Cholewinski 1998: 251; Wyrzykowski 1999: 257).

One might say that only by means of the implementation of the 1997 Constitution did the latter acquire the status of higher law; also because the independent Constitutional Tribunal obtained the 'final word' on constitutionality and constitutional interpretation. The Polish 1997 Constitution is relatively difficult to amend (more difficult than the Hungarian one, but less so than the Romanian one)[20] and could therefore be seen as relatively well entrenched. Article 235(4) of Chapter XII on 'Amending the constitution' stipulates a majority in both chambers of the parliament, that is two-thirds in the Sejm and an absolute majority in the Senate. Amendment can be initiated by both chambers of the parliament and by the senate (but not by civic initiative). There is a reinforced procedure for specific parts of the constitution, where a confirmatory referendum may be required. The referendum may be called for by both houses of the parliament and by the president. The relevant parts of the constitution are Chapters I, II and XII, related to the organization of the state, rights and amendment respectively.

In terms of the entrenchment of rights, the Polish constitution is relatively protective of some rights. In Chapter II, article 30 the 'inherent and inalienable dignity of the person' and its inviolability are invoked, thereby constituting a kind of 'meta-right' (Sadurski 2008: 128), which can be used for the protection of more specific rights from limitation. Wyrzykowski has argued in this regard that '[h]uman dignity and liberty were constitutionally recognized as the unalterable foundation of the Republic' (Wyrzykowski 1999: 258–9). The Polish constitution further allows for the (statutory) limitation of rights only when necessary in cases of protection of security or public order, protection of the natural environment, health or public morals, or the freedoms and rights of other persons (31(3)). Also in the Polish constitution the impossibility of the violation of the 'essence' of rights is referred to.

Constitutional Court

From the 1970s onwards, a heightened interest in constitutionalism and constitutionality could be noticed in communist Poland. Puchalska speaks of a 'fundamental turn in constitutional thinking by the main political powers in Poland at that time' (2011: 42). In 1976, for instance, a constitutional amendment introduced the necessity to 'see the law's conformity with the constitution' (Czeszejko-Sochacki 1996: 26; Klich 1996). This did not entail anything like a form of judicial review as within a Kelsenian system, but it did reflect a growing emphasis on constitutionalism and legality from the part of the regime. This became even more evident in the wake of the emergence of Solidarnosc and its repression in 1980–81, in particular in terms of the amendment of the Constitution by the Polish parliament (Diet) in 1982 to establish a Constitutional Tribunal. The statute was, however, enacted only in 1985. While the prerogatives of the Tribunal seemed to correspond to a West-European, Kelsenian model of judicial review, in reality it was mostly a façade institution, as the communist authorities were 'without any intention to make these institutions work to guard the integrity of constitutional principles or to protect citizens' rights' (Klich 1996: 37). The establishment of the Tribunal provided the only example in Central and Eastern Europe of the institution of something like a constitutional court before the events of 1989 (cf. Sadurski 2008).

The establishment of the Tribunal under communism meant, however, that it was the result of a compromise, and, as mentioned, differed in this from the Kelsenian tradition in important ways. The most conspicuous difference was that originally the court's decisions were not final but could be overruled by a two-thirds majority in the Polish parliament (until the adoption of the new constitution in 1997; the only other case in the region was that of the Romanian court). The new 1997 Constitution 'rectified' many of the weaknesses of the Tribunal, *inter alia* by introducing finality of the court's decisions and the introduction of the procedure of constitutional complaint (Garlicki 2003: 267). The main role of the court is the review of legal norms on their constitutionality. In this, the court has the power to put to review legal norms, including statutes. *Ex ante* or preventive review is rather exceptional, and can only be initiated by the President in relation to international agreements and statutes of Parliament before these are signed. Most of the court's decisions regard *a posteriori* review of an abstract kind, which can be initiated by a wide range of actors, including 50 members of parliament, 40 members of the senate, the Ombudsman and local government units, as well as trade unions, and churches and religious organisations (article 191(1)). Concrete review can be initiated by courts which doubt the conformity to the constitution of legal provisions which are at the basis of specific judgements (cf. Garlicki 2003: 274). Constitutional complaints are understood in a relatively limited sense in the Polish case, in that a complaint can only be raised against a legal provision but not against a specific legal ruling (Garlicki 2003: 275).

Romania

Sovereignty

The constitution-making process in Romania in the early 1990s strongly emphasized a classical understanding of sovereignty. Conspicuous in the 1991 Constitution is the establishment of an independent nation-state, grounded in the constituent power of a sovereign, homogeneous people, and exclusively linked with a distinct territory (cf. Albi 2005: 30). The emphasis is on a Romanian constitutional-democratic state that is an equal sovereign on the international level, and that fully expresses the political sovereignty of the Romanian people. Such a view is well reflected in two articles. The first (article 1(1)) states that 'Romania is a *sovereign, independent*, unitary and indivisible National State' (emphasis added). The second article (2(1)) articulates that 'The national sovereignty shall reside within the Romanian people, that shall exercise it by means of their representative bodies, resulting from free, periodical and fair elections, as well as by referendum'.

The constitution grounds state sovereignty in the 'majority ethno-nation' and not in individual citizens regardless of their ethnic origin. Such a definition of the nation as an ethno-cultural understanding of the nation, grounded in shared traditions and history, can be reconstructed by means of various relevant articles (2(1), 2(3), 3(1), 4(1), 30(7) and 50). As argued, among others, by Renate Weber, these articles express a unitary, majoritarian vision of the Romanian nation, and its principal ethical outlook was not shared by various national minorities, who had reservations about consequentially reinforced tendencies towards assimilation by the national majority (see Weber 2001: 233–4).[21] Article 50, stipulating 'faithfulness towards the country', can also be found in many other constitutions, but in the Romanian constitution, where there is a diffused conflation of the notions 'people', 'nation' and 'country' (see Lungu 2002: 402; Preda 2002: 393), the reference to the country seems not necessarily as neutral as might be the case in other constitutions. It can be argued that in particular in the first decade of transformation, a distinct emphasis was placed on a form of 'constitutional nationalism', which prioritized the national majority through politics, understood as a homogeneous Romanian people, including in constitutional politics. Indeed, one observer has classified the Romanian constitution of 1991 as reflecting a form of constitutional nationalism in its identification of the constitution with unitary nation with a singular language and culture (Lungu 2002: 400).

Higher law and fundamental rights

The idea of the constitution as a 'higher law' has played an important, even if not uncontested, role in the Romanian constitution-making process. For instance, in the Romanian Constitutional Assembly of 1991 the president of the constitutional commission Antonie Iorgovan argued that the 'fundamental idea that has been at the basis of the elaboration of these theses [regarding the structure and principles of the new constitution, pb] is to provide the definition of a charter of citizens' rights and liberties, . . . to which the whole system of state powers will be subordinated as well as public life in general'.[22] But throughout the constitutional assembly, the ideas of a rigidly entrenched constitution and an independent constitutional guardian remained contested. In general, then, the Romanian Constitution's status as a higher law has continued to be surrounded by ambiguity and political conflict.[23]

Nevertheless, and in a paradoxical way, the constitution-makers did entrench the 1991 Romanian Constitution significantly, in that it is very difficult to amend (articles 150–152) (cf. CoE 2010: 15). According to one observer, revision entails a 'very rigid amendment process, requiring both extraordinary concurrent majorities – two-thirds in both Houses and, in case of a divergence, three-fourths in joint plenary session – and a referendum ratification of amendments (to safeguard in perpetuity the initial arrangement)' (Iancu 2010: 194). This entrenchment was, however, weakened by the fact that – until 2003 – the parliament could *de facto* override Constitutional Court rulings, as stipulated in article 145 of the 1991 Constitution (see below).

A case for the entrenched nature of the Romanian Constitution is further corroborated by the fact that the Constitution 'declares certain provisions to be absolutely unamendable' (CoE 2010: 41). These provisions regard the special protection of the definition of the state as well as of fundamental rights, as stated in article 148(1):

> (1) The provisions of this Constitution with regard to the national, independent, unitary and indivisible character of the Romanian State, the Republican form of government, territorial integrity, independence of the judiciary, political pluralism and official language shall not be subject to revision.
>
> (2) Likewise, no revision shall be made if it results in the suppression of the citizens fundamental rights and freedoms, or the safeguards thereof.

In general, then, and in contrast to continuous political contestation and disregard, the Romanian Constitution is relatively well entrenched.

This formal entrenchment emerges from its extraordinarily rigid amendment procedure, the protection of important parts, including the definition of statehood, from revision, the protection of fundamental rights and, last but not least, the enhanced status of the Constitutional Court since 2003 (and even further so since 2010).

Constitutional Court

As mentioned, the idea of a Constitutional Court constituted one of the most important conflicts in the debate on the new Constitution. As argued by Renate Weber, '[m]any were either reticent or sceptical about the Constitutional Court by the time of its establishment' (Weber 2001: 215; cf. Weber 2002). During the constitutional debates in 1991, it was, for instance, feared that the Constitutional Court would become a 'fourth power' within the architecture of the Romanian state (Geneza Constituţiei 1998: 876). Others argued, in contrast, that constitutional control was not only a 'sinecure for lawyers, but an irrepressible necessity and [something] unanimously acknowledged' (Geneza Constituţiei 1998: 854). To add to the complexity, in Romania there was something of a tradition of judicial review by the High Court of Cassation and Justice, while the new Constitutional Court seemed to clash with the role of the already existing Supreme Court. Ultimately, then, and as argued by Ion Muraru, president of the Romanian Constitutional Court in the 1990s, '[i]n our country, in the debates in the Constituent Assembly, it was hard to convince even the lawyers that we needed a distinct authority of this sort'.[24]

It is not surprising in the light of its contested nature that the Romanian Constitutional Court played a rather secondary role in the Romanian democratization process, at least until the early 2000s. Some observers argue that it held a marginal and largely irrelevant position during the 1990s, in which the Court issued only one decision of public impact, related to the legitimization of a third consecutive presidential mandate of Ion Iliescu.[25] As observed above, until the amendment of 2003, the Romanian Court was the only court in the region (with the Polish Constitutional Tribunal until 1997) that was not considered the final arbiter in constitutional matters. Indeed, article 145 of the 1991 constitution allowed a two-thirds majority in parliament to override its rulings.[26] In addition, as argued by Sadurski, the Romanian Court was less strong than some of its counterparts in the region, because prior to the 2003 revision it could not arbiter conflict between public institutions. Up until 2003, it could then be argued that the Romanian case did not constitute a form of legal constitutionalism all the way, but allowed for a form of legislative supremacy. The parliament formally held a final say in constitutional matters, which in reality, however, it never successfully used.

In general, throughout the 1990s there seems to have been little parliamentary acceptance of Constitutional Court rulings as mandatory, also due to the Court's apparent openness to political interference (cf. Gilia 2012a). Weber argues that 'silence and ignorance' characterized the first decade of the Court's operation (Weber 2002: 284). As another observer puts it more staunchly:

> [f]or a very long time after the adoption of the 1991 Constitution, neither public debates nor political disputes were framed in the language and logic of constitutionality or constitutionalism. The local "Guardian of the Constitution" was relegated to a marginal, almost irrelevant position.
>
> (Iancu 2010)

Be that as it may, the powers of the Constitutional Court as established in the 1991 Constitution (article 144) do conform to a wider pattern in Central and Eastern Europe (cf. Constantinescu *et al.* 2004; Gâdiuţă 2012; Weber 2002). This is particularly clear since the revision of the Constitution in 2003. The Court's competences include both abstract *a priori* and concrete *a posteriori* review (144a). The constitutionality of a draft law may be challenged before the Constitutional Court, after the adoption of the law, but before its promulgation (abstract review). Such a challenge can be initiated by the president of Romania, by the president of either chamber of parliament, by the government, the Supreme Court of Justice, by a number of at least 50 deputies or at least 25 senators. In the 2003 revision of the Constitution, an Advocate of the People or Ombudsman was also included. The Constitutional Court further has concrete *a posteriori* review powers, as stipulated in article 2003/146d (1991/146c). The procedure entails bringing to the Courts of law the suspicion of the unconstitutionality of a law or a (governmental) order (the so-called *excepţie de neconstituţionalitate*) (cf. Constantinescu *et al.* 2004: 323).

Additional powers of the Court now include *inter alia* the control of constitutionality of international treaties (2003/144b), the solution of legal disputes of a constitutional nature between public authorities (2003/144e), the observation of the procedure for the election of the President of Romania (2003/144f), and the observation of the procedures regarding referenda and citizens' legislative initiatives (2003/144i and j). The main novelties introduced by the 2003 revision included the role of the Ombudsman, the extension of the Court's prerogatives regarding the constitutionality of international treaties and intermediation in inter-institutional conflicts, and the *erga omnes* status of the Court's decision. The revision, further specified by Law no. 232/2004, has effectively abolished the parliamentary right to override decisions of unconstitutionality, bringing the Romanian system in line with new constitutionalism.

In this, the 2003 revision has contributed to a peculiar and fairly drastic change in the status, visibility and activity of the Court since the early 2000s. What is more, the Court has made various decisions with significant political clout and conflictive potential, such as its decision in 2008 on the commission for investigation of the archives of the Securitate (see Iancu 2010). The Court became increasingly the object of referrals, while also 'many public and political debates have suddenly started to be carried out within constitutional parameters' (Iancu 2010; cf. Sadurski 2010). In particular in the second half of the 2000s, the Court has attempted to mediate in cases of high-level political conflict (predominantly between the President and the government) and constitutional crisis (I will discuss this further in Chapter 6).

One of the most problematic and controversial decisions, in particular with regard of the Court's interference in issues of high political salience and in terms of a potential political bias was its ruling on a proposed reform of the judicial system in the light of EU accession in July 2005. The Court struck down a legislative package for which the government had taken responsibility, on a number of referrals by the political opposition in particular. The declaration of unconstitutionality of some provisions of this legislative package was met by the government as well as society at large by strong criticism, and was portrayed as a way of blocking reform and endangering EU accession. Prime Minister Tăriceanu even threatened to resign, while the Minister of Justice questioned the neutrality of the Court and criticized the Court for invalidating modifications explicitly asked for by the European Commission. Some even called for the abolition of the Court and the transfer of its powers to the Senate (Sadurski 2010).

Slovakia

Sovereignty

The main elements of dispute in the 'Velvet Divorce' between the Czech and the Slovak Republics in 1992 were sovereignty and national self-government (Nedelsky 2009: 190), and the Slovak Constitution entrenches these concepts extensively. External sovereignty is invoked in the preamble in terms of the '*natural right* of nations to self-determination' (emphasis added). And the preamble begins with: 'We, the Slovak nation, mindful of the political and cultural heritage of our forebears, and of the centuries of experience from the struggle for national existence and our own statehood.' The main text invokes the idea of Slovakia as a 'sovereign state' in article 1, while article 34(3) relates the rights for minorities to an absence of 'jeopardizing the sovereignty . . . of the Slovak Republic' (see Albi 2005: 28).

Internal sovereignty is related to a homogeneous and ethnic understanding of Slovak nationhood. As Nedelsky observes, the Czech Republic opted for a largely civic orientation of the new democratic state in the wake of the divorce, while the Slovak Republic followed an ethnic idea of the nation-state and of national sovereignty. Such a reading is to some extent corroborated by relevant constitutional principles enshrined in the relative texts (cf. Přibáň 2007: 89–90). It seems reasonable to argue that the Slovak Constitution provides instruments for the pursuit of a communitarian type of politics, which emphasizes a strong link between sovereignty and the political will of the Slovak majority. Such a communitarian view is visible already in the preamble, which refers to the 'Slovak nation' (and not, such as in the Polish preamble, to the 'nation and its citizens'), and invokes a specific national tradition, that is the 'political and cultural heritage of our forebears, and of the centuries of experience from the struggle for national existence and our own statehood, in the sense of the spiritual heritage of Cyril and Methodius and the historical legacy of the Great Moravian Empire'.

Higher law and fundamental rights

The Slovak Constitution is relatively weakly entrenched, in that a three-fifths majority of all members of parliament (the Slovak National Council) can revise or amend the Constitution (art. 84(4)). In other words, formally speaking the Slovak parliament has a relative hold over the Constitution by means of an accessible power to revise the Constitution and therefore to trump Constitutional Court decisions. And indeed, the Constitution has been amended five times since its adoption in 1992 (in 1998, 1999, 2001 and twice in 2004),[27] with the most important amendment being in 2001.

From a different perspective, the Constitution tends to be well entrenched in that it is difficult or even impossible to revise some of its parts (cf. CoE 2010). Some see this as a form of 'absolute entrenchment' in that distinct parts of the constitution are deemed not open to revision. This dimension is particularly relevant with regard to fundamental rights. The Slovak Constitution does contain such a safety zone of fundamental rights that is (nearly) impossible to revise. In article 12(1), it argues that fundamental rights – as laid out in Section Two of Title Two on Fundamental Rights – are 'sanctioned, inalienable, imprescriptible and irreversible'. At the same time, parts of the fundamental rights laid out in Title Two are to be further stipulated in statutory law, thereby making entrenchment less absolute, such as in the case of the freedom of thought, conscience, religion and belief, which 'may be restricted only by a law, if it is regarding a measure necessary in a democratic society for the protection of public order, health and morals or for the protection of the rights and freedoms of others' (article 24).

Constitutional Court

As observed, Czechoslovakia was the only country in the region that had had some experience with a Kelsen-inspired constitutional court prior to the communist period and 1989, that is in the interwar period. In the post-communist period, a Constitutional Court was initially set up in the federal context of Czechoslovakia, in 1991. Indeed, some have suggested that in the case of Czechoslovakia, there exists a certain tradition of the 'protection of constitutionality' (Broest *et al.* 2001: 13, 144–6). Also Radoslav Prochazka has stated that '[i]n Czechoslovakia, tradition informed the establishment of constitutional review in more immediate ways than it did elsewhere in the region'. He goes on, 'it was relatively easy for the Czechoslovak post-1989 drafters to press for the incorporation of constitutional review by emphasising indigenous tradition rather than import from abroad' (Prochazka 2002: 59). Indeed, Prochazka claims that in the drafting process the 'provisions on the Constitutional Court were virtually uncontested' (ibid.: 68). Other observers are, however, more sceptical and have argued that the Slovak Constitutional Court is largely an 'untraditional institution' (Malová 2001: 371).

Be that as it may, the Slovak Court was set up after the 'velvet divorce' and became operative in March 1993. The Court follows a general pattern – as identified by Sadurksi – in terms of powers of 'concentrated' or 'centralized' constitutional review by an independent and specialized institution (Sadurski 2008: 5). As also argued by Broest *et al.*:

> Currently prevailing trends indicate that the protection of constitutionality should be invested in permanent and special court

> authorities, which have the indispensable system of guarantees of their independence and impartiality . . . Just as other countries of Central and Eastern Europe, the Slovak Republic has also accepted this prevalent trend, and in its Constitution of 1992 it created a permanent specialized authority of constitutional protection.
> (2001: 13)

The general role of the Slovak Court is expressed in article 124: 'The Constitutional Court of the Slovak Republic is an independent judicial body charged with protecting constitutionality.' In order to perform such a protective role, the Slovak Court has a number of explicit powers, including the power of abstract judicial review, which means that it can examine the constitutionality of any law, statute, or regulation passed by parliament, council of ministers, or local governments (art. 125). Abstract review can be initiated in Slovakia by at least one-fifth of the deputies of parliament, the president of the republic, the government, any court, the general prosecutor, and by any individual in the case of the presumed violation of rights (constitutional complaint) (article 130). In the latter case, review is of the concrete type, in that it regards distinct cases of rights violations. In this regard, the Slovak system of judicial review appears as fairly accessible for both institutional and individual recourse. The court has additional powers, for instance in terms of mediation in inter-institutional conflict, verifying the mandates of parliamentarians, receiving complaints regarding referendum results and overlooking elections (article 129).

An enhanced status of the Constitutional Court became visible in the Slovak reforms in 2001 that were initiated in the light of EU accession. According to Broestl *et al.*, the amendments involved the 'strengthening of the position and legal powers of the Constitutional Court' (2001: 169). The strengthening and autonomization of the Constitutional Court's powers included the increase of number of judges and the extension of their terms (Constitution Watch 2001; Lastic 2006; Malová and Láštic 2001: 25; Ucen 2002: 1078). In this, the amendment Law 90/2001 has been described as a 'significant amendment of the basic law of the country', not least because of the implications for the constitutional order itself (Broestl *et al.* 2001: 169).

Concluding remarks

In Central and Eastern Europe, a version of legal constitutionalism emerged prior to 1989, and can only partially be explained by reference to a global convergence to 'juristocracy' or 'new constitutionalism'.

Both the legalistic language of the dissidents and the reform attempts of the communist regimes invoked elements of legalism (the rule of law, fundamental rights) in order to endorse significant changes to the existing system (the dissidents) or, in an attempt to 'change everything, so that everything could remain the same'. The availability and impact of a legalistic language has not been the same everywhere (for instance, even if in Romania some references to legalism were made prior to 1989, their impact (also after 1989) was relatively modest). At the same time, it seems hard to deny that more or less robust forms of legal constitutionalism have emerged in all five countries under study.

As most forcefully argued by Albi, all countries originally showed a relatively disproportionate attachment in their constitutional orders to a concept of modern sovereignty, both in an insistence on national self-determination and to different extents to a closed, homogeneous understanding of the 'nation' (exceptions, at least on a formal-constitutional level, here are the Czech Republic and Hungary, prior to 2012). In terms of constitutional entrenchment (related to amendment procedures and the unamendability of parts of the constitution), varieties of intensity are visible (ranging from the Czech Republic and Hungary, on one side, to Romania, on the other). The role of constitutional courts has been more conspicuous in some countries than others (Hungary and Poland probably stand out), and is in some countries the subject of high-level political conflict (especially Hungary and Romania; see Chapter 6), but in all cases a clear attachment to a role of guardianship can be discerned.

In the following two chapters, I will engage with the question of whether the legal-constitutional tendency in these countries is a singular one, or whether 'antidotes' can be observed that point to a different, more democratically informed tradition. While the latter might be relatively weak and underdeveloped, its importance might lie in its capacity to inform (future) attempts at significant correction of one-sided legal constitutionalism.

Notes

1 An earlier version of this account can be found in Blokker (2012).
2 For instance, in the Romanian constitution of 1965, in article 28, the constitution grants the 'citizens of the Romanian Socialist Republic . . . freedom of speech, press, meeting, association and demonstration'.
3 Cited in Kurczewksi and Sullivan (2002: 257).
4 For the constitutional debates, see *Geneza Constituţiei* (1998).
5 As Adam Michnik suggested: 'To believe in overthrowing the dictatorship of the party by revolution and to consciously organize actions in pursuit

of this goal is both unrealistic and dangerous' (1985a: 142). Regarding the legal nature of new evolutionism, Baker has suggested that an emphasis on civil liberties and human rights was a 'by-product' rather than priority in Michnik's strategy of 'new evolutionism' (1998: 129).

6 Mentioned in: Markovits (2007: 237).

7 Cf. Preuss who identifies three historical phases of the concept of sovereignty, a first phase characterized by exclusive territorial control, a second phase characterized by collective self-rule of a multitude which is constituted through the constitutions, and a third phase that reconceptualises the idea of collective self-government as the 'capacity of a collective to interact with other communities and share with them the control of their life conditions on a global scale irrespective of territorial boundaries' (2010: 39). The first phase is related to absolutism, the second to modern constitutionalism and the third might emerge in an age of constitutional pluralism.

8 It can be argued that this is only in part, because new constitutionalism is equally close to the idea of 'universal constitutionalism', which consists of an understanding of constitutionalism that is universally valid and hence supersedes the national; the national and universal dimensions are obviously in tension.

9 Albi's distinction between independence and sovereignty coincides with the distinction between external and internal sovereignty. In Albi's view, the emphasis on both external and internal sovereignty has to do with historical reasons, not least of all experiences related to the Soviet era.

10 There was, however, also the probably less significant Hungarian experience with a Constitutional Council, which was set up in 1983 (Csink and Schanda 2012: 161).

11 The Constitutional Tribunal had been strongly in favour of the abolishment. As argued by Marek Safjan, the former Chief Justice of the Polish Constitutional Tribunal, the abolishment of parliamentary influence is a 'final victory of the Constitution over politics and recognition that nothing can justify keeping unconstitutional legal provisions within the legal system' (cited in Sadurski 2008: 30).

12 Article 9(2) was for instance invoked by the Czech Constitutional Court when it ruled on a Constitution Act which sought to shorten the term of office of the chamber of deputies. The Court ruled that in particular a core principle of the rule of law, that of generality, had been violated (2009/09/10 – Pl. ÚS 27/09).

13 Here, the Hungarian Constitution thus also indicates possibilities for more direct civic participation. See further Chapter 5.

14 It cannot be excluded that the available English translations are problematic in this respect.

15 The Constitutional Court's understanding of the Constitution as a higher law is reflected – *inter alia* – in decision 11/1992. The decision conveys an emphasis on the ordering and higher nature of the constitution as well as on the need for 'radiation' of the higher principles throughout society:

> That Hungary is a constitutional state is both a statement of fact and a statement of policy. The constitutional state becomes a reality when the Constitution is truly and unconditionally given effect. For the legal system the change of system means, and a change of legal systems can

> be possible only in that sense, that the Constitution of the constitutional state must be brought into harmony – and so maintained, given new legislative activity – with the whole system of laws. Not only the regulations and the operation of the state organs must comply strictly with the Constitution but the Constitution's values and its "conceptual culture" must imbue the whole of society. This is the rule of law and this is how the Constitution becomes a reality. The realization of the constitutional state is a continuous process. For the organs of the State, participation in this process is a constitutional duty.

16 This is in contrast to what seems to be sustained by some scholars (Jakab 2012: 6).

17 In decision 30/1992, the Court elucidated restriction in a more detailed way, in terms of necessity and proportionality (cf. Balogh and Hajs 2012: fn. 12):

> The State may only use the tool of restricting a fundamental right if it is the only way to secure the protection or the enforcement of another fundamental right or liberty or to protect another constitutional value. Therefore, it is not enough for the constitutionality of restricting the fundamental right to refer to the protection of another fundamental right, liberty or constitutional objective, but the requirement of proportionality must be complied with as well: the importance of the objective to be achieved must be proportionate to the restriction of the fundamental right concerned. In enacting a limitation, the legislator is bound to employ the most moderate means suitable for reaching the specified purpose. Restricting the content of a right arbitrarily, without a forcing cause is unconstitutional, just like doing so by using a restriction of disproportionate weight compared to the purported objective.

18 See further below and Chapter 6.

19 The Court has been criticized for its activism and its judges labelled 'activist human rights fundamentalists' or 'parliamentary legal allies' (Halmai 2003: 196).

20 Sadurski notes that before 1997, when the Constitutional Tribunal's decisions could be overridden by parliament, such overriding was tantamount to a constitutional amendment in that it required the same supermajority as for amendment (2008: 82).

21 Weber further underlines this identitarian perception of the Romanian nation – as historically and ethno-culturally bound – by pointing to the statement of six experts of the Drafting Committee that invokes a vision of a 'common ethnic origin, language, culture, religion, psychological characteristics, life, traditions, desires, and above all the history and aspiration to last on its territory' (cited in Weber 2001: 235; see also Preda 2002 for the constitutional debate). In the 2003 amendment, the Hungarian minority party attempted to change article 1(1), by proposing the elimination of 'national' in the definition of the state. This amendment was, however, rejected by reference to article 148(1), which prohibits the revision of the character of the state, and which, so it was argued, 'corresponds to the

project of the Constitution of the European Union, according to which the EU respects the national identities of the member states' (Romanian Commission 2003: 2).

22 *Geneza Constituției, supra* note 26, p. 56.

23 This emerged in particular in a number of constitutional crises, in 2007 and 2012. See Chapter 6.

24 Mungiu-Pippidi (1997: 79). Valea mentions other critical positions that were articulated during the constitutional debate, including an outright rejection of the idea of a constitutional court as a 'superpower', and 'alien body', and an 'extra-parliamentary body' 'situated above the parliament' (Valea 2010: 58; cf. *Geneza Constituției* 1998: 856–64).

25 Decision 1/1996. See Iancu (2009: 187).

26 The original article 145 stated:

> In cases of unconstitutionality, of the in accordance with Article 144 Constitutional subparagraphs a) and b), the law or Court standing orders shall be returned for reconsideration. If the law is passed again in the same formulation by a majority of at least two thirds of the members of each Chamber, the objection of unconstitutionality shall be removed, and promulgation thereof shall be binding.

27 The Romanian constitution, arguably the most difficult to amend constitution in the region, has been amended once, in 2003.

4 Rudiments of civic constitutionalism

The argument in this book is that legal constitutionalism risks being a counterproductive project: while the primary objective of legal constitutionalism is to induce political stability and the rule of law, in reality its strong emphasis on a separation between constitutional law, on the one hand, and political and civil society, on the other, potentially limits the diffusion of constitutionalism as a primary political language in political and civic interaction. In the terms of Richard Albert, legalistic forms of constitutionalism (Albert speaks of 'counterconstitutionalism'), while consistent with the purpose of constitutionalism of creating the structures of the state and setting the boundaries between the state and the citizen, risk '[r]ather than breathing life into participatory democracy, [to smother] the possibility of creating the possibility of participatory democracy because counterconstitutional constitutions do not create a constitutional culture that is conducive to participatory democracy' (2008: 4). In other words, if constitutionalism is about both order creation *and* participation and autonomy (cf. Cohen and Arato 1992), legal constitutionalism falls short in terms of the second dimension. One could go further by arguing that without a satisfactory fulfilment of the second meta-dimension of constitutionalism – democratic participation – the first meta-dimension is at risk. A too wide gap between a formal constitution and a constitutional culture, which embeds the constitution, entails the risk of reducing the constitution to an elite instrument. It might have little to no relevance in political and civic matters and/or is largely perceived in instrumental-strategic terms, not least by political actors.

The preceding chapter illustrated the way in which legal constitutionalism plays a predominant role in the political and constitutional transformations in Central and Eastern Europe. Four criteria were deemed relevant here: an emphasis on politico-legal autonomy and state sovereignty, the constitution as primary law, the fundamental nature of rights and the independent role of constitutional courts. Using these criteria, all five new democracies show a strong leaning towards legal constitutionalism (even if in the case of Romania this has been a rather recent phenomenon, which is now anyhow much under stress). The argument in this, and the following, chapter is that legal constitutionalism is, however, not the only constitutional language that is available in the region. The complexity of the constitutional semantics that have informed constitutional trajectories since 1989 include 'authoritarian constitutionalism' and legal constitutionalism, but also communitarian and democratic constitutionalism (Blokker 2010a, 2010b; Přibáň 2007; Skapska 2011: 120–1).

In this study, the tension between the emergence of legal constitutonalism as the predominant constitutional language and the availability of democratic constitutionalism as an alternative forms the primary focus.[1] In this, it is possible to observe some rudimentary elements of more democratic or civic forms of constitutionalism in the new democracies. The latter include emphases on multiple channels of civic participation and self-government (cf. Arato 2000: 71–2), and can, in some ways, be related to a republican-democratic view. In part, and as I will discuss below, I believe these elements can be related to oppositional views of self-government and more participatory forms of democracy that emerged in the 1970s and 1980s. The suggestion is that dimensions of civic constitutionalism do play a role – even if a rather variegated one – in all countries under study. In some countries these dimensions – also due to external factors – have taken on a more important status over time, even if they remain object of significant political conflict. Admittedly, in some countries, notably Hungary and Romania, recent developments have seen strong setbacks for *both* legal and civic constitutionalism.

I understand civic constitutionalism as operating both on the level of constitutional and of normal politics (see Ackerman 1991; Colon-Rios 2012). It is important, I believe, to understand robust constitutional democracy in terms of multiple channels of democratic engagement. In this, the argument is that in the drafting of the constitutions 'all too often the main concern was the legitimacy of the constitution related to [a] 'vote-centric' . . . concept of political participation', rather than substantive and continuous civic engagement (Puchalska 2011: 15). As Albert has argued, 'participation must not be geared solely towards national institutions. Participatory democracy exists only if individuals press upon disparate points of access and engagement, from community-based local sites of activity to the highest echelons of government administration' (2008: 10). My argument also follows some of Andrew Arato's (2000) regarding the importance of the existence of constitutional arrangements that facilitate civil society and civic participation and initiative for a robust constitutional-democratic order. The idea is that for constitutionalism to become a viable and socially embedded language, the constitution should not be strongly disembedded from society and politics (cf. Albert 2008), and operate merely from a meta-level onto society. Rather, it should endorse various forms of social and political interaction with the fundamental norms. Following Sadurski (e.g. 2005), my concern is that a too strong emphasis on constitutional entrenchment and independence of constitutional norms, in particular, but not only, in a context of 'weak civil society' and a 'weak party political system', might perpetuate the weakness of political and social actors, and therefore undermine the long-term objective of establishing a robust constitutional democracy based on the idea of civic self-government (Sadurski 2005: 23).

The importance of robust constitutional arrangements that provide possibilities for political and societal interaction with the constitution are a *conditio sine qua non* for a viable democratic order grounded in the idea of autonomy. Such constitutional arrangements provide counter-tendencies, or perhaps better, civic-democratic additions to (cf. Arato 2000: 70–3), a closed legal constitutionalism. Below, and in the following chapter, I will identify such arrangements in, first, possibilities of civic participation in constitutional amendment and revision; second, civic participation beyond representative channels, such as through referenda; and third, forms of decentralization and self-government (in terms of local and regional democracy, and both in terms of representative and more direct channels).[2]

Before turning to a comparative analysis of these dimensions in the five constitutional orders under study, I turn to the intellectual and cultural traditions that can be related to the institutionalization of democratic forms of constitutionalism in the region. The suggestion is that such traditions might have re-emerged in endorsements of such forms after 1989, and nurtured and facilitated civic and political action. A comprehensive study of constitutionalization and constitutional politics in the region cannot do without such a historical analysis, in order to acknowledge the different legacies that have influenced the specific form and shape constitutional regimes have taken (cf. Arato 2000). In the rest of this chapter, I will therefore briefly engage with the emergence of a complex set of constitutionalist languages in the last two decades of communism, and emphasize an emancipatory language that was articulated by some, even if not all, of the dissident movements. This emancipatory discourse tended to emphasize self-government and proximity of politics, civil society and civic engagement.

Constitutional languages before and after 1989

The legal and constitutional changes that in part preceded the negotiated revolutions of 1989 involved complex tendencies that do not merely point to the straightforward emergence of the rule of law and constitutionalism, replacing the highly pseudo-legal structures of post-totalitarian communism. Constitutional changes that emerged already prior to 1989 were informed by various ways of approaching the law and constitutionalism. The different interpretations were available at the moment of regime change, and include positivist, substantivist, nationalist/traditionalist and democratic conceptions (cf. Skapska 2011). In different ways, these languages have played and continue to play a role in post-1989 constitution-making. The complexity regarding available and emergent understandings of legality and constitutionalism was also reflected in the highly important dissident language. The variegated dissident discourse included an emphasis on rights and the rule of law but equally stressed civic emancipation.

A more generalized invocation of rights and the rule of law, as well as the language of constitutionalism, emerged most visibly in the 1970s. This legal language, used by movements such as the Polish Committee for Social Self-Defence (KOR) and the Czechoslovak Charter 77, involved an attempt to hold the communist regimes up to their constitutional promises as enshrined in the communist constitutions. But it is important to realize that communist regimes themselves not only responded by means of harsh repression.[3] At least in some cases, the communist regimes also increasingly sought recourse to legal instruments in an attempt to regain legitimacy for the communist regimes. This recourse to law was equally stimulated by different forms of international pressure. As remarked by Skapska, communist regimes were increasingly vulnerable to the foreign financial world because of their growing indebtedness, and the 'states had to seek legitimization of their activities wherever possible in order to justify the system they represented' (2011: 109).

Visible instances of the change in the constitutionalist language of communist regimes were the establishment of a Constitutional Tribunal in Poland in 1986, resulting from pressures from the Solidarnosc movement, as well as a Polish ombudsman (the Commissioner for Citizens Rights) in 1987 (Boulanger 1999: 2; Skapska 2011: 109). As Jacek Kurczewksi has remarked:

> [t]he Communist regime was already so interested in legalistic legitimation throughout the 1980s that constitutional lawyers were pressing towards legalizing every change. After all, the constitutional

> court itself had already been set up before 1989 in the attempt to develop the 'socialist state of law' as it was then called.
>
> (2003: 164)

Also in the case of Hungary, breaches in the old-style Stalinist approach to constitutionalism became visible in the early 1980s, for instance by means of the establishment of a Constitutional Council in 1983:

> Politicians had found the institution [the constitution, pb] suspicious until the middle of the 1980s, when the idea of establishing an organ formally separated from the Parliament emerged in order to institutionalise 'efficient' protection of the Constitution. This organ was the Constitutional Council that was established in 1983. It was a new and significant step towards constitutional protection, even though it could not act as a real 'protector' in the political atmosphere.
>
> (Csink and Schanda 2011: 161)

While the idea of a legalistic 'socialist state of law' pointed in particular in the direction of a more formalistic understanding of legality, the legal language of dissidents was richer and went beyond a merely formal, positivistic understanding of the law. This more variegated understanding of the rule of law and constitutionalism is important for my analysis in that it points to both the significance of dissidence for the emergence of legal constitutionalism *and* its contributions towards the endorsement of forms of democratic constitutionalism. The argument is that the dissident influence, however complex and variegated in its own right (see, e.g., Renwick 2006), has played at least a dual role in promoting constitutionalism from the post-totalitarian period onwards. In this, dissident 'anti-politics' contained both a descriptive and a normative component. In its descriptive sense, anti-politics pointed to the really emerging 'parallel societies' and civil society activities in some communist countries, which went 'beyond the limits of the "obsolete" contract on which the communist system rested – the negative constitutional consensus' (Skapska 2011: 112). In this descriptive sense, it can also be argued that the endorsement of the actual implementation of formally existing rights contributed to a pragmatic strategy of ameliorating the existing situation. In a normative sense, anti-politics has a different, and in ways more powerful, thrust in that it insisted on the false, distorted nature of existing reality and the need for 'living in truth'. The normative vision informed ideas of 'new evolutionism' (Michnik) and peaceful resistance, but it also stressed ideas of civic engagement, self-government and the opposition to a 'politicization of life-worlds' (Skapska 2011: 113). This dual language is somehow visible in the programme of Solidarnosc, adopted during its first national congress in October, 1981. In the chapter called 'The Self-Governed Republic', the programme invokes the need for a democratized state as well as independent civil society and self-government, a constellation which is to guarantee a correspondence of public institutions with human needs and social aspirations:

> Public life in Poland requires deep reforms which should lead to the definitive establishment of self-government, democracy and pluralism. For this reason, we shall struggle both for *a change in state structures and for the development of independent, self-governing institutions in every field of social life*. Only such a course can guarantee that *the institutions of public life are in harmony with human needs and the social and national aspirations of Poles*. Such changes are also essential if the country is to find a way out of the economic crisis. We consider that pluralism, democracy and full enjoyment of constitutional rights provide the guarantee that the workers' efforts and sacrifices will not be wasted once again.
>
> (Solidarity 1981: thesis 19; emphasis added)

As argued in slightly different terms by Přibáň, the dualistic objectives of dissident forces pointed to an emphasis on, first, a stable order grounded in the rule of law and the fundamental protection of civil society and, second, in a related sense, the possibility of civic engagement and emancipation. The constitutionalization of the new democratic orders in Central and Eastern Europe was therefore not merely about entrenching the ground rules of the democratic political game, but also about ensuring a continuing influence of civil society on politics and the safeguarding of some of the key values of civil society that had emerged in the 1980s. The latter included avoidance of suppression (by the state), public engagement, solidarity, critique and dissent (Přibáň 2007: 76–7). In this regard, the dissident language was not merely legalist, as pointed out by Přibáň, but had a more fundamental, in some ways opposed, character. In this latter, more fundamental sense, the dissidents questioned the ideas of legality and the rule of law as merely formalistic concepts. Thus, according to the dissidents,

> neither the legal procedures, nor the legal rules of communism could be squared with the principle of legality and the rule of law. So far as the principle of legality and the rule of law is concerned, legal

> rules and procedures must represent certain values, political principles and procedures supporting the separation of political power.
>
> (Přibáň 2002: 168)

In this, they pointed to the idea that legal institutions by themselves are not sufficient, but need the active engagement and civic endorsement to be viable and democratic.

As promoters of both the rule of law and civil society, dissidents therefore played a highly significant role in post-communist constitution-making (Arato 2000: 70–80; Přibáň 2007: 78). As again Přibáň argues, '[t]he constitutional transformations in Central Europe then both promoted the institutional rebuilding of civil society and derived their legitimacy from the civil society tradition and virtues' (2007: 77). Also according to Arato, the constitutional dimension to the making of democracy in terms of institutionalizing civil society and facilitating civic participation is crucial. At the end of the 1990s, Arato observed that civil society, despite many notifications to the contrary, had not disappeared in Central and Eastern Europe. According to him, civil association and practice survived both because of a politico-cultural legacy and constitutional institutionalization:

> The answer [as to the spread of civil society discourse, pb] lies both in the survival of the conception both in the region as well as (importantly) abroad and even more in the structural characteristics of the liberal democratic systems established in the region. Indeed, the discourse might have lost its social context, *had not the constitutional arrangements facilitated* in various ways and degrees the reemergence of civic associations and initiatives and their reinsertion into national politics.
>
> (2000: 71; emphasis added)

In the following chapter, I will engage with this constitutional facilitation by comparatively analysing the three dimensions of civic constitutionalism indicated above: possibilities of civic participation in constitutional amendment and revision; civic participation beyond representative channels; and forms of decentralization and self-government in the five constitutional orders. But first, I will briefly revisit some of the relevant dissident legacies in the various countries under study, to explore the conception of civil society and engagement that was elaborated during communist times, and to highlight the relevance of this conception to the changes after 1989 and to a participatory-democratic dimension of such changes.

Possible roots of civic constitutionalism: the dissident past[4]

The changes of 1989 have been – for a good part rightly so – identified as both 'rights revolutions' as well as 'legal revolutions', indicating the emphases on the retrieval of fundamental rights and radical change taking place within the existing legal context. The changes demonstrated a strong desire to establish liberal, constitutional democracies. But it can be shown that the changes were about more than the establishment of a liberal, representative type of democracy grounded in the rule of law. Depending on one's interpretation, it can be argued that an alternative democratic dimension in the changes of 1989 entailed either a republican complement to liberal, representative democracy or indicated the importance of a more radically distinct view of participatory republicanism. In this, it is often overlooked that democracy is better understood in a multiple way, as it builds on both the liberal and the republican traditions. The latter can be regarded as a significant alternative model, which – through its emphasis on public participation – can in itself be related to participatory as well as more direct forms of democracy. The post-1989 assessment of democratization in Central and Eastern Europe has seen a one-sided emphasis on liberal-representative democracy, while the earlier recognition of the more radical sides to dissident thought, as expressed in notions such as civil society, self-government and anti-politics, has been 'tamed' in the predominant liberal reading of democratization (Baker 2002). The significance of bringing out a republican dimension lies in its re-evaluation of the continuing importance of an alternative understanding of democratic politics, and in enhancing our understanding of political conflict over the *finalité* of democratic politics.

The essence of republican thought – which can in many ways be understood as a distinct, alternative tradition of democratic thought (Skinner 1990) – lies in its priority for 'public engagement' and 'self-government', in contrast to ideas of private, individual interest and representative politics of liberalism (Dagger 2004). Public engagement is concerned with politics being a public, openly conducted affair, with equal access for all; with a civic attitude – civic virtue – that transcends the self-interest of liberal individualism and indicates a citizen's concern for the public good; as well as with a distinct type of public sphere. Self-government refers to the ability of citizens to give themselves their own rules. Self-government can then take the form of direct democracy in terms of direct participation in self-rule (in contrast to mere representation), but in modern democracies it can also be translated into the endorsement of more decentralized, local forms of participation in government (closer to the citizen) as well as the positive evaluation of engagement in civic association. A sensitivity to smallness was probably more prominent in classical republicanism, in the idea that the proximity of the citizens to matters of the public good makes politics purer and easier to conduct, but it can still be seen as underpinning modern ideas of self-government and civic engagement. In this, the recent revival of republicanism shows its continuing relevance for modern democratic polities (Dagger 2004: 174).

The significance of a republican view of democracy in the Central and Eastern European region can be traced back to dissident discourse in a variety of significant ways (cf. Dryzek and Holmes 2002).[5] A republican dimension was clearly part of the dissident ideas that emerged in the 1970s and 1980s. As argued above, a good part of the dissident discourse and practice took a legalist guise, that is its main objective was to uncover the arbitrary and political nature of 'socialist legality' and to establish a genuine type of rule of law based on fundamental rights. But legalism was clearly not the only objective informing the discourse of dissident movements in the region. The idea of dissidence containing a republican dimension has remained fairly marginal to debates on dissidence and its post-1989 significance,[6] despite ample discussion of related notions such as anti-politics and civil society. Its relevance can, however, be easily shown by reference to the various debates in Czechoslovakia, Hungary and Poland, but much less so in the case of Romania.

Czechoslovakia

In the Czechoslovakian context, at least three dimensions of dissident discourse indicated a republican view of democracy, that is ideas of civic engagement and the civic scrutiny of formal politics, ideas of civic association, and endorsements of (local) self-rule and autonomy. Instead of an attempt to overthrow the existing regime by revolutionary violence and overtake political power, the emphasis in much dissident thought was on 'civic activation' and a 'gradual pressure from below'. One important aspect that was articulated, not least through Václav Benda's notion of a 'parallel polis' to existing power structures (Benda *et al.* 1988), was the need for the limitation, and critical scrutiny, of official politics. This can be related to a republican view of civic virtue and engagement as a counterbalance to the arbitrariness, corruption and abuse of formal centres of political power. As Isaac has shown with regard to Charter 77, a significant part of its oppositional activities was about the revival of active citizenship (Isaac 1996: 308).

The attempt to create a parallel polis was not merely prompted by the idea of the retrieval of rights in the face of a repressive, (post-)totalitarian state, and the creation of a civil society based on such rights.[7] An all-important inspiration for creating a public sphere was the endorsement of publicly inspired civic action in favour of the common good, as well as the possibility to 'live in truth'. The idea of 'civic responsibility' was in this a critique of the civic apathy and alienation of both post-totalitarian and liberal-democratic systems (Isaac 1996: 313; Kis 2008: 303). Civic apathy and consumerism were to be overcome by forms of civic engagement, based on a 'spiritual orientation', 'which includes ethical postulates, sensitive creation, analytical and synthetic processes of learning and self-discovery in openness and progress' (Batek 1985: 97).

As for the idea of civic association, the notions of 'anti-political politics' (Havel) and 'self-organization' (Uhl) were 'envisaged on a local level . . . [as] a call for the recovery of a more self-determining and less alienating political order' (Baker 2002: 38). The main critique here – shared among dissidents holding ultimately very different ideological backgrounds – was one of the immanent alienating tendencies in large-scale, centralized bureaucracies (Havel 1985; Uhl 1985). Thus, in dissident discourse, as in republican thinking, one could find a distinct sensitivity for smallness and the need for the proximity of democratic politics: '[t]here can and must be structures that are open, dynamic and small; beyond a certain point, human ties like personal trust and personal responsibility cannot work' (Havel 1985: 93). This points to a need for direct forms of democracy, civic association and the enhancement of possibilities for civic self-management. In contrast to notions of a centralized, unitary and bureaucratized state, citizens should be able to form their own associations that form an important counterweight to official government, in a form of 'informal politics' and 'politics from below', while official politics needs to be sufficiently open to such civic voice (see Cohen and Arato 1992).

Collective autonomy in the republican vein of giving oneself one's own rules was a key dimension in dissident thought. Much of the spirit of dissident thought and the idea of a 'parallel polis' was essentially about the renewal of 'relationships that, in return, give its members the dignity of participating in decisions that concern the community, and creating that community's structures' (Jirous 1988: 227). In the words of Jiří Dienstbier, an important spokesman of Charter 77, '[t]he basic aim of the self-organization of civil society, of independent and parallel activities, is the preservation and renewal of normality . . . the renewal of civic awareness and interest in the affairs of the community'

(1988: 231). It was realized, though, that civic engagement with politics could only be effective if the right institutions and means for self-rule were available. Thus, Petr Uhl, a thinker situated on the radical left, argued for a combination of representation and direct democracy:

> Social (not merely economic) self-management is . . . a combination of direct and indirect forms of democracy. Indirect (representative) democracy means a system of workers (and other) councils, horizontally co-ordinated, which would invest authority in a general council to replace today's legislative and executive state organs. It would be a democracy of the productive forces complemented by the territorial principle. The indirect democracy would be complemented by elements of direct democracy: referenda, even at the local level, public opinion polls whose results are binding, the direct administration of things by groups of people, and so on.
>
> (1985: 190–1)

In Uhl's view, however, '[s]ocial self-management is not a panacea: it is only worthy of support if it guarantees the continual expansion of direct democracy in favour of the gradual dismantling of representative democracy' (ibid.: 191). His argument is thus one for a radicalized, republican democracy from below as the only way of 'democratizing democracy' and guaranteeing genuine self-rule. Also Rudolf Battěk, one of the later founders of the Movement for Civil Freedom (HOS), argued in favour of forms of self-management, and the need for fragmenting or pluralizing sovereignty. Equally, however, he perceived the impossibility of fully doing away with state structures:

> Social structures can be democratized by expanding the elements of self-management, limiting institutional growth, making allowance for ideas as a motivating factor, and strengthening direct democracy by eliminating priorities and privileges. On other hand, however, we must avoid political leaps into the dark and shun those fascinating social utopias with their visions of the elimination of power, government, and the state . . . But political power, the highest form of decision-making power, must be prevented, both through law and through 'power', from becoming totally concentrated in a single place.
>
> (Battek 1985: 108)[8]

In addition, the Civic Forum, established in 1989, argued in favour of a bottom-up process of democratization, starting from the local level:

> Politics begins in communities [municipalities] whose members feel sufficient co-belonging that it is worth their while complying with democratic procedures . . . Along with economic reform we must come up with, for example, new territorial arrangements in which it will be abundantly clear where the sphere of citizens' self-government ends and the competences of the authorities begin . . . The state has to be built organically, gradually . . . through the expansion of our homes and our communities . . . [W]hat we lack most of all today is community, and without living, self-governing communities politics and democracy are mere figments.
>
> (*Fórum* 1990, cited in Smith 2003: 47)

Much attention in the literature has gone to the Czech manifestations of dissidence, in particular as embodied by the figure of Havel (see, e.g., Tucker 1999). Differences in dissident manifestations can, however, be observed with regard to how dissidence developed and the forces that were behind it in the cases of the Czech Republic and Slovakia. Barbara Falk has argued that '[w]ithin Slovakia dissent proceeded at lower decibel levels and with less attention than in Prague, but paradoxically was more broad-based' (2003: 96). Distinct elements in Slovak dissidence were related to its make-up, which, for instance, included the Hungarian minority which invoked human rights in order to endorse self-government, as well as the Catholic Church. The latter, the Hungarian minority and the Church, together with Slovak adherents to the Charter 77 movements, formed the democratic movement that emerged at the end of the 1980s and formed Public Against Violence (VPN). The latter invoked, in a similar way as the Civic Forum, forms of local self-government in contrast to centralized communist rule:

> The alternative is decentralization, self-government in every region . . . the division of the res-publica into thousands of individual publics, making competent decisions about their environments . . . That is why VPN supports the emergence of the most varied fora . . . These fora, and particularly those at the local level, can become the source of a genuinely cultured local or regional milieu, the activisers of local life, local administration, local culture in the broadest sense of the term.
>
> (*Verejnost* 1990, cited in Smith 2003: 47)

Hungary

Ideas of self-organization and civic engagement were clearly less central in the Hungarian debate, where the intellectual elite engaging in dissidence was relatively small and less organized,[9] and where an intellectualist, 'avant-garde' mentality prevailed (Bozóki 2009). It can be argued that the Hungarian oppositional movement – in particular the intellectuals around the samizdat journal *Beszélő* – followed primarily a liberal-legalist strategy, based on fundamental rights and notions of a Rechtsstaat, and pluralism. This was formulated by János Kis, one of the most prominent dissident voices in Hungary, as the 'idea of dual mobility: in the sphere of public law towards the constitutional state, and in the sphere of civil law towards pluralism' (Kis 1989: 125). Kis argued in *Beszélő* against the 'legal anarchy' of the communist regime, as '[t]his practice destroyed the public mores of political life and has started to eat away private morals as well. One of our very first tasks is to make it understood that only people who are conscious of their rights and ready to defend them may become citizens with self-respect' (Kis 1989: 121, 123). It can then be argued, as observed by Renwick, that '[t]he language of the 'ethics of truth' or the 'ethical nation' was less prominent in Hungary's political opposition' (Renwick 2006: 313).

But despite a more legalist, pluralist, and liberal-democratic inclination (Baker 2002: 47–50), and a certain distance to notions of moral politics and the idea of 'living in truth' (Kis 1999, 2008), it is clear that ideas of a 'parallel polis' or 'secondary society', grounded in some idea of the authenticity of civic voice, were not wholly absent or altogether insignificant in the Hungarian debate (Hankiss 1988). Indeed, János Kis later recognized a variety of dissident ideas, but also indicated two decisive concepts as a commonality among the opposition: 'human rights' and 'civil society' (1999: 19). The same Kis had stated in the early 1980s – in a joint article with György Bence – that they had 'reached radical reformism coming from Marxism' (Bence and Kis 1980: 295). Radical reformism was for Bence and Kis a 'Polish phenomenon', in which '[t]he autonomous self-organisation of society is an end in itself' (ibid.: 286). And in the best-known dissident statement and evidently more civic-minded 'Antipolitics', György Konrad argued that the 'idea of delegated authority has become problematical'.[10] He continued,

> [t]here is less reason all the time why grown, educated, intelligent people should transfer their powers of decision to distant, unknown, and scarcely accountable individuals, as if selecting guardians to make their decisions for them. It would seem more natural if authority and labor, administration and everyday life were to be separated as little as possible.
>
> (1984: 133)

Konrad understood ideas of civic engagement, the need for civic voice and for civic proximity as essential antidotes to centralistic decision-making, be it of a communist or liberal-democratic kind:

> Workplace or local community self-government, based on personal contact, exercised daily, and always subject to correction, have a greater attraction in our part of the world than multiparty representative democracy because, if they have the choice, people are not content with voting once every four years just to choose their deputy or the head of the national government. That somehow seems very little when people hope that, by taking part in the affairs of the community, *they can gain a voice in their own destiny*.
> (Ibid.: 137; emphasis added)

Central to the Hungarian oppositional views was the idea of a compromise between dissident forces and society, on the one hand, and the party state, on the other (Kis 1989a: 95–6). In this, a primary demand was that for associational freedom and a functioning civil sphere. As argued by Kis, '[i]n the political sphere institutions are needed such as [those that] can regulate and resolve conflict: trade unions, a functioning parliament, legally defined freedom of press, and effectively safeguarded civil rights' (1989b: 239). Such a development would 'take us closer to the ideal of citizens' equality; it would provide individuals and minorities with greater autonomy and legal protection vis-à-vis the state; it would widen the spectrum of available life alternatives' (ibid.). In addition, György Gadó (2008), editor of the samizdat journal *Magyar Zsidó*, argued along these lines:

> Regardless of under whose aegis they exist or function, any press organ, debating forum, organizational framework through which public opinion is informed in a manner true to reality, and which enhance the organization of society in the interest of reform and democracy is useful. But this can take place only if alongside the organs and organizational forms which exist as functions of those in power, there are organs and organizational forms which function independent from those in power, and in response to which the former do not unequivocally become the manipulative tools of those in power, and the dynamic emergence of which forces the former to take steps in the direction of democracy.

Associations were predominantly understood from a liberal-pluralist, interest-based perspective, although notions of self-governance and autonomy were also evident. According to Miklós Haraszti, editor of

Beszélő, reforms of the socialist system were an impossibility 'without the workers and all others involved having the possibility to freely articulate their interests and to negotiate them' (1983). In the second political programme issued by the opposition in the 1980s, demands for democratization then not only referred to a 'multi-party system, and representative democracy in state policy', but also to 'autonomy in the workplace and in the municipalities'.

It can then be argued that also in the Hungarian case – even if to a much more modest extent than in Czechoslovakia and Poland – there was an appreciation of the need for civic participation in any genuinely democratic order, the need for independent civic organizations to guarantee substantive civic participation, and the need for actual civic voice in co-defining the common good. During the 1980s, opposition movements called for the introduction of popular initiatives (Pallinger 2012: 113). It was probably Konrad who articulated ideas of civic participation most clearly: 'The message is clear in the resolutions drawn up by the workers' councils during the Hungarian revolution of 1956: multiparty parliamentary democracy is essential; self-governance in every concrete community is essential. Democracy is essential at every level' (1984: 138). Konrad went on by arguing: 'Democracy is needed in factory management, in the government, and in relations with other governments. We need it in self-defense, so that others will not be able to humiliate, ruin, occupy, and terrorize us' (ibid.).

Poland

The most evident case of a republican dimension to dissident thought is probably that of Poland. Here, there was a strong critique in dissident thought of the denial of politics in the post-totalitarian regimes, as well as the recognition that civic engagement in political activity is of primary importance for the democratization of society. In Adam Michnik's famous essay 'A New Evolutionism', he already admitted to so much by arguing that '[f]aith in one's ability to exert influence on the fate of society is an absolute prerequisite for political activity' (1985: 137). Michnik indeed ended that essay by arguing:

> In searching for truth, or to quote Leszek Kołakowski, "by living in dignity", opposition intellectuals are striving not so much for a better tomorrow as for a better today. Every act of defiance helps us build the framework of democratic socialism, which should not be merely or primarily a legal institutional structure but a real, day-to-day community of free people.
>
> (Ibid.: 148)

It has indeed been argued that Polish dissidents came up first in the region with a 'society first' strategy, that is society as the main 'locus of political change' (Baker 2002: 17). In Polish dissident thought, one dimension included, then, not merely a search for a parallel or alternative society, free from state oppression, but the insight that democratization needs the 'rebuilding of autonomous social structures from below' (Kuron 1981).

Central in the ideas of some dissidents was the idea of individual action supporting the common good, which came through in particular in the writings – and arrived at from very different angles – of Jacek Kuroń and those of Father Tischner (Wesolowski and Gawkowska 2004). In the latter's Catholic perspective, solidarity 'establishes specific interpersonal bonds; a man binds himself to another man in order to protect the one who needs care' (Tischner 2009: 41). It can be argued that in the Polish case, partially under the influence of Catholic ideas on solidarity, a communitarian dimension of civic engagement was more evident, in terms of a stronger emphasis on references to the Polish community, and a certain emphasis on duties and unity (Wesolowski and Gawkowska 2004).

This is corroborated by the fact that much of the '*etos*' of Solidarity in the 1980s evidently took the form of a discourse of civic resistance. One element in this '*etos*' was that of 'self-determination', which can be interpreted as involving the 'recovery of agency and control from the state through participation in *etos*' (Holc 1995: 4). Michnik's idea of a 'politics of activism' – which he derived from the very different ideas of the Polish nationalist Dmowski and the socialist Abramowski – resonates fully with the idea of self-determination and civic virtue. Following Abramowski, any 'new captivity' inherent in statist structures was to be prevented by 'building up self-determination in civil society by creating associations from below and avoiding the intermediary role of state institutions in public life' (Michnik 1985: 303). But self-determination was not only about the republican idea of the value of participation in politics in its own right, but was further linked with notions of 'unity', that is society united against the state as well as sharing moral duties, a nationalist ethos, and a gender outlook (Holc 1995: 4), in this reflecting a more communitarian and exclusionary streak.

A significant and related aspect in Solidarity's ethos was a form of 'associationalism', that is the idea of the construction of an autonomous community or set of communities from below.[11] This emphasis on self-government and self-organization was famously expressed in the Solidarity programme presented in October 1981, which, not by coincidence (Glinski 2006), has been referred to mostly by means of the title of the sixth chapter: 'The Self-Governing Republic'. From both a normative-democratic and a more pragmatic stance, the self-governing republic was understood as a complement, or even an alternative, to centralized state structures (cf. Gawin 2008: 39). That is to say, in addition to the normative prioritization of society there was also a recognition, in particular expressed through the influence of early twentieth-century ideas on leftist cooperative movements, that modern society is too complex to be managed by a central state, and that only flexible autonomous associations were able to combine efficiency, creativity and sentiments of the common good (Gawin 2008: 40).

The most important republican notion – that of collective autonomy, self-determination or self-rule – was intimately related to Solidarity's endorsement of civic education and virtue, and civic organization in associations from below. Kuroń's notion of 'self-organization' expressed this particularly well. This idea included the project of creating a public sphere in which free deliberation about matters that are common to all can take place. The aim of the dissidents was thus not merely the creation of a sphere untouched by state interference, in which people could then be free to engage in individual activities (as in a liberal, rights-based view), but much more importantly, the endorsement of collective engagement in self-determination. In the words of David Ost, the 'goal of the opposition in the 1970s was to get people to do things – anything – just as long as they did it on their own, with no official mediation . . . [this was] felt to produce an ethos of self-determination, a belief in one's ability to act publicly' (Ost 1990: 70). The emphases on workers' self-management as well as on territorial and local self-government were further instances of the 'ethic of self-rule' and the idea of an 'authentic voice of local communities' in dissident ideas (cf. Zielonka 1989: 73). Indeed, in Adam Michnik's words, it permitted breaking the 'psychology of slaves' (Zielonka 1989: 77). This was inter alia reflected in thesis 21 of Solidarity's programme of 1981: 'Regional self-government structures, legally and financially autonomous, should genuinely represent the interests of the local population' (Solidarity 1981). According to Jan Zielonka, the idea of a self-governing republic was predominant over any initiatives aiming at the strengthening and expansion of a liberal, parliamentary democracy in Poland (1989: 74).

Romania

Communist Romania is often described as an exception. This is equally true with regard to phenomena of dissidence. As seen in the previous chapter, some dissident action invoking legality and human rights emerged also in Romania, in response to the Helsinki Acts and the Czechoslovak experience with Charter 77. In general, however, collective forms of protest and in particular intellectually driven dissidence were largely absent or at most isolated actions in the Romanian context. As one Romanian scholar has argued, '[u]nlike Central Europe, communist Romania had no equivalent to KOR or Charter 77, no collective action, no coalition between intellectuals and workers, no *samizdat* publications' (Tănăsoiu 2011: 324). Many Romanian intellectuals were engaged in a 'resistance through culture' rather than an open confrontation with the regime. The rather limited Romanian phenomenon of explicit dissidence was largely related to Paul Goma, a writer,[12] and the relatively sizeable collective protest he was able to mobilize (Cătănuş 2011a). This was not least expressed in the most important moment of the Romanian equivalent of post-Helsinki dissent, which led to an open letter addressed to the 1977 Belgrade conference (a follow-up to the Helsinki event), with some 200 signatories (Petreşcu and Petreşcu 2005: 339). In this letter, various – civic and social – rights enshrined in the Romanian constitution were invoked, in particular the rights to free movement of people, ideas and information. It further argued that the 'right to citizenship is transformed into an obligation which does not serve the cause of progress' (Goma 1979: 46–7).

As observed in Chapter 3, to some extent the legalist, rights-based dimension can also be identified in the Romanian context, even if in a much weaker form than in the Czechoslovak or Hungarian cases. Very few signs of a substantial and elaborated critique on the communist system as such in terms of 'anti-political politics' and related notions of self-government and civic engagement can, however, be detected in the Romanian communist experience. Recently, one Romanian scholar has argued that in the case of the (isolated) dissident efforts of Mihai Botez, a mathematician and dissident thinker, some parallels with Central European concepts can be identified (Cătănuş 2011b). This scholar argues that Botez not only emphasized the need to resist the communist regime with legal means but also developed an alternative discourse which pointed to the 'solitary dissident' as a figure that attempts to live in truth and inspires others to speak the truth publicly. Moreover, Botez invoked a notion of a 'parallel society' in which a diversity of views was to co-exist and which could exercise societal pressure on government strategies by means of a 'mass critical opinion' (Cătănuş 2011b: 346, 355). Botez did not, however, manage to mobilize other intellectuals and a wider audience with these ideas. Further examples of civil society-kind of approaches are the work of philosopher

Mihai Şora, who advocated a generalized dialogue between social actors, and that of Doina Cornea, who engaged in a self-critical examination, echoing in some ways Havel (Tănăsoiu 2011: 333–4, 336).

Only from 1987 onwards did more explicit attempts at criticizing the Romanian communist system emerge, and it was only really by 1989 and the December Revolution that dissidents started to play an important role in provoking an anti-communist and democratically oriented revolt. This culminated in the Timişoara declaration of 20 December 1989. According to Petreşcu and Petreşcu, in the Romanian case 'dissidents clearly had only a very limited influence in structuring the public sphere in the long run' (2005: 346). This is probably true, but it can also be sustained that after 1989 in particular intellectuals started playing a role more similar to their Central European counterparts. Thus, Tănăsoiu argues:

> Similar to their Central and Eastern European peers, Romanian intellectuals have argued for a 'return to Europe', decommunisation, civil society, political (i.e., separation of powers, minority rights, freedom of speech), economic (i.e., privatization, property law), and judicial (i.e., independence of magistrates) reforms.
>
> (2008: 81)

The same scholar argues that the Romanian intellectuals acted as belated dissidents in endorsing civil society as well as a form of 'anti-political politics' in the post-1989 setting. It is interesting to see that, in this, they used a similarly dualistic language as the 1980 dissidents had invoked elsewhere. On the one hand, 'Romanian intellectuals [were] particularly concerned with the functioning of the judicial system, the law, and the rule of law. Thus they became vocal advocates of judicial reforms securing the independence of magistrates from the realm of politics'[13] (Tănăsoiu 2008: 89). On the other, they pursued a form of belated 'anti-political politics', a discourse 'characterized by contempt towards politics and politicians' and in favour of a 'politics of people'. This evolved into a 'watchdog type of discourse adequate for a country on the road to democratization where the acts of the political elites and of the political establishment have to be continuously monitored by representatives of civil society' (ibid. 93).

To sum up, the dissident discourse in the various Central and Eastern Europe nations was rich, critical, but also variegated and often displaying internal tensions. In relation to legal and constitutional narratives, though, it seems clear that in all cases sustained references to legalism and respect for the values and rights that were formally enshrined in the communist constitutions was made. Even in the highly closed national communism of Romania such legal demands and claims emerged. But while this – in certain ways – precursor to the legal-constitutionalist views of the 1990s was extremely important in the post-1989 constitutional trajectories of the new democracies, in this chapter I have tried to show that in all cases, except for Romania, an important alternative narrative was also articulated. This democratic-constitutional narrative was related to the idea of civil society, which became subsequently so much associated with the dissident experience. This narrative clearly emphasizes a different role of democratic and legal institutions and their relation to politics and wider society. In the next chapter, I will explore to what extent such a narrative is actually reflected in the constitutional orders of the new democracies.

Notes

1 I have discussed the role of communitarian constitutionalism in the region at some length elsewhere (Blokker 2010a, 2010b).
2 Arato in his endorsement of the institutionalization of civil society includes in his list of relevant institutions: the guarantee of fundamental rights, the establishment of a recognized constitutional order with independent courts, 'political and economic decentralization, involving independent local and regional self-government', 'acceptance and recognition' of civic associations and their financing (2000: 71–2).
3 Amongst victims of repression were the Czechoslovak philosopher Jan Patocka (who died after a police interrogation) and the Romanian writer Paul Goma (who was forced into exile).
4 An earlier and more concise account appeared in Blokker (2011a).
5 This clearly does not mean it was the *only* dimension, nor that dissidence thought constituted a homogeneous set of ideas, as also attested by the idea of a dual language of rights and civil society (cf. Přibáň 2002). Rather, the dissident discourses contained a variety of dimensions and nuances (cf. Gawin 2007; Renwick, 2006), of which republican ideas were a significant, but since 1989 often neglected, part (cf. Isaac 1996).
6 For exceptions, see Carter (1999); Falk (2003); Isaac (1996); Żółkoś (2004).
7 See in particular the first public statement of Charter 77 (1977); cf. Patocka (1981).
8 See also Dienstbier (1988: 230).
9 Referred to by the sociologist Gyorgy Gado in an interview for the university journal *Szazadveg* as the 'civil disobedience manifested by the *Beszélő* circle and by other members (this truly informal, lose group)' (Gado 1988).
10 Konrad (1984: 133). Renwick indeed relates Konrad's ideas to those of Havel, defending spiritual values and an ethical civil society (2006: 289–90).
11 For an analysis of the events at the Gdansk Lenin shipyard in August 1980 from a classical republican lens, i.e. as the self-constitution of a 'sphere of free political community', see Gawin 2007.

12 In the Romanian context, it seems fair to say that at most some eight intellectuals did fit the designation of dissident, in the sense of a 'person in [public] disagreement with the ideological, political and economic fundaments of the society in which her or she lived' (Petreşcu and Petreşcu 2005: 338).

13 Interestingly, an important civil society group, the *Group for Social Dialogue* (GDS), criticized the referendum on the constitution in 1991 as a way of 'legalizing republicanism', whereas the GDS believed Romania should have returned to the constitutional monarchy of the 1930s, as this had been illegally abolished in 1948, and a return to this system would mean safe-guarding legality (Tănăsoiu 2008: 85).

5 Searching for civic constitutionalism

A comparative analysis

The emergence of constitutional democracy in the region of Central and Eastern Europe is not reducible to the adoption of the legal-constitutional or 'new-constitutional' model predominant in the contemporary world (cf. Stone Sweet 2008). As argued in the preceding chapters, the legal and constitutional changes that in part preceded the negotiated revolutions of 1989 involved complex tendencies that do not merely point to the straightforward emergence of the rule of law and liberal constitutionalism, replacing the (post-)totalitarian structures of communism. The complexity of legal and democratic change was also reflected in the highly important dissident language, which involved both an emphasis on rights and the rule of law, and on civic emancipation. In this regard, a comparative analysis of (the potentials of) civic or democratic constitutionalism seems overdue[1] and of high significance for a more comprehensive understanding of democratization and legal change in the post-communist countries.

What the dualistic objectives of dissident forces point to are an emphasis on both a stable order grounded in the rule of law and the fundamental protection of civil society (and hence the possibility for durable civic engagement). In this regard, the constitutionalization of the new democratic orders in Central and Eastern Europe was not merely about entrenching the ground rules of the democratic political game, but also about ensuring a continuing influence of civil society on politics and the safeguarding of some of the key values of civil society that had emerged in the 1980s, such as avoidance of suppression (by the state), public engagement, solidarity, critique and dissent (Přibáň 2007: 76–7). As promoters of both the rule of law and civil society, dissidents therefore played a highly significant role in post-communist constitution-making (Arato 2000: 70–80; Přibáň 2007: 78; cf. Puchalska 2011). As Přibáň argues, '[t]he constitutional transformations in Central Europe then both promoted the institutional rebuilding of civil society and derived their legitimacy from the civil society tradition and virtues'. He also remarks that '[a]s those principally responsible for instituting the democratic rule of law were dissidents committed to civil society, they were able to exercise great influence over post-communist constitution-making' (2007: 77, 78).

Post-communist constitution-making included the institutionalization of a capitalist market and a democratic regime, but also the creation of an institutional framework for civil society and what I would like to call a plurality of democratic channels (cf. Arato 2000). Constitution-making has thus included both legal and democratic constitutional dimensions, but to what extent these can be said to be robust, and even more importantly to be in balance with each other, remains an open question. In order to comparatively explore the salience of a democratic dimension to constitutionalism in the region, I will not so much focus on the tracing of forms of dissident influence on post-1989 constitutional structures (in itself a most interesting but arduous task), but, much more modestly, try to see to what extent the prevalent emphasis on legal constitutionalism has been countered by the three dimensions of civic constitutionalism I outlined, that is a civic influence on constitutional amendment or constitutional reform, the existence of channels of direct democracy on various levels, and decentralization and local self-government.

Constitutional revision

As argued in Chapter 2, the emphasis in legal constitutionalism on an entrenched constitution, which is protected from political and social interference, is in tension with the idea of democracy. If democratic self-rule is to be understood as the possibility for those subject to rules to be able to (co-)formulate those rules, a form of constitutional rigidity prevents such self-rule from taking place. Constitutional amendment 'provides a way for framers to share some of their authority over the constitution with future generations', and, in this, 'trenches upon core issues of democracy and sovereignty' (Holmes and Sunstein 1995: 276). Amendment plays a crucial if ambiguous role in constitutional democracies in that it 'inhabits a twilight zone between authorizing and authorized powers'. Stephen Holmes and Cass Sunstein refer to amendment power as '*le pouvoir constituent constitué*', that is a kind of institutionalized revolutionary power (1995: 276).

No constitution is in reality fully entrenched or unalterable. Constitutions contain rules of revision that stipulate how they should be changed if an imperfection is recognized (Levinson 1995). The revision of the constitution can be understood as a way to re-open the door to political and social interference. In this sense, revision becomes relevant for our discussion of civic constitutionalism, in that more accessible revision rules could be said to enhance dimensions of political and civic influence on the foundational rules. In the most radical, civic sense, this might include civic constitutional assemblies and civic constitutional initiatives, as for instance described by Colon-Rios (2012). Holmes and Sunstein make a case for the particular importance of amendment in the case of societal transformation. They argue that in the context of the post-communist states (in the 1990s), it would be advisably to set 'relatively lax conditions for amendment' so as to allow for constitutional adaptation to rapid change and new social input.

Carlos Closa has recently distinguished two 'competing theoretical approaches on constitutional reform, a Jeffersonian and a Madisonian view (2012: 283–7). The Jeffersonian view can be related to what we have referred to as democratic constitutionalism. As Closa argues, on this view 'law is the codified rule of past generations, and as such its effects on the present generation could be arbitrary and even despotic. Viewed in this light, a constitution becomes especially suspect if it is made difficult to amend' (2012: 283). A Jeffersonian view understands (regular) amendment as an 'essential mechanism to counteract a potentially fallible document' (ibid.). While Closa relates the Jeffersonian view largely to federal systems, we might add that there is an additional reason why one might want to endorse such a view of constitutional reform. From a democratic constitutional view, amendment provides a crucial democratic instrument which (potentially) provides citizens and their representatives with a means to influence the fundamental rules which make up their political community. Albert states this in a way when he argues '[unamendability clauses] are counterconstitutional because they place the constitution beyond the reach of the people, and therefore undermine participatory democracy' (2008: 25).

The Madisonian view of constitutionalism understands constitutional reform in a rather different way. It understands constitutions as containing special areas (in particular fundamental rights and institutional architecture and democratic procedures) that need special protection. Such special areas relate to fundamental issues that are best settled in special moments, and in this create a distinction between constitutional and normal politics (Closa 2012: 285; cf. Ackerman 1991). The creation of such 'pre-commitments' leads to a form of constitutional rigidity in which these special areas are protected by entrenchment (for instance, in the form of an *Ewigkeitsklausel*) and/or difficult amendment procedures. Closa argues that ultimately most theorists agree that constitutions need to balance between flexibility and rigidity, depending on specific circumstances. Be that as it may, the global trend of new or legal constitutionalism seems to prioritize the Madisonian rather than the Jeffersonian view, while more marginal countertrends indicate more propensity to Jeffersonian understandings (cf. Colon-Rios 2009).

As already becomes clear from the above, amendment or revision is not a straightforward matter. As argued by Francesco Palermo, revision can be related to both a change of the constitution (for instance, into a direction as desired by political and civic actors) and a (simple) maintenance of the constitution. In the latter case, revision would be largely about the conservation of the original text, and closer to a legalistic understanding of change. Conservation (the preservation of the existing text by incorporating relevant changes) tends towards a logic of preserving the status quo, while an adjustment (a modification to respond to changed circumstances) entails a political logic (Palermo 2007: 2; cf. Lutz 1995). Explicit formal revision entails a revolutionary element (Levinson 1995: 4), which points to an attempt to change the character of the constitutional text.[2]

Below, I will briefly explore the way in which revision is perceived in the constitutional texts of the five Central and Eastern European cases. The focus is in particular on the dimension of what could be called a 'pluralism of actors' (Palermo 2007: 12), that is the access of the different actors to the instrument of revision (such as parliaments, presidents, as well as civil society). In the line of my argument, an increase of channels of revision open to various actors might increase the democratic potential of constitutions.[3] A further complexity is the role of affirmative referenda, which according to some potentially involves a positive instance of popular influence on constitutional change (Tierney 2012), whereas others contest its positive nature (Holmes and Sunstein 1995).

Czech Republic

In the Czech case, the emphasis of the dissident tradition on self-government and civic engagement seems not reflected in a lasting civic-democratic influence on constitutional design, at least not with regard to the revision rules. In the Czech Constitution, revision initiatives – referred to as 'constitutional acts' (see art. 9(1), Constitutional Court ruling 27/09) – can be started only by the Czech parliament. In this regard, the Czech Constitution continues the parliamentary revision procedure as already part of the communist constitution of 1968 and retained in the changed Czechoslovak structures of the early 1990s (Arato

2000: 309, fn. 41). One could speak in the Czech case of a limited pluralism or parliamentary monism. The centrality of the parliament in revision is further stipulated in article 39(4): 'The concurrence of three-fifths of all Deputies and three-fifths of all Senators present is required for the adoption of a constitutional act or for giving assent to the ratification of treaties referred to in Article 10a para. 1.'

In this regard, the revision procedure is similar to the Polish parliamentary-driven procedure (cf. Holmes and Sunstein 1995: 292, 293), in that it needs supermajorities in both parliamentary chambers. The dual approval by both houses of Parliament indicates a 'more demanding constitutional amendment procedure' (Albi 2005: 70). At the same time, from the point of view of some scholars, this revision procedure entails a fairly low level of rigidity or entrenchment of the Czech Constitution, as no other requirements such as a popular referendum or the dissolution of the chambers are needed (Tomoszek 2010). In a comparative analysis of post-communist countries, Roberts (2009: 104) classifies the Czech Republic among easy to amend constitutions. In this parliamentary-driven procedure, however, no possibility for citizen-driven constitutional change is available, neither in terms of initiation nor in confirmatory, referenda terms. Limitations for constitutional acts are stipulated in article 9(2) (a kind of *Ewigkeitsklausel*; see Tomoszek 2010[4]): 'Any changes in the essential requirements for a democratic state governed by the rule of law are impermissible.' Since 1991, the Czech parliament has adopted eight constitutional acts, beginning in 1991 with, among others, the act related to the Charter of Fundamental Rights and Freedoms which supplements the Czech Constitution (cf. Slosarcik 2001).[5]

Hungary

Revision played a particularly central role in the Hungarian constitutionalization process after 1989. Up until 2012, the regime transformation from a communist to a constitutional-democratic system was enacted through the amendment of the existing 1949 constitution. In this regard, the constitution was 'completely revised by the parliament' (Drinoczi 2007: 447).[6] As argued by Arato and Miklosi, 'In the strict legal sense, the method of constitution making that achieved this result was one of parliamentary constitution making through legal continuity, utilizing the amendment rule of the old regime, a rule that survives to this day' (2005: 350). The period of 1989–1990 was particularly intensive regarding revision, and is referred to as the 'constituent process for regime change' (Drinoczi 2007: 448). Only with the adoption of the Basic Law in 2012 was this incrementalist pattern replaced by a more radical rupture (in a formal sense) with the preceding regime.

In terms of the revision procedure, the revision of the Hungarian Constitution (both before and after 2012) is equally a case of restricted pluralism or parliamentary monism (Arato speaks of the 'monopoly of a purely parliamentary revision rule', 2000: 153). Even if the constitutional text (again, both that of before and after 2012) does not explicate the relevant institutions, also the Constitutional Court has confirmed that only the parliament has the right to revision initiative. In the pre-2012 constitution, the rules for amendment are laid down in article 24(3), which applies the 'two-thirds' rule to constitutional amendment, meaning that only two-thirds of the parliament can introduce a constitutional change.[7] The constitutional right to the holding of referenda on citizens' initiative does not apply to the amendment of constitutional rules. Even though the Constitution does not explicate this, this became clear in a 1993 ruling of the Hungarian Constitutional Court (Arato 2000: 154; Deszo and Bragyova 2001: 75–6).[8] In the new Constitution of 2012, the monistic revision procedure is replicated: 'The approval of a motion to ratify or amend the Constitution shall require the support of at least two-thirds of the Members of Parliament' (R article). What is more, the absence of a national referendum related to constitutional revision is now made explicit in article 8 on the 'National Referendum'.

Poland

The Polish Constitution of 1997 arranges for amendment procedures in chapter XII. As stipulated in article 235(1), there is no citizens' initiative for constitutional amendment,[9] but constitutional change is not purely parliamentary-driven either, in that not only the Sejm and Senate, but also the president can initiate an amendment (cf. Rytel-Warzocha 2012: 214). Similar to the Czech and Hungarian procedures, constitutional amendments need a supermajority in parliament, that is they shall be 'adopted by the Sejm by a majority of at least two-thirds of votes in the presence of at least half of the statutory number of Deputies, and by the Senate by an absolute majority of votes in the presence of at least half of the statutory number of Senators' (article 235(4)).

Citizens' involvement only takes an ex post, confirmatory form, in that the Polish Constitution codifies the citizens' right to direct participation through referenda in constitutional matters, that is in the form of an affirmative referendum (cf. Gebethner 2001). Thus, in contrast to the Hungarian constitution, and similar to the obligatory referendum in the Romanian case, the Polish Constitution grants the possibility of a popular, affirmative referendum on constitutional amendments. Such a referendum is, in contrast to the Romanian case (see below), not obligatory, and can only be initiated by the Sejm, the senate, or the president. Moreover, a referendum can be held only in case of an amendment dealing with particular chapters (art. 235(6)).[10] In addition, citizens have the possibility to appeal to the Constitutional Court in case they presume that their constitutional rights and freedoms have been infringed by statutory law or decrees (art. 79; cf. Arato 2000: 225).

Romania

The revision of the Romanian Constitution is arranged for in article 150, which argues that revisions can be initiated by 'the President of Romania on the proposal of the Government, by at least one quarter of the number of Deputies or Senators, as well as by at least 500,000 citizens with the right to vote'. In contrast to, for instance, the Hungarian and Polish cases, the Romanian constitution provides for civic initiatives to constitutional revision. At the same time, the amendment procedure as such is relatively rigid, and substantially reduces possibilities for effective public participation in constitutional politics. According to Andrew Arato, the Romanian Constitution's 'revision rule is the most difficult in the region' (2000: 163; cf. Banciu 2001: 404–5; Roberts 2009: 104). Not only are specific geographical-distributional criteria stipulated for the civic initiative (article 150 (2)),[11] and it is difficult to succeed in having the revision adopted (two-thirds majorities in both chambers), and to arrive at final ratification (which includes a confirmatory popular referendum), but also the substance of revision is limited[12] (see also Chapter 3).

Initiatives to revise the constitution have been undertaken six times since 1991 (see Valea 2011). Two times (in 2000 and in 2007) the revision initiative was undertaken by Romanian citizens, but both times the initiatives were found unconstitutional by the Romanian Constitutional Court on procedural grounds (ibid.: 99–100).

Slovakia

The Slovak Constitution, as in the cases of Hungary and Poland, provides for a parliamentary-driven revision process. Article 84(3) states that 'The agreement of at least a three-fifths majority of all deputies is required to pass and amend the Constitution and constitutional laws, to elect and recall the president, and to declare war on another state.'

The Slovak Constitution is therefore less stringent in that it requires a smaller majority than the supermajority in the Hungarian case. In fact, Albi argues that the Slovak Constitution is 'one of the easiest to amend amongst the countries in question' (Albi 2005: 67). While the Slovak system is centred on the parliament as the institution with exclusive amending power, at the same time a channel for direct popular participation has emerged. A popular initiative to constitutional amendment has developed in a highly interesting way, in particular because this channel is not explicitly provided for in the Constitution. It was in the context of an expected political crisis that opposition parties started a popular initiative that called for a referendum on Constitutional amendment with regard to the direct election of the president. The initiative was justified by means of reference to article 2 of the Constitution, which refers to direct popular involvement. Further relevant constitutional provisions are article 93, which refers to the possibility of referenda on 'issues of the public interest', and article 95(1), which stipulates that at least 350,000 citizens can submit a petition for a referendum. The Constitutional Court ruled that an 'amendment of the constitution was eligible as a subject of referendum' (Lastic 2012: 161). At the same time, the Court argued that an amendment was to be enacted by parliament:

> it is not possible to directly amend the Constitution merely based on the outcome of the vote. The adoption of a proposal through the referendum has constitutional relevance only to the effect that the citizens who took part in the voting have thus demonstrated to the National Council of the Slovak Republic that they want the Constitution of the Slovak Republic to be amended in line with the outcome of the referendum.
>
> (US 31/97)

The Slovak Constitution thus follows a formally monistic revision pattern, but with the possibility for a citizens' initiative based on the right to petition (cf. Holmes and Sunstein 1995: 293).

To briefly resume, from the point of view of a 'pluralism of actors' able to initiate review, a parliamentary monistic approach is the dominant mode in the five countries under study. The Czech Republic, Hungary and Slovakia only indicate parliament as the constitutional subject for revision of the fundamental rules. Poland and Romania follow a more pluralistic pattern, in that in the former the president also has the right to initiative, while in Romania the president as well as citizens have this right, next to parliament. From the point of view of democratic constitutionalism, the picture is thus not bright, in that only Romania and (in an interesting way) Slovakia allow for civic initiative, even if in the former case this entails a highly complex procedure whereas in the latter the ultimate gravity remains with parliament.

Overall, Closa's general remark on a certain balancing between Madisonian and Jeffersonian constitutional views in constitutional realities seems also relevant in Central and Eastern Europe, in terms of different combinations of constitutional rigidity and revisionary inclusiveness. Some of the least rigid revision procedures are balanced by parliamentary monism (Hungary and the Czech Republic), thus making revision fairly easy but also exclusivist, while the most difficult to amend constitution, that of Romania, formally allows for presidential and civic initiative. The Slovakian case is at least on paper the most participation-conducive, in that its amendment procedure is probably the easiest of those under review here (a three-fifths majority in parliament), while also a citizens' initiative emerged from below.

Instruments of direct democracy[13]

As I have argued throughout the book, a purely legalistic view of democracy – as reducible to representation, liberal institutions and stability – is problematic from the point of view of civic participation, self-government, and the diffusion of constitutional culture. In the context of the post-communist countries, it is true that an alternative, radical idea of democracy, as a concept and institutional beacon, became of much less importance after 1989, not least because of the prioritization of the institutionalization of liberal institutions in the form of a constitution and the rule of law (cf. Přibáň 2007). It is probably also true that the direct influence of the dissidents and their ideas on post-1989 politics diminished rapidly, and that some dissidents seemingly radically changed ideas or estranged the public by taking an elitist-intellectualist stance (but see Isaac 2004). However, it is not clear that this justifies the widespread inattention as to what extent alternative ideas, models, concepts and attitudes – in many cases directly related to dissident thought – have had an influence on the new democratic orders (cf. Rytel-Warzocha 2012).

In contrast to a liberal reading, it can be shown that the civic-republican dimensions of democracy are of significance when discussing the relation of dissident legacies to democratization. This can, for instance, be sensed from Vladimir Tismăneanu's recent estimation: '[t]he events of 1989 had world-shattering revolutionary consequences. They brought about a new vision of the political based upon a rediscovery of democratic participation and civic activism.' And he goes on: '[t]he importance of these revolutions cannot therefore be overestimated: they represent the triumph of civic dignity and political morality' (2009).

One significant political-institutional dimension of the republican legacy of dissident ideas involves the relatively extensive attention – admittedly in particular in the early years of transformation, but with important consequences, and in some cases with revivals later on – for forms of direct democracy. As I will argue below, ideas of direct democracy have had a visible impact on the post-1989 constitutional and legal orders of the Czech Republic, Hungary, Poland, Romania and Slovakia. This is significant, even if such an impact has been uneven and changing over time. Constitutional and legal developments demonstrate a variegated impact of dissident ideas, as well as the multiple democratic dimensions to the post-1989 regimes, and problematize both a narrative of the absolute insignificance of radical dissident ideas for the institutional architecture of the new democratic regimes, and that of a necessary convergence of these democracies with a liberal, representative model.

Czech Republic

In the Czech case, while admittedly quite a number of attempts to promote a civic-participatory vision of democracy throughout the 1990s has foundered (Hadjiiski 2001), the same attempts have also left some constitutional and legal-institutional 'traces' as well as embedded a democratic narrative in the region that might potentially be, and on some occasions has been, re-activated (Pontuso 2002).

In terms of a dissident legacy of direct democracy, the institutionalization of institutions of civic participation seems particularly compromised in the Czech Republic (cf. Tucker *et al.* 2000). Thus, in a fairly stark contrast to the intensity of republican ideas of the 1980s, post-1989 Czech democracy appears to display the least extensive form of constitutional and legal institutionalization of forms of direct democracy – at least regarding direct democratic instruments, such as civic consultation through referenda – in the region.

Elements of direct democracy are then not prominent in the Czech Constitution. And while, as a result of a compromise, the 1992 constitution does entail the formulation that '[a] constitutional law may stipulate the cases when the people exercise state power directly' (art. 2(2)), to date no related statutory law has been adopted, despite repeated attempts by pro-referendum groups (cf. Smith 2011: 34). Discussions on the inclusion of direct democracy into the constitutional framework were held in the early 1990s, not least in the context of a Constitutional Act proposed by Vaclav Havel, which envisaged the usage of the referendum instrument in the case of legislative bills and proposed Constitutional Acts, as well as on essential state questions. Indeed, the Act included a binding citizens' referendum with the status of a Constitutional Act, thus providing a confirmatory amending power to the citizenry. The Act was ultimately, however, not adopted (Adamova 2010: 48–50). The Act that was adopted instead, and which stipulated a referendum in case of the break-up of the federation, was ignored in the actual federal split-up, sealing in a way with it the fate of the referendum instrument.

On a closer look, however, while it is clear that political forces sceptical of referenda and direct democracy have so far prevailed, the issue is clearly not settled yet and continues to re-emerge in Czech political debate (see, for a detailed overview, Adamova 2010). For instance, in 2002, in the context of debates over the referendum on EU accession, a constitutional act for a general right to referendum was proposed, but was (once again) rejected by right-wing parties. Particularly the Civic Democratic Party (ODS) of Vaclav Klaus has been consistently against direct democratic instruments (see Smith 2011: 34; Adamova 2010: 53). Ultimately, an act on referendum was adopted that related only to EU membership. This resulted in the only national referendum that was held in the Czech Republic, on matters of EU accession (Smith 2011: 34).

But while a constitutionally guaranteed right to the holding of national referenda is still absent, referenda on the local level have been arranged for and seem to have become much more consequential since the early 2000s (see below).

Hungary

In Hungary, institutions of direct democracy are fairly well entrenched, and became important already before 1989, not least due to dissident pressure on the communist authorities (Pallinger 2012: 113–14). In general, 'demands for referendums were part of the movement for democracy' and since the transition, 'no political party has denied that at least certain forms of direct democracy should be part of the Hungarian constitutional and political order' (Dezsö and Bragyova 2001: 63). In the late 1980s, the reaction of the Communist Party to the opposition's demand for referenda resulted in Act XVII, adopted unilaterally in June 1989. This legal act was the basis for referenda and popular initiatives until 1997, when it was renewed and partially replaced by the constitutional articles 28B-E.[14] In 1997, a new set of rules was constitutionalized through a constitutional amendment, while statutory law further arranged for details on referenda and citizens' initiatives (as part of Act C of 1997 on Electoral Procedure). The direct democratic tendency can be regarded as at least partially the outcome of initiatives related to the democratization movement of the 1980s.[15] Even if the 'scope and conditions of referenda were gradually restricted since (Sajó 2006: IV-14)', the amendment of the constitution enhanced the status of direct democracy considerably. This constitutional status of referenda was reiterated by a ruling of the Constitutional Court in which it argued that the 'institution of referendum is closely related to the provisions of the Constitution. Referendum, as a typical form of direct democracy, is related to the sovereignty of the people, and the practice of the Court interprets *the right to referendum as [a] fundamental right*' (website Hungarian Constitutional Court; decision 52/1997; emphasis added; available at: www.codices.coe.int/NXT/gateway.dll/CODICES/precis/eng/eur/hun/hun-1997-3-009?fn=document-frameset.htm$f=templates$3.0).

At the same time, Pallinger is right when he argues that in Hungary the 'primary mode of exercising popular sovereignty is representative democracy', and '[d]irect citizen involvement is only an exceptional possibility' (2012: 117). This could be reformulated as that the Hungarian democratic system is in general a representative one, and the constitutionalization of instruments of direct democracy has created a tension between direct democracy and the predominantly liberal, representative idea as constitutional principles. As observed by other scholars, 'direct democratic institutions already have a foothold in Hungarian constitutional thought', even if the institutions are perhaps not sufficiently well defined (Deszö and Bragyova 2007: 82).[16]

The Hungarian Constitution allowed for three types of initiatives and referenda: a full-scale initiative or national referendum (to be initiated by at least 200,000 voting citizens) and with binding results for parliament; an agenda initiative with the possibility of a referendum (initiated by at least 100,000 voting citizens, or by the president or one-third of the parliament); and a 'proper' agenda initiative, in which 50,000 voters can ask parliament to place a subject on the agenda (Pallinger 2012: 118). In 1997, a 25 per cent threshold for national referenda was installed. Furthermore, the constitution foresaw various subjects that cannot be part of a referendum (article 28C). Overall, six national initiatives have taken place in post-1989 Hungary, including referenda on the NATO and EU accessions, and of which two were initiated by citizens. Eight 'proper' agenda initiatives have taken place, mostly promoted by civic movements, of which only two were found valid (Pallinger 2012: 121).

With the 2012 Basic Law, generally the fundamental principles related to direct democracy have not changed, but at the same time it is true that the favourable tendency towards direct democracy since 1997 has been reversed (the relevant article for national referenda is now article 8). This has become particularly clear in the return to a 50 per cent threshold for participation in referenda as well as the abolishing of the 'proper' agenda initiative (articles 8(1) and (4)). As argued by Pallinger, 'it seems possible that the use of the direct democratic instruments will be more restricted in the future than it has been to date' (2012: 114).

Poland

In terms of direct democracy as a dimension of post-1989 Polish democracy, it is clear that it has become a 'common element of democratic decision-making' (Přibáň and Sadurski 2006: 218). It can obviously not be denied that in the early 1990s, the 'Solidarity leadership as a whole supported representative, rather than direct democracy as the most stable and efficient form for government' (Cirtautas 1997: 214) and that most of the democratization process was about the institutionalization of the structures of representative democracy. But it is equally clear that dimensions of participatory democracy have taken on a certain significance in the Polish democratic architecture in their own right. In this, although clearly not dominant, a 'civic republican' political culture, which can be regarded the 'most direct successor to the 'politics of truth' pursued by Solidarity' (Dryzek and Holmes 2002: 233–6), and in which forms of direct democracy have to some extent become a commonplace, is clearly reflected in the Polish constitutional and legal structures. In the words of Anna Rytel-Warzocha, '[t]he lack of confidence in the purely representative democracy and the overall deficit of democracy in the country . . . were the reasons for emphasizing the need to provide citizens with direct opportunities to exercise power' (Rytel-Warzocha 2012: 212).

The institutionalization of instruments of direct democracy started early on in the Polish transformation. Two constitutional amendments in late 1989 and early 1990 introduced a change of the 1952 constitution so that sovereignty was now vested in the nation, and could be exercised in a representative as well as a direct way. In 1992, a mandatory constitutional referendum as well as the instrument of a national referendum regarding issues of particular significance for the state were instituted, while in 1990 the instrument of local referenda was arranged for by law.

Instruments of direct democracy were articulated forcefully in most constitutional drafts proposed throughout the early 1990s, and in the newly adopted Constitution in 1997 even gained somewhat in importance. It seems fair to argue that the 1997 Constitution, 'unlike all its predecessors, contains a relatively wide range of provisions concerning direct democracy', which is a 'fact worth stressing, especially as such solutions are rare in Polish history' (Szmyt 1999: 128–9). This is confirmed by the legal scholar Ewa Popławska, who has argued that the 'increasing value of direct democracy is reflected in its extended forms, in particular in the extension of the scope of facultative application of a referendum to include matters of fundamental importance to the state' (Popławska 1999: 187).

Indeed, the Polish constitution invokes a notion of direct civic participation already at the beginning, in article 4(2), as well as in the preamble. The 1997 constitution codifies the citizens' right to direct participation through referenda in constitutional matters, national referenda regarding ordinary legislation (on 'matters of particular importance to the State', article 125(1)). Referenda can be initiated by the Sejm or the Polish president, with consent of the Senate (article 125). A popular initiative to hold a national referendum is not provided for in the constitution, but has been subsequently introduced in the Act on nationwide referendum of 2003. The national referendum instrument has, however, not often been used; that is, since 1989 only three proposals to call a referendum have been submitted to the Sejm (Rytel-Warzocha 2012: 215). Referenda on the local level are referred to in article 170 (see further below).

The constitution further grants the possibility of a popular, confirmatory referendum on constitutional amendments, even if it can be held only in case of an amendment dealing with particular chapters (art. 235 (6)). What is more, a citizens' initiative has been introduced by a law on referenda of 1995 (replaced by the Act on National Referenda in 2003), and is confirmed in the 1997 Constitution. In addition, Polish citizens have the right to legislative initiative, which can be related to the notion of subsidiarity, according to article 118(2) (see, for an extensive overview, Rytel-Warzocha 2012).

Admittedly, as argued by a current judge of the Constitutional Tribunal, Stanisław Biernat, the 'instruments of direct democracy, at least on the level of the state, are only of limited significance in Poland' (Biernat 2005: 88). While the existing constitutional and legal structures do allow for more substantive civic participation, a civic political culture seems not developed sufficiently to result in widespread participation.

The legal scholar Ewa Popławska (2008) comes to similar conclusions with the specific regard to civic participation in constitution-making through pre-constitutional referenda. But it can be equally put forward, as also Biernat admits, that the referendum instrument does have greater significance on the local level. In the early 2000s, for instance, Paweł Swianiewicz observed some positive trends in terms of more frequent and widespread use of local referenda, and a higher success rate (Swianiewicz 2001). Furthermore, since its institutionalization, the instrument of citizens' initiative has had some impact on legislation, even if hardly ever in the original form proposed, but rather in amended legislation (IDEA 2008: 90).

Romania

Forms of direct democracy play a relatively restricted role in the Romanian Constitution. Direct democracy has not been at the centre of political debate since 1989 (see APD 2008a). In contrast to the experiences of Central European countries, Romanian dissidents did not forcefully promote citizens' self-governance before 1989, and after the changes, even if belatedly adopting 'anti-political politics' (see Tănăsoiu 2008), pro-democratic forces mostly invoked a liberal, representative view of democracy (cf. Blokker 2004).

But the Romanian constitution does contain some, mostly general, references to direct democracy, which point to a form of 'semi-representative' or 'semi-direct democracy' (cf. Băisanu 2011).[17] In this, it can be argued that article 2 – which gives the Romanian people the possibility to exercise national sovereignty both through representative bodies and by referendum – invokes a clear 'political project, at least on the theoretical level, . . . to encourage civic participation in the taking of decisions of national interest' (Carp and Stanomir 2008: 246). In reality, on the one hand, direct and participatory democracy are relatively marginal in the Romanian context; a significant pro-democratic movement has argued that 'participatory democracy' is 'little discussed', but is 'without doubt important for the growth in quality of Romanian democracy' (APD 2008a: 35). On the other hand, some have recently argued that the usage and importance of referenda has increased in the Romanian context, most evidently in the 2000s.[18]

In contrast to the prominent constitutional invocation of a form of direct democracy in article 2, overall the codification of participatory rights is relatively limited and one-sided in the Romanian Constitution. Stanomir claims that the 'Romanian legislator has demonstrated extreme reservation with regard to the perspective of enlarging the framework of effective civic engagement' (Carp and Stanomir 2008: 252–3). It can be argued that the constitution contains a tension between direct and representative democracy, and that the absence of a right for abrogatory referenda strengthens the representative dimension (Carp and Stanomir 2008: 253). There is further a risk of plebiscitary forms of civic participation (Stanomir identifies both the referendum on the constitution of 1991 and that on the amended constitution of 2003 as having demonstrated plebiscitary features, mostly due to the conspicuous lack of public debate; Carp and Stanomir 2008: 250).

The constitution allows for national referenda[19] on 'national problems' on initiative of the president (art. 90): 'The President of Romania may, after consultation with Parliament, ask the people of Romania to express, by referendum, their will on matters of national interest.' No possibility for civic initiative exists in the Romanian context. A referendum is also to be held in the case when the President is suspended by Parliament (as has occurred in May 2007 and in July 2012): 'If the proposal of suspension from office has been approved, a referendum shall be held within 30 days, in order to remove the President from office' (art. 95 (3)). A third type of referendum involves constitutional amendment (as referred to above). Amendment needs popular approval by referendum within 30 days of the passing of a proposal (art. 151(3)).

Additionally, citizens are provided with the instrument of 'legislative initiative', similar to the Polish case:

> A legislative initiative shall lie, as the case may be, with the Government, Deputies, Senators, or a number of at least 100,000 citizens entitled to vote. The citizens who exercise their right to a legislative initiative must belong to at least one quarter of the country's counties, while, in each of those counties or the Municipality of Bucharest, at least 5,000 signatures should be registered in support of such initiative.
> (74(1))

> A legislative initiative of the citizens may not touch on matters concerning taxation, international affairs, amnesty or pardon.
> (74(2))

In contrast to the Hungarian and Polish constitutions, in the Romanian constitution no referenda are provided for on the local level (this is arranged for in organic law, as stipulated in art. 73(3d)) (see below).

Slovakia

Also in the Slovakian case, direct democracy constitutes only a modest feature of the constitutional-democratic architecture.[20] The relative weak tradition of direct forms of democracy is indicated by one scholar as follows: 'The dissolution [of Czechoslovakia, pb], over which the voters had no say, symbolically envisaged the future of direct democracy in both [the Czech Republic and Slovakia]' (Lastic 2012: 152). The same scholar argued elsewhere that as a 'consequence of an uninspiring constitutional text and as an instrument in the hands of political parties, the national referendum has yet to convince Slovak voters about its unique role' (2011: 237). Nevertheless, in contrast to the Czech Constitution, as well as the tradition of the Czechoslovak state, the Slovak Constitution does contain clear references to referenda (cf. Schmid and Horsky 1995: 51). Part of this is related to dissidence of the 1980s and the emphasis on citizens' participation in anti-communist movements after 1989. The citizens' initiative in the form of the 'right to petition was considered to be an essential part of a democratic regime' after 1989 (Lastic 2012: 154). This was not least due to the demands of the Czech Civic Forum and the Slovak Public against Violence, two dissident-based movements that initiated public action by means of bottom-up claims-making for a political dialogue with the authorities (Lastic 2012: 154). The Movement for a Democratic Slovakia, an offshoot of Public against Violence, played an important role in drafting the Constitution that was adopted in 1992 (Malová and Lastic 2001). Be that as it may, the debate on the constitution in the early 1990s was heavily influenced by the question of Slovak independence, and Lastic suggests that little attention was paid to specific constitutional design (Lastic 2012: 155). This might have had its effects on the relative ambiguity regarding the instrument of referendum, not least with regard to the status of the outcome of referenda.

The Constitution refers to the possibility of a national referendum in the case of a union with other states as well as secession, as well as in a more general sense (article 93(2)): 'A referendum may also be used to decide on other crucial issues of the public interest.'[21] In contrast to, for instance, Romania, a national referendum is not only the initiative of the parliament, but can also be initiated by (at least) 350,000 citizens.[22] As observed above, the right to initiate a national referendum by citizens also pertains to constitutional matters (as emerged from a referendum on the election of the president).

The most significant problems with the referendum instrument in the Slovak includes unclear provisions in the constitution, but more importantly, the dominance of political parties in taking the initiative and a relatively high quorum. As reported by Lastic, none of the popular initiatives has been valid (Lastic 2012: 164).

To resume, few of the constitutions of the countries in question provides for very extensive instruments of direct democracy (for instance, only the Polish constitution allows for an 'agenda initiative', while the Hungarian Basic Law has eliminated the agenda initiative of the Constitution (article 28C/4), which granted the right to introduce a subject onto the political agenda). At the same time, however, most systems do by now contain a fairly robust set of participatory channels in the form of (different types of) referenda. In this, as also recently argued by Stephen Tierney in an extensive analysis, the Central and Eastern European countries share in a trend of a growing number of constitutions that mandate the usage of referenda (2012: 7–8). The Czech constitution only hints at the possibility of national referenda, but such an instrument has not (yet) been legally created due to strong resistance. In the case of Hungary, the constitution provided for significant instruments (one might argue, including the instrument of *actio popularis*), but the new Basic Law has significantly restricted such instruments. The Polish constitution allows for different modes of direct democracy (including a confirmatory referendum), while a legislative Act (2003) has included a citizens' initiative to hold national referenda. In Slovakia, both parliament and the citizens can initiate referenda, while in Romania, referenda can be initiated only by the president, whereas mandatory referenda are held in the case of suspension of the president (as occurred in 2007 and 2012) as well as constitutional amendment.

Local and regional democracy

The importance of local government and democracy in the post-totalitarian context of Central and Eastern Europe is self-evident. The highly centralized systems of communism – indeed coined 'democratic centralism' in Leninist systems – did not allow for any significant participation or voice by either stakeholders or the citizenry at large (cf. Smith 2003). What is more, the far-going centralization of communist political systems meant that no form of sub-national autonomy or territorial self-government was allowed for. Not by coincidence the discourses of protest of many dissident movements in the region contained a strong dimension of civic participation, decentralization and local self-government (see Blokker 2011a; Renwick 2006; Smith 2003).

The past communist systems were detrimental to any idea of formal sub-national self-government[23] in at least two ways. First, sub-national forms of government were always strictly controlled by the central state, and therefore merely consisted in institutions for the execution of centrally imposed policies, lacking any kind of space for autonomous action in the interest of local populations. Second, not only did democratic centralism mean that no democratic channels were available for civic participation, but also any kind of political pluralism within the communist political institutions was reduced as far as possible, in that the state was subjected to the communist party with its homogeneous programme and ideological principles, while alternative voices were stifled under the banner of 'enemies of the people'.

In addition, the 'socialist legality' that underpinned the political structure of communist regimes was based upon 'paper constitutions' that did have very little to do with the rule-of-law and were rather a fiction or form of symbolism (in a pejorative sense) that displayed a large discrepancy with the arbitrary nature of political-legal reality (cf. Skapska 2011). Rather than contributing to social integration and the constitution of political communities, the 'paper' communist constitutions helped to enhance existing traditions of 'us and them', or, in other words, a deep distrust of society against the ruling elites.

The 1970s and 1980s, as well as the early 1990s saw a fierce backlash against the centralism and political party-monism that had been imposed with communism. In particular in the early 1990s, radical steps were undertaken to undo the hypercentralization of the past. However, such reforms tended to run out of steam fairly quickly, not least due to increased disagreement about the exact nature of reforms. At any rate, the sub-national reform process has continued in a more gradual manner in most societies in the post-communist region.

Ideas of local self-government and local (representative and direct) democracy have had a visible impact on the post-1989 constitutional and legal orders, and while the initial radicalism of changes of the early 1990s did not continue in later years of transformation, the five democracies analysed here all display significant levels of decentralization. At the same time, though, the constitutional and legal developments demonstrate a variegated impact of ideas of local democracy and direct forms of democracy.

Czech Republic

The constitutional state in the Czech Republic can best be defined as a predominantly centralized, unitary state, based on a parliamentary-democratic system (cf. Illner 2010, 2011). However, this does not mean that the local and regional levels of government are not important, nor that more direct forms of democracy or active citizenship are inexistent or not part of the constitutional order. A thrust towards participatory and decentralised forms of politics came indeed from dissident forces, in the early 1990s loosely organized in the Civic Forum and Public Against Violence (for a rich discussion of the role and influence of these movements, see Smith 2003). The importance of civil society becomes already clear from the symbolic–substantive reference to civil society in the preamble of the 1992 Constitution: 'a free and democratic state based on the respect for human rights and the principles of civic society'.

However, some have argued that while some forms of decentralization and self-government are part and parcel of the Czech system, its main logic is that of 'state administration' (Bryson 2008; cf. Smith 2011). The Czech state as it emerges from the 1992 Constitution is a sovereign, unitary and democratic state: 'The Czech Republic is a sovereign, unitary and democratic, law-abiding State, based on respect for the rights and freedoms of man and citizen' (art. 1(1)). At the same time, the constitutional state allows for decentralization at the local and regional levels. The 1992 Czech Constitution states in Chapter 1 on 'Basic Provisions' that '[t]he autonomy of units of territorial self-administration shall be guaranteed' (art. 8), while Chapter 7 on 'Territorial Self-Administration' stipulates the decentralized, 'basic units of territorial self-administration' as municipalities, and higher units in the form of lands and regions (art. 99). Article 100 states that 'communities of citizens, inhabiting a particular area . . . have the right of self-government', while article 101(3) underlines local autonomy in that '[s]elf-governing territorial divisions are public-law corporations which may have their own property and which operate according to their own budget'.

While the value of sub-national self-government and civil society, and related institutions, are entrenched in the Constitution, significant (political as well as social) obstacles to the realization of principles of local self-government seem not to have been overcome in two decades of transformation, and the centralistic nature of the Czech state can only partially be said 'corrected' by local and regional autonomy. However, at the same time, it would be hard to deny the continuing importance of decentralization and ideas of self-governance for democratization in the Czech Republic.

Throughout the 1990s, the latter was particularly visible in the form of a conflictive debate between Václav Havel (and the Czech left) and Václav Klaus (and the Civic Democratic Party or Občanská demokratická strana (ODS)) on the role and form of especially the regional level of government (cf. Myant 2003). Klaus opposed issues of reform and decentralization on grounds of neo-liberal scepticism towards bureaucracy and intermediary institutions, and held off the implementation of article 99 of the Constitution. Eventually, though, at the end of the 1990s, significant decentralizing steps and the creation of a regional layer were effected, not least due to EU pressure (cf. Calda 1999). The Constitutional Act of 3 December 1997 on the 'Creation of Higher Territorial Self-Governing Units' changed article 99 into '[t]he Czech Republic is subdivided into municipalities, which are the basic territorial self-governing units, and into regions, which are the higher territorial self-governing units'. And indeed, there are indications that the regional level has grown in importance since its establishment. Recently, Baun and Marek have argued that the 'new regions have begun establishing themselves as legitimate and important political actors' (425).

The constitutional status of sub-national self-government was further entrenched by a number of rulings by the Czech Constitutional Court. For instance, in 2003 the Constitutional Court ruled:

> The guarantee of territorial self-government in the Constitution is laconic. Alongside the differentiation of the local and regional levels of self-government (Art. 99) territorial self-government is conceived as the *right* of a territorial association of citizens, arising from its characteristics and abilities, as the Constitutional Court stated in its finding of 19 November 1996, file no. Pl. ÚS 1/96.
>
> (Collection of Decisions of the Constitutional Court, volume 6, p. 375)
>
> The Constitutional Court considers local self-government to be an *irreplaceable component* in the development of democracy. Local self-government is an expression of the capability of local bodies, within the bounds provided by law, to regulate and govern part of public affairs on their own responsibility and in the interest of the local population.
>
> (CC 2003/02/05 – Pl. ÚS 34/02: Territorial Self-Government; emphasis added)[24]

As mentioned above, the Czech Constitution defines Czech democracy in a predominantly representative, parliamentary manner. This is, however, paralleled by constitutional foundations of sub-national representative democracy as well as more direct forms of civic participation.

It should be noted that the 1992 Constitution was predominantly designed by a government commission dominated by the ODS, which squarely favoured a centralist state without intermediary levels. The articles on local self-government that were ultimately included in the 1992 document were the result of a compromise between the ODS, its coalition members (more favourable to local government) and the opposition. The compromise led to a fairly vague and open-ended formulation, and the regional level was not implemented before 1999, but the Czech Constitution does go some way in qualifying a fully centralistic as well as liberal-representative view of the Czech state. The Constitution arranges for representative democracy on the sub-national level in article 101, which states that both municipalities and regions are administered by councils, which are 'elected by secret ballot on the basis of universal, equal, and direct suffrage' (art. 102). The political status of sub-national democracy is enhanced by the fact that, even if the turn-out rates for both the elections of regional and municipal councils are generally not very high, in particular the municipal institutions enjoy a very high level of political trust among the Czech citizens, much more so than those on the national level (Illner 2010: 519).

References to sub-national democracy can be further found in the Czech Bill of Rights, – the 'Charter of Fundamental Rights and Basic Freedoms' – which can be considered part of the constitutional constellation. The Charter invokes the Czech 'nations' traditions of democracy and self-government', and also refers to the fact that '[c]itizens have the right to participate in the administration of public affairs either *directly* or through the free election of their representatives' (art. 21(1)) (emphasis added).

As argued above, the issue of direct democracy is not settled yet in the Czech context, and continues to re-emerge in Czech political debate. And while a constitutionally guaranteed right to the holding of national referenda is still absent, referenda on the *local* level have become much more consequential (on the regional level, referenda are not permitted, cf. Illner 2011: 518). As argued by Adamova, '[t]he attitude of the Czech political representation to local referenda has been rather different' (2010: 53). During the 1990s referenda were only used for questions of secession from existing municipal arrangements. And while the original legislation regarding local government – the 1992 Law on Local Elections and Referendums – notably stems from the Civic Forum period, no referendum of general import took place on its basis in the first decade of democratization. However, following the amendments of the law in 2004 and 2008, clearing a number of ambiguities and strengthening the position of referenda proposers, local referenda have become a much more significant – and binding – civic instrument in Czech democracy, and are used for much wider purposes than before (see Smith 2011; Adamova 2010: 53–4).

Hungary

Also the democratic opposition in Hungary had endorsed a civic-democratic narrative of local autonomy, even if decisively less vigorous than in the cases of Solidarność or the Civic Forum (cf. Pallinger 2012). This becomes for instance clear in the political programmes of the government and opposition parties in 1989, in which local self-government was a recurrent theme. The Hungarian Democratic Forum, which formed the first post-communist government under József Antall, stated that the HDF was in favour of promoting the autonomy of communities, enhance the communities' property base, the autonomous handling of community matters by communities and the set up of a national body of local governments within Parliament. And as stated in the programme 'for changing the system' of the Alliance of Free Democrats,

> [s]elf-governments will have an important part to play in public life. Set up by citizens on functional or territorial grounds, they will differ from associations in that they will exercise executive power under the supervision of the law. It is in the capacity of self-government and not as a local executive instrument in state power that local councils will operate.

Some of the calls for decentralization and self-government are reflected in the development of the post-1989 Hungarian state. At least until 2012, the Hungarian democratic state could be defined as a 'decentralized unitary' one, with a 'strong and decentralized system of county governments' (Soós and Kakai 2010: 530). Local government has been strongly entrenched since 1989, and has enjoyed (until recently) a high level of autonomy in decision-making. Local democracy is mostly focused on representative, party-based democracy, while civic input and NGO participation are so far limited.

In the constitutional changes of the early 1990s, local self-government enjoyed a high priority in that it was seen as an indispensable way of undermining the centralist institutions of 'democratic centralism'. Thus, 'the replacement of the council-based public administrative system with a sphere of independent local self-government was a key concern in administrative reform' (Balázs 1993: 76). The amended Constitution of 1949 dedicates chapter IX to Local Governments, in which article 42 on the 'Right to local government' states: 'Eligible voters of the communities, cities, the capital and its districts, and the counties have the *right to local government*. Local government refers to independent, democratic management of local affairs and the exercise of local public authority in the interests of the local population' (emphasis added).

The main sub-national distinction is between the local level (villages, cities, capital districts, capital) and the county level. A regional level was added in 2000 to be able to attract EU Structural Funds, but its status so far is weak (Soós 2010: 113–14). In contrast, local governments of the municipal type, and to a lesser extent counties, have since 1989 been the entities with most political significance on the sub-national level.

Democratic reforms towards decentralization mainly involved two stages. In 1990, the parliamentary Act No. LXV on Local Governments was adopted, which 'established the legal foundation for the process of democratization and reform of the political system'. The Act LXV is introduced as follows:

> Following the progressive local government traditions of our country, as well as the basic requirements of the European Charter on local governments, Parliament recognizes and protects the rights of the local communities to self-government. Local self-government makes it possible, that the local community of electors – directly, and/or through its selected local government – manage the public affairs of local interest independently and democratically. Supporting the self-organizing independence of local communities, Parliament assists the creation of the conditions necessary to self-government, it promotes the democratic decentralization of public authority.
>
> (Act No. LXV)

Moreover, the Act No. LXIV on Local Elections was adopted, arranging for local democracy to start functioning. In a second stage, in 1994, the existing local system was reformed by means of the Act on Local Governments (No. LXIII). These reforms included a call for broader constitutional guarantees of local government, steps towards more direct participation (the direct election of mayors), and the regulation of civic participation and publicity.

These reforms have led some observers into saying that '[w]ithout doubt, the 1990 local government reform established one of the most liberal systems of local government in Europe' (Balázs 1993: 85). Also others have argued that in 1990 legislation was adopted that established a 'very high degree of autonomy for the lowest, local level of government', while the constitution enshrined the right to self-government at local and county levels as a constitutional principle (Fowler 2001: 8).

Local democracy as a citizens' right – in both indirect and direct ways – was until 2012 entrenched in the Hungarian constitutional order, in that article 44 (1) stipulates that '[e]ligible voters exercise the right to local government through the representative body that they elect and by way of local referendum' (see also article 42).[25] In Act no. LXV, a similar idea is expressed in art. 1(4) as '[t]he local government may – through the elected local body of representatives, or with the decision of local plebiscite – undertake independently and voluntarily the solution of any local public affair, which is not referred by a legal rule to the jurisdiction of another organ'. As seen above, the constitutionalization of instruments of direct democracy importantly complements the representative democratic system. Direct democracy on the local level has been since 1989 become more strongly legally entrenched, in particular through the constitutionalization of the general right to referenda, and the stipulation of the local right in statutory law, that is in Chapter XV on local referendums and Chapter XVI on local initiative of Act C/1997.[26] It can be argued that local democracy has so far enjoyed a relatively high standing in terms of civic political trust in Hungary. Local governments (with the institutions of the president and the constitutional court) tend to score significantly higher than both the parliament and the government (Soós and Kákai 2010: 541).

As mentioned, since 1 January 2012 Hungary has adopted a new 'Basic Law', of which the implications are not yet entirely clear at the time of writing, also because some of the relevant legislation has become valid from January, 2013. The Basic Law contains regulations regarding local self-government that are not entirely new, that is '[m]any of the rules are the same or almost the same as before'. At the same time, at least one observer has argued that the 'leading philosophy or conception behind them is fundamentally different' (Patyi 2012: 219). This becomes, for instance, visible in the absence of a general right to self-governance, as was stipulated in article 42 of the Constitution. In contrast, the Basic Law merely mentions the managing role of local governments regarding public affairs (articles 31 and 32) (cf. Patyi 2012: 219). The absence of an 'explicit mention' of the 'principle of local self-government' was also criticized by the Venice Commission of the Council of Europe in its comments on the draft Basic Law. It argued that the European Charter of Local Self-Government stipulates as a 'starting point' the principle of local self-government (CoE 2011: 24).[27] The changed philosophy also comes through in the absence of mention of explicit democratic engagement of citizens on the local level. While the Constitution refers to a citizens' exercise of the right to local government by both representative and direct democratic means, in the Basic Law such a reference is absent. Relevant matters are now part of a 'cardinal law' (of a semi-constitutional nature) or, to be precise, the Act on Local Self-Government adopted in December 2011

(Act No. CLXXXIX). Patyi formulates this as '[t]he local referendum is not the (seldom-used) alternative method of exercising the collective right to self-government anymore, but a method of deciding each case within the competence of the local government' (2011: 221).

Further concerns include the autonomy of local authorities. This involves not least the fact that the Basic Law provides the possibility for parliament to dissolve elected municipal councils on the grounds of a breach of the constitution, without mediation of the Constitutional Court (cf. CoE 2011: 24). Furthermore, the Basic Law provides the opportunity to 'nationalize' local authorities' property, while a new law on local government, approved by parliament in December 2011, importantly restricts and recentralizes important competences of local authorities. As stated in a report of the Assembly of European Regions, the new law on Local Self-Government substantially redefines the distribution of competences of central and local self-governments, and generally reduces the 'autonomy of the local self-governments' leading to a 'far more centralized system than the one set up in 1990' (AER 2012: 1).

Poland

The Polish constitutional state is also defined as a unitary and centralized state, even if allowing for sub-national government on the regional and local levels. In other words, while, as expressed in article 3 of the 1997 Constitution, Poland has without a doubt a centralized system, its constitutional order allows for 'relatively strong local autonomy' and tendencies towards strengthening regionalization are visible (Swianiewicz 2011: 482). The latter becomes already clear from the preamble – '. . . [h]ereby establish this Constitution of the Republic of Poland as the basic law for the State, based on respect for freedom and justice, cooperation between the public powers, social dialogue as well as *on the principle of aiding in the strengthening the powers of citizens and their communities*' (emphasis added).

In the Polish case, local self-government was a prominent focus in the constitution-making process, and has been amply arranged for in the 1997 Constitution. The process of decentralization already started in the early 1990s, and had in many ways been prepared by the political struggle of the Solidarność trade union for decentralized government (cf. Benzler 1994; also Blokker 2011a). The Local Government Act of 1990 provided the fundamental legal underpinnings of the right to self-governance of local authorities. In addition, almost all of Solidarność's demands for territorial self-government were enshrined in the articles

43–47 of the amended 1952 constitution, while these were later re-confirmed in the so-called Small Constitution of 1992.

The 1997 Constitution has often been criticized as being rather unspecific with regard to notions of local self-government and decentralization, but it can at the same time be argued that the dimension of local self-government is strongly anchored in the text. As noted above, the symbolic–substantive dimension of self-government and subsidiarity is reflected in the preamble, indicating their status as foundational-constitutional values. The constitutional text itself introduces local self-government as early as article 15 – '[t]he territorial system of the Republic of Poland shall ensure the decentralization of public power' (1) – and 16 – '[t]he inhabitants of the units of basic territorial division shall form a self-governing community in accordance with law' (1) – and '[l]ocal self-government shall participate in the exercise of public power. The substantial part of public duties which local self-government is empowered to discharge by statute shall be done in its own name and under its own responsibility' (2). The constitution arranges for local self-government in a detailed way in chapter VII. It should be noted (cf. Swianiewicz 2011: 484), however, that only the local, municipal level (*gmina*) is arranged for in the constitution (art. 164(1)), while the other, regional and county, levels are to be arranged for by statute (164(2)). In constitutional terms therefore, local self-governance at the municipal level is prioritized. In 1998, a decentralization reform of the county and regional levels saw the creation of elected self-government.

The process of decentralization and the creation of local self-government has arguably been a success in Poland,[28] and is one of the most effective – even if continuously contested – reforms in the region (contestation regards in particular the status of the sub-national levels other than that of municipalities). The attention for local self-government and civic participation can be clearly related to the dissident legacy of Solidarność, even if the latter's original idea of a 'self-governing republic' has never been realized in any extensive way. On the one hand, it can then be argued that 'local self-government in Poland found a permanent place within the post-transformation political landscape', not least through its constitutionalization, but at the same time, it can be said that there are clear tendencies towards recentralization and state disregard for local autonomy (Regulska 2009). What is significant, though, is that tensions and contestations over the desirable form of local self-government, and appropriate relations between the centre and periphery, continue to exist, indicating the unsettled nature of local democracy and the continuous relevance and discursive force of the notion of self-government. As argued by Swianiewicz, in 2007 the new

Civic Platform government announced plans for further decentralization, which constituted a 'clear difference with the previous (2005–7) government, which did not believe in the value of local autonomy and was focused on hierarchical control rather than on creating an environment for larger discretion of sub-national units' (Swianiewicz 2011: 495).

Local government is underpinned by both representative and direct forms of democracy in Poland: '[e]lections to constitutive organs shall be universal, direct, equal and shall be conducted by secret ballot. The principles and procedures for submitting candidates and for the conduct of elections, as well as the requirements for the validity of elections, shall be specified by statute' (169(2)), and '[m]embers of a self-governing community may decide, by means of a referendum, matters concerning their community, including the dismissal of an organ of local government established by direct election. The principles of and procedures for conducting a local referendum shall be specified by statute' (170). Local elections are arranged for by the 1998 Local Election Law. Also in the Polish case, turnout for local elections tends to be relatively low (it has never been higher than 50 per cent since 1990; see Swianiewicz 2010: 497), but public opinion polls show consistently higher civic trust in local institutions than in central political institutions.

In terms of direct democracy as a dimension of post-1989 Polish local democracy, it is clear that it has become a 'common element of democratic decision-making' (Přibáň and Sadurski 2006: 218; cf. Piasecki 2011: 136). Dimensions of participatory democracy – in particular through the form of referenda – have taken on a certain significance in the Polish democratic architecture in their own right, and already from the late 1980s onwards (see Piasecki 2011).

The institutionalization of instruments of direct democracy started early on in the Polish transformation. Two constitutional amendments in late 1989 and early 1990 introduced a change of the 1952 Constitution so that sovereignty was now vested in the nation, and could be exercised in a representative as well as a direct way. The Local Government Act of 1990 included the option of popular vote, next to that of regular elections, and identified three types of referenda: mandatory (recall), mandatory (self-taxation) and facultative (matters of importance to the commune (Piasecki 2011: 126–7). The Local Referendum Act of 1991 further stipulated the implementation of referenda.

Romania

Romania has a centralist and unitary state tradition, which has continued into the post-1989 era, even if contrasting with demands of regional and local autonomy by its sizeable Hungarian minority.[29] Article 1 of the Romanian constitution famously underlines this tradition in its definition of the Romanian state as 'unitary and indivisible', an article that has not been changed in the 2003 amendment, even if strong calls for change were present at the time (cf. Blokker 2010a).

The centralist idea of the state has, however, given some way to a more decentralized one by means of local government reforms since 1989 (Dobre 2011: 686), 'transferring much of the power to manage local interests from the central to the local level' (Coman *et al.* 2001: 356). The Romanian decentralization process, which was partially stimulated by anti-communist, pro-democratic movements[30] as in other Central and Eastern European countries, initially put emphasis on the level of municipalities and counties (articles 121 and 122 of the 1991 Constitution). The Constitution bases local public administration – in chapter V, section 2 – on the principles of 'decentralization, local autonomy, and deconcentration of public services' (art. 120).

It was only in 1998 that a further sub-national tier of government, a regional level, was introduced, establishing eight regions that correspond to the EU NUTS 2 level, partially also as an attempt to respond to EU criteria for membership and regional policy (cf. Coman *et al.* 2001: 358). The peculiarity in the Romanian case is that the regional level knows no legal personality and no direct or indirect participation of citizens. The regions are rather managed by agencies and subsequently ministries with the primary objective of regional development in mind, while also the Regional Councils play a role (and are made up of elected representatives from the county and municipal levels), but the emphasis remains on a technocratic rather than a participatory decision-making process (Dobre 2011: 700–1). Dragoman argues that the 'new macro-regions were designed only as a development tool, and because they were not territorial-administrative units settled by the constitution, they were not legal entities, but only formal associations between counties' (2011: 652). In this light, Dobre states that '[i]f the [local authorities] have gradually become important actors in the framework of political and financial decentralization, this is not the case for the regional institutions', as the latter suffer from a 'democratic deficit' (ibid.: 704–5).

The democratization and autonomization of sub-national political structures in Romania were in part a response to the 'democratic centralism' of the communist period, even if according to some scholars a 'centralist mentality' has subsisted on the local level during the post-communist years (Cernicova 2004: 40). As seen above, the Romanian sub-national democratic architecture puts the emphasis on the local and provincial (county) levels, whereas the regional level remains a technocratic rather than democratic level. Sub-national democracy includes both representative democratic dimensions (the elected nature of local councils, county councils as well as the direct election of mayors and county council presidents) and direct-democratic ones (chapter V, section 2 and statutory law). The latter are arranged for in section 13 of the Referenda Act (No. 3/2000), which allows citizens to directly participate in local decision-making by means of local referenda. These can be organized regarding matters of special importance to local authorities on the initiative of a third of the members of local or county councils or of the mayor or chair of county councils (and thus not by citizens themselves, cf. CoE 2009: 13). Another relevant law that elaborates on local self-government is the Law of Public Administration 215/2001, which widened the competences of local authorities and 'diversified the possibility of citizens to participate in local administration', arranging not only for referenda, but also for citizens' legislative initiatives, and the organization of citizens in consultative bodies (Cernicova 2004: 43; Chiper 2011: 82).

It is in particular since the early 2000s that more emphasis is put on civic participation in local government, also under influence of the EU and integration into European structures such as the Council of Europe (including the European Charter of Local Self-Government, to which Romania adhered in 1997) and ideas of 'good governance' (Cernicova 2004: 43–4). Apart from the laws mentioned above, this dimension comes through in the law on access to information and on transparency in decision-making processes (the laws 544/2001 and 53/2003 respectively).

Despite a stronger embedment of local self-government and forms of civic democratic participation in the Constitution (in particular since the 2003 amendment) and in statutory law, a more intense civic participation seems to be lagging behind in the Romanian case. Apart from a few more advanced cases,[31] civic participation is not robust and does not seem to be taking advantage of legally institutionalized channels of participation. For instance, in a recent analysis of civic participation in local council meetings in Eastern Romania, very few instances of actual participation were found (Chiper 2011), while De Graaf *et al.* find a 'rather well-structured legal base of . . . participatory practices in local government in Romania', but at the same time large differences in participation rates between Bucharest (the main case study) and the Dutch city of Eindhoven (De Graaf *et al.* 2009: 9, 15).

Slovakia

Slovakia is a centralized, unitary state, and its democracy a representative, parliamentary one. The Slovak Constitution strongly grounds the primary role of the parliament, the Slovak National Council (Capkova 2011: 554). But also in the Slovak case, the immediate post-1989 period saw strong demands for the 're-establishment of freely elected local councils with a substantial degree of local autonomy' (ibid.: 556). As argued by Capkova, 'self-government at the local level has remained a strong characteristic of the country' (ibid.: 569). Demands for local self-government were closely related to experiences with the 'second society' or 'islands of positive deviation' as a parallel or civil society was referred to in the Slovak case (Smith 2003: 1). Above, I already mentioned the idea that self-government was an important anti-dote to centralistic, authoritarian government, in particular in terms of the social energy it was supposed to release. Smith has aptly stated that in the early 1990s

> [h]opes were invested in renewed self-government as a forum for the realization of latent civic potential . . . , and the continuation of a relatively centralized public administration following the passage of laws on municipal administration and municipal property was interpreted as an institutional barrier to the proper development of local citizenship in Slovakia.
>
> (Smith 2003: 10)

In post-1993 Slovakia, a dualistic system has prevailed with regard to local government (in some ways in line with long-standing traditions), in that both local state administration and local self-government form distinct dimensions of local government. In other words, both a centrally controlled dimension of local government and a more grassroots-based dimension are relevant. Local self-government has been evaluated as strongly entrenched in the Constitution, in that '[a]s long as [municipalities] respect the constitution and laws, they are left with almost absolute autonomy when it comes to their decision-making' (Lastic 2011: 237). But this situation only came about in the early 2000s, when a far-going decentralization process transferred significant competences to the local level. It can be argued that the reforms of the early 2000s have shifted the Slovak republic from a strong unitary state to a more decentralized one, and 'massively increased the importance of local affairs' (Lastic 2011: 237, 2012). In the same constitutional amendment of 2001, the regional level became an important 'higher territorial unit', further adding to the decentralization of the Slovak state.[32] Both municipalities and regions are considered 'independent self-governing and administrative units' (Capkova 2011: 558, 569). In title four of the Slovak constitution, on territorial self-administration, the articles 64 and 64a refer to the municipal and regional units (higher territorial units) as 'independent territorial and administrative units'.

In terms of local democracy, the Slovak Constitution indicates both representative and direct forms of democracy, in that it recognizes elected (local and regional) authorities, as well as public assemblies and local and regional referenda (Lastic 2011: 237). Article 67 indicates both referenda (further stipulated by law) and elected authorities. As argued by Lastic, the instruments of direct democracy have changed and been restricted over time, not least through three amendments (in 1998, 2001 and 2006). The subjects that can be referred to in local referenda have been restricted as well as the percentage needed to call for referenda increased (to 30 per cent of registered voters). On the local level, the law allows for obligatory and facultative referenda (in the case of changes in municipal territorial change, when called for by the local assembly, or by petition of citizens) and for the recall of the major (Lastic 2011: 239–40). On the regional level, both referenda and the recall procedure are available.

In general, it seems fair to argue – despite, as stated by Lastic, the lack of available and accessible practical evidence – that direct democracy on the local level is hampered by high turnout and quorum requirements (2011: 243). As also argued by Capkova, '[a]lthough legislation allows for referendums, these rights are rarely exercised either by local governments or by citizens'. At the same time, in recent years an increased interest – both by authorities and citizens – in participatory forms of decision-making can be observed (2011: 567, 570). What is more, local government enjoys higher citizens' trust.

All the countries discussed display important tendencies towards the institutionalization of sub-national forms of government as well as some forms of participatory democracy on the local level. The most conspicuous problem in the Czech Republic regards the issue of the regional dimension, whose institutionalization has been long obstructed by rightist political forces. Local, rather than regional, democracy has become much more consequential in recent years, even if local referenda have not been constitutionally arranged for. In the case of Hungary, local government was constitutionalized as a right, but this right has now disappeared in the new Basic Law. The latter involves a fairly radical change in conception of the role of decentralized government in Hungarian democracy, emphasizing recentralization. The change in conception is also evident in the more restricted nature of local direct democracy. In Poland, local self-government and participatory democracy are well entrenched, and there are signs that this trend might be deepened. In contrast, Romania largely follows a centralist tradition, even if since the later 1990s a trend towards more decentralization has become visible. A peculiarity is that the regional level has no democratic but rather a purely administrative status. Regions do not enjoy constitutional status. The 2003 amendment of the constitution has strengthened the autonomy of local government, and ordinary law has increased possibilities for participation through local referenda and legislative initiatives. Slovakia's constitution entrenches local government strongly, while the constitutional amendment of 2001 created the regional level as 'higher territorial units'. But the trend in local democracy is a restriction of civic access.

Notes

1 The predominance of legal constitutionalism is the object of recent, highly interesting and critical studies, such as Puchalska (2011), Skapska (2011) and Parau (2012).
2 One should keep in mind that formal revision is only one – probably the most cumbersome – way of changing a constitution. Informal change can occur through judicial interpretation or extra-constitutional changes, which nevertheless significantly touch the character of a constitution (see Palermo 2007: 3; Closa 2012). Lutz lists the following ways of altering constitutions: formal amendment, periodic replacement of the entire document, judicial interpretation and legislative revision (1995: 248). Lutz also interestingly observes that 'formal amendment, legislative revision, and judicial interpretation reflect, in the order listed, a declining commitment to popular sovereignty' (ibid.: 241). Palermo interestingly holds that there are signs of an increasing use of formal revision in various constitutional contexts, a phenomenon which he refers to as 'constitutional acceleration' (2007: 15).
3 Palermo, however, warns that an increased pluralism could be understood as a 'crisis of revision', in that increased, pluralistic calls for a possibility of changing the constitutional pact indicates its decreasing hold on society (2007: 12).
4 Williams suggests that the *Ewigkeitsklausel* – a form of constitutional entrenchment – might have actually originated with Vaclav Havel, who supposedly has inserted limitations to amendment in article 9 in order to prevent changes in the democratic basis of the Czech state (2011: 36).
5 See the website of the Czech Constitutional Court: www.concourt.cz/clanek/other_acts.
6 The most substantial change was constituted by Law XXXI of 1989, which changed some 80 percent of the communist constitution of 1989 (Drinoczi 2007: 441).
7 The two-thirds majority does not refer only to constitutional revisions, but also to other special legislative cases. There are some provisions that regard inviolable norms in the pre-2012 Hungarian constitution (see Chapter 3; in contrast to what is affirmed in Drinoczi 2007: 453). In the Basic Law, article I and II stipulate those parts of the Constitution that are inviolable.

The Basic Law further mentions that some laws require a supermajority to be changed, such as provisions related to family protection or local government issues.

8 At later stages, the Hungarian Constitutional Court confirmed parliamentary monism, for instance in 1999, when it argued that 'The Constitution cannot be amended trough a national referendum initiated by voters, since amending the Constitution falls within the exclusive competence of Parliament. The national referendum, whose aim is to amend the Constitution, would deprive Parliament of its constitutional competence, and would therefore be unconstitutional' (Headnotes of decision 25/1999, available at: www.codices.coe.int/NXT/gateway.dll/CODICES/precis/eng/eur/hun/hun-1999-3-007?fn=document-frameset.htm$f=templates$3.0).

9 Interestingly, in 1994 a (temporary) possibility for citizens' involvement was given through a citizens' right to draft a new constitution. The draft needed to be backed up by at least 500,000 voting citizens and one citizens' draft was indeed presented (for details, see Rytel-Warzocka 2012: 212).

10 The article reads: 'If a bill to amend the Constitution relates to the provisions Chapters I, II or XII, the subjects specified in Paragraph (1) above may require, within 45 days of the adoption of the bill by the Senate, the holding of a confirmatory referendum' (Article 235(6)).

11 150(2): 'The citizens who initiate the revision of the Constitution must belong to at least half the number of the counties in the country, and in each of the respective counties or in the Municipality of Bucharest, at least 20,000 signatures must be recorded in support of this initiative' (2003).

12 Article 152(1) stipulates that '[t]he provisions of this Constitution with regard to the national, independent, unitary and indivisible character of the Romanian State, the republican form of government, territorial integrity, independence of justice, political pluralism and official language shall not be subject to revision', and 'no revision shall be made if it results in the suppression of the citizens' fundamental rights and freedoms, or of the safeguards thereof' (152 (2)). In addition, the 'Constitution shall not be revised during a state of siege or emergency, or at wartime' (152(3)).

13 Earlier versions of parts of the discussion here – on direct and local democracy – can be found in Blokker (2011a) and Blokker (2012a).

14 The earlier act – according to András Sajó a 'very poorly drafted document' (2006) – was widely contested because of various lacuna, not least in procedural terms. What is more, there was a strong suspicion of its unconstitutionality.

15 A direct trigger to lower the threshold from 50 to 25 per cent of the electorate was the upcoming referendum on accession to NATO.

16 As these scholars further indicate, one of the main problems in the Hungarian context is the conflict between 'plebiscitarian' and 'referendarian' understandings of direct democracy, i.e. between visions that understand direct democracy as a populist alternative to representative democracy, and those that see it as a complementary, deliberative instrument. This became particularly acute with a referendum on questions of healthcare in 2008, initiated by *Fidesz* and the *Christian Democratic People's Party*.

17 The execution of referenda is guarded by the Constitutional Court (art. 144g), while the constitution leaves the specific regulation of referenda to organic law (art. 72(3c)).

18 Six referenda have been held in the 'post-December' (1989) context, the first in 1991 regarding the Constitution, the second in 2003 regarding constitutional amendment, the third in 2007 on the suspension (*demitere*) of President Băsescu, the fourth in 2007 on the uninominal vote, the fifth in 2009 on a unicameral parliamentary system, and the sixth in July 2012 on the suspension of President Băsescu. Turnout for the referenda was 67, 55.70, 44.45, 26.51, 51.50 and 46.24 per cent respectively (see Glodeanu 2011).

19 The detailed prescriptions for holding referenda are found in Law 3/2000.

20 According to one analysis, the institute of referendum in the Slovak case has weakened democracy: 'the institute of referendum has become one of the important instruments (mis)used by parties in political competition. Its use by other – non-party – participants proved to be unrealistic. Its legal regulation in the Slovak Constitution led to the situation when its application produced more problems than it resolved' (Belko and Kopecek 2003).

21 The Constitution does not arrange for citizens' legislative initiatives, which is regulated in ordinary law. The law lacks, however, in clarity on the terms of registration of initiatives as well as the time period involved (Lastic 2012: 170).

22 To date, of seven popular initiatives, two were truly citizens' initiatives, while the others were started by political parties rather than civil society (Lastic 2012: 162–3).

23 In the informal reality of 'socialist realism', there were different ways of circumventing central control.

24 Later in 2003, the Constitutional Court further underlined the importance of fiscal autonomy of regions and municipalities:

> According to the starting thesis, on which the concept of self-government is built, the foundation of a free state is a free municipality, then, in terms of regional significance, at a higher level of the territorial hierarchy a self-governing society of citizens, which, under the Constitution, is a region. With this concept of public administration built from the ground up, the following postulate must be immanent to self-government, as an important element of a democratic state governed on the rule of law: that a TSU must have a realistic possibility to handle matters and issues of local significance, including those which by their nature exceed the regional framework and which it handles in its independent jurisdiction, on the basis of free discretion, where the will of the people is exercised at the local and regional level in the form of representative democracy and only limited in its specific expression by answerability to the voter and on the basis of a statutory and constitutional framework (Art. 101 par. 4 of the Constitution). Thus, territorial self-governing units representing the territorial society of citizens must have – through autonomous decision-making by their representative bodies – the ability to freely choose how they will manage the financial resources available to them for performing the work of self-government. It is this management of one's own property independently, on one's own account and own responsibility which is the attribute of self-government. Thus, a necessary prerequisite for effective performance of the functions of territorial self-government is the existence of its own, and adequate, financial or property resources.
>
> (2003/07/09 – Pl. ÚSD 5/03: Territorial Self-Government Unit; emphasis added)

25 In the new Basic Law, unilaterally adopted by Fidesz in April 2011, the representative dimension of local democracy is articulated, but not in relation to a right to self-government: '[t]he members of the local representative body and the mayors are elected by the citizens on the basis of universal and equal suffrage, with direct and secret ballot, at elections articulating the free will of the people in a manner defined by super majority law' (art. 35(1)). The instrument of local referendum is mentioned once in the draft text, but not in the section on local government, and without further stipulation.

26 Schiller classifies Hungary's procedures of local direct democracy as of 'medium' quality, together with the Czech Republic and a majority of the German states (2011: 19). Schiller further argues that in a comparative context, Hungary, at least in contrast to Belgium, Luxemburg, and Spain, displays 'substantial rates of activity' of local direct democracy (ibid.: 22).

27 Hungary adheres to the European Charter of Local Self-Government and thus the Charter is binding.

28 Although some experts note that the funtional role of local governments is overshadowing any democratic role (cf. Swianiewicz 2011: 484).

29 The post-1989 trajectory of Romanian democratization has been importantly influenced by strong tensions between 'nationalists' and 'regionalists', for a good part overlapping with representatives of the Romanian majority and Hungarian minority respectively. As argued recently by Dragoman, this has meant that 'regional design was characterized as anti-constitutional behavior and was banned from the public discourse for several years' (2011: 649; see also Maxfield 2012).

30 One of the most important thrusts towards democratization in Romania, the movement around the 1990 Timişoara declaration, included a call for 'economic and administrative decentralization' (Dobre 2011: 704). Also later in the Romanian democratic transition, calls for an increasingly regionalized and decentralized state gained importance, as in calls for 'civic regionalism' (Molnar 2000; cf. Dragoman 2011: 655).

31 A more general picture is lacking because of the unavailability of detailed comparative work. More specific, in-depth studies are available, however. Cernicova, for instance, relates to the experimental experience with citizens' self-organization and interaction with public authorities in the city of Timişoara (Cernicova 2004).

32 In the Constitution prior to 2001, only the municipality was seen as the key local self-governing unit (see Schmid and Horsky 1995: 53). Similar to the Czech case, it took until the end of the 1990s (not least due to EU pressure) to develop an explicit second tier of regional government.

6 Constitutional democracy under strain

Europeanization and legal resentment

The analysis so far has focused on the predominant pattern of constitutionalization in the new democracies, informed by legal constitutionalism, and a latent but not insignificant counter-pattern of civic constitutionalism. It is undeniable that the former has been supreme in the post-1989 years of transformation, even if not uncontested. But if we agree that the legal-constitutionalist view is generally grounded in a distrust of democratic politics, and an institutional bias towards judicial supremacy, entrenched rights and rigid constitutions, then constitutional forms that invoke (the importance of) civic participation, civic access to (constitutional and democratic) institutions on a variety of levels and constitutional openness towards (civic) politics, can be taken as counter-trends of civic constitutionalism (cf. Albert 2008). At the same time, it is hard to deny that these trends of civic constitutionalism remain fairly weakly institutionalized in all countries discussed (even if some relevant and significant traditions exist, as indicated in Chapter 4). In this, while potentially providing the basis for a further deepening of democratic constitutionalism in the region, civic constitutionalism is subject to various pressures, including external as well as domestic ones.

The focus of this chapter is on such external and domestic pressures, in the form of, first, a legal-constitutionalist and rather monistic democratic bias in European integration, and, second, in the form of domestic reactions against legal constitutionalism in the form of what I call 'legal resentment'. In the first part of the chapter, I will discuss a few forms of 'perverse' impact of the European integration process, in particular in the form of EU accession, on the constitutional structures of the new democracies. This 'perverse' impact includes a legal-constitutionalist bias, a technocratic-instrumental view of democracy and the rule of law, and a monist view of democracy that reduces democracy to representative, liberal forms. In the second part of the chapter, I will look at legal resentment in depth, focusing on the cases of Hungary and Romania. In both countries, a strong backlash against legal-constitutionalist institutions has emerged, not least visible in political attacks on the constitutional courts.

Constitutionalism under pressure

Complex, multi-faceted processes such as globalization and the emergence of supranational as well as sub-national political and legal regimes (including those with constitutional relevance) undoubtedly affect the status of the idea as well as practice of modern constitutional democracies. While national legal systems become increasingly intertwined and connected, and democratic and constitutional ideas have become available beyond borders, as particularly evident in the diffusion of the idea of constitutional democracy, the dynamic nature of political and legal processes also provides many challenges to the idea of modern constitutionalism as deeply tied up with the triptych of territory, jurisdiction and people. Frishman and Muller recently argued that 'in some respects, states may find it increasingly difficult to offer constitutional protection, when such a large amount of policy and decision-making power originates outside the state's legal order, thus placing it beyond the reach of national constitutions'. They go on: 'while the concepts of constitutions and constitutionalism undeniably emerged in the context of the nation-state, any contemporary discussion of the dynamics of constitutionalism cannot be confined to this framework' (2010: 2).

In this regard, the democratization projects in the East-Central European (ECE) region heralded in a particularly complex and dynamic era. It could be argued, with Dick Howard, that 'the revolutions of 1989 have to "catch-up" with the Western model of the nation-state, just at the moment when, according to Habermas's notion of "constitutional patriotism", that traditional model has supposedly lost its hold!' (1995: 1428). One of the ironies involved in the emergence of constitutional democracies in the region is that of a 'sovereignty conundrum', as Wojciech Sadurski (2012) has coined it. This conundrum consists of the tension in the post-1989 democratization processes between the emancipation from a totalitarian empire and the integration into supranational structures of different kinds. In other words, if one of the driving forces of democratization has been the will to become self-governing, the conditions under which democratization is evolving impose important limits on the space for self-government. As formulated by Sadurski:

> countries with a proud national history, only just emerging from several decades of oppressive domination by the Soviet Union, at best suffering all the burdens and disadvantages of limited sovereignty, and at worst being subjected to forceful integration into Soviet statehood (as was the case of the Baltic states), were about to embark on the surrender of their sovereignty to a foreign body again – admittedly benign, but foreign nevertheless.
>
> (2012: 3)

But the region-specific tensions have a more general nature; they can be equally related to modern constitutionalism in general (see Walker 2002). A key question is: how to understand the confirmation of the global rise and expansion of constitutionalism in the 'legal revolutions' of 1989, at the very moment that an increasing disenchantment with and various challenges to modern constitutionalism have become visible? Constitutional democracies on the national level are affected by productive and destructive energies that 'are being unleashed in social spheres beyond the state' (Teubner 2012: 1–2). If modern constitutions were originally about the 'release of the energies of political power in nation states and at the same time to limit that power effectively', this model seems now in crisis (ibid.: 1).

Developments beyond state borders significantly affect the make-up and capacities of constitutional democracies in the process of democratization. It is without doubt true that transnational developments – including the process of European integration and the emergence of transnational regimes, as well as the transfer of political power to non-public actors – erode some of the bases of modern constitutional democracy. Peters has argued that '[g]lobalization puts the state and state constitutions under strain: global problems compel states to co-operate within international organizations and through bilateral and multilateral treaties'. She speaks indeed of 'deconstitutionalization on the domestic level' in that 'typically governmental functions, such as guaranteeing human security, freedom, and equality, are in part transferred to 'higher levels' and 'non-state actors' (acting within states or even in a transboundary fashion) are increasingly entrusted with the exercise of traditional state functions' (2006: 580). She concludes from this that '[t]he hollowing out of national constitutions affects not only the constitutional principle of democracy, but also the rule of law and the principle of social security. Overall, state constitutions are no longer 'total constitutions' (ibid.). Teubner even goes so far as to claim that globalization is not causing but rather making visible a 'basic deficiency of modern constitutionalism' (2012: 5).

At the same time, in particular in the case of the countries in ECE, there has been clearly a 'democratic dividend' that resulted from engagement with transnational processes, most clearly in the form of a 'return to Europe', particularly in terms of accession to the EU, but also resulting from membership of the Council of Europe (Sadurski 2004). The most important development beyond national borders for the ECE countries is evidently the European integration project, and the latter can be said to have a profound impact on national constitutional democracy. But it is exactly in this entanglement between new constitutional democracies and the evolving European project that significant dilemmas and tensions for democratic constitutionalism emerge.

In this chapter, I will be particularly interested in the general question of how national constitutional orders are affected by international and supranational tendencies with regard to their democratic sovereignty and democratic capacities. Below, I will first explore to what extent it can be said that the EU accession process and subsequent EU membership have had specific influence on the constitutional nature of the new democracies (not least with regard to a legal-constitutionalist 'template'), and how such influence might have effected elements of democratic deliberation and participation in the new democracies. I will focus on a specific set of aspects, related to what I call substantive (rather than procedural and strategic) dimensions of the EU accession process. This substantive dimension includes an influence on the substantive make-up of constitutionalism in the new democracies (not least, an emphasis on strong, independent constitutional courts), a one-sided emphasis on an instrumental-technocratic approach to constitutionalism and the rule of law (to the detriment of moral issues and matters of justice) and, finally, a predilection for a rather minimalist, representative-liberal understanding of democracy, without due concern for alternative, participatory dimensions. All three dimensions can be said to have adversely affected civic-democratic constitutional potential in at least some of the new EU member states.

In the second part of the chapter, I will discuss a domestic form of reaction against EU integration and legal-constitutionalist understandings of democracy, a reaction I will call 'legal resentment' or resentment against legal constitutionalism. The cases explored will be Hungary and Romania, two democracies that have recently displayed a strong backlash against both EU integration (and the primary role of the EU in establishing the rules for constitutional democracy) and legal constitutionalism as a template for domestic democracy. The turn away from legal constitutionalism in both countries consists in a complex reaction to external imposition as well as distinct understandings of democracy and the rule of law. The orientation of legal resentment is worrisome, in that it is both moving away from legal constitutionalism with an emphasis on judicial supremacy and away from democratic constitutionalism with its emphasis on civic engagement and participation, and public deliberation.

Europeanization and domestic democratic capacities

In the context of my discussion of constitutionalism and democracy, the EU accession process of the former communist countries constituted a very distinct dimension in the establishment of new constitutional democracies.[1] As observed, the constitutionalization of the post-communist societies occurs in a very specific historical period, in which modern constitutionalism in its state-centric version is subject to complex, multifaceted and intense change. One of the implications of European integration is the emergence of a new type of sovereignty, 'divided sovereignty' (Přibáň 2010). As observed, the prospective member states thus faced the conundrum of reinforcing their recently re-won national sovereignty by means of integration into a supranational constitutional structure.

In general, it can be argued that EU accession enhanced democratic structures in the new member states. It seems beyond doubt that the EU accession – in terms of a preparatory process with attached conditionality as well as the role of the EU as a 'democratic anchor' in a wider sense – has played a very significant role in the democratic transformation of the former communist countries. Many observers agree that the EU accession of the Central and Eastern European countries has involved the strengthening of democratic structures, at least in a formalistic-institutional sense. Thus, Spendzharova and Vachudova have argued that

> [t]he tremendous benefits of EU membership created political incentives to satisfy the EU's extensive membership requirements. These incentives, along with certain characteristics of the pre-accession process to reward progress and publicise shortcomings, create the EU's leverage on domestic reform. EU leverage has helped compel candidates to *reform the state and the economy, improving the quality of democracy and the efficiency of state institutions* in various ways.
>
> (2012: 39; emphasis added)[2]

Sadurski has referred to this as a 'democracy dividend' of EU accession, while paying due attention to the diverse impact of EU conditionality on the various candidate countries. As he has argued,

> [t]he interaction between the 'external' factors of conditionality and the domestic calculus of the costs and benefits of transforming an institution (or adopting a rule) provides the best lens through which to evaluate the impact of 'conditionality' on the speed, depth and resilience of adoption and maintenance of particular democratic rules or institutions in the candidate states.
>
> (2004: 69)

But other observers, while acknowledging the positive results, have also called attention for how EU accession has in some ways compromised democratic practices and the emergence of a constitutional-democratic political culture. As Přibáň argues, the 'conditionality process weakened democratic deliberation but strengthened democratic institutional designs' (Přibáň 2010: 21). In other words,

> [f]rom the perspective of democratic constitutionalism, the Copenhagen criteria and the Commission's progress reports (designed with conditionality in mind) had very mixed results. EU membership was considered such a political priority in all candidate stataes that the laws were approximated without appropriate democratic deliberation and then justified as a historical necessity. The candidate states did not participate in the creation of the EU *acquis* and their contribution to the Europe agreements and conditionality documents was very limited.
>
> (Ibid.: 16–17)

Puchalska also brings into relief the problematic sides to external democratization through Europeanization. She points to the asymmetric and top-down relations between the old and prospective member states, the lack of a clearly defined democratic template, a general absence of transparency and accountability in the process, the technocratic nature of the accession process, and an unproportional financial support for Western NGOs (2011: 103, 107–116).

Below, following this critical argument, I will suggest that in a number of ways the EU accession process has compromised the emergence of democratic constitutionalism in the region, which, to put it in Tully's terms, would balance the constitutional and democratic dimensions of constitutionalism. A problematic institutionalization of constitutional democracy relates to both procedural and substantive aspects. In procedural terms, many have argued that the EU accession process itself has been asymmetric, in that the EU mostly imposed its (rather vague) norms and values, without allowing for democratic interaction between the prospective states and the EU, nor within the domestic political arenas of the candidate countries (cf. Albi 2005; Iancu 2010; Puchalska 2011). Also, the accession process was dominated by the governments of the candidate states, whereas the parliaments were largely side-lined, and public debate was largely avoided, even in the context of the referendum on EU accession.

Much of the attention in scholarly debates has gone to the procedural (and strategic) side of enlargement, and perhaps less consideration has been given to the substantive aspects of democratization (cf. Haukenes and Freyberg-Inan 2012: 2). It has often been argued – and rightfully so – that the conditionality of the EU enlargement process is based on vague criteria, which in practice were often applied in non-homogeneous ways with regard to the various applicant countries (Kochenov 2008). But at the same time, it can be argued that distinct dimensions have been and are present in the EU's approach towards the institutionalization of constitutional democracy in candidate countries, even if often articulated only in an implicit way (cf. Haukenes and Freyberg-Inan 2012). Below, I will briefly discuss three of such substantive dimensions, which include a certain emphasis on legal constitutionalism and judicial supremacy, at least in the cases of Romania and Slovakia, an instrumental-technocratic relation to the law, as well as delineations of a specific democratic model that the EU seeks to promote.[3]

Regarding the first dimension, the EU accession process has in some cases clearly contributed to the promotion of a distinct vision and 'template' of constitutionalism, that is what I have called legal constitutionalism. This becomes visible not least through an emphasis on judicial independence, including that of constitutional courts. It can therefore be argued that at least partially the European integration process of the new member states has strengthened the 'constitutional' rather than the 'democratic' side of constitutionalism, in emphasizing the importance of independent, non-political institutions that safeguard the primacy of the constitution and of fundamental rights. One of the concerns of the EU regarded that of domestic judiciaries having the capacity to nationally enforce the EU legal system or *acquis* (Parau forthcoming, 2013a: 2). In this regard, the EU is part of a wider constellation of international actors (notably including the Council of Europe) that promotes a 'certain institutional-design template' (Parau forthcoming, 2013b: 1), in which a rigid separation of politics and law, not least through judicial independence, plays a significant role. The EC further endorsed active constitutional courts that could play the role of arbiter in the often very conflictive form of parliamentary politics in the region (Haukenes and Freyberg-Inan 2012: 12). In two cases such external, EU influence is particularly evident,[4] that is in the case of Romania, and to a lesser extent that of Slovakia.

In the Romanian case, the European Commission noted in its first 'Opinion on Romania's application for Membership of the European Union in 1997' that 'the Court's ruling that an act is unconstitutional is without effect if Parliament upholds its original decision by a two-thirds majority (Article 145 of the Constitution), which limits considerably the scope of the supervision exercised' (EC 1997a: 14). The Commission in general stated: 'The fact that the Constitutional Court's rulings can be overturned by a two-thirds majority of Parliament is a major obstacle to genuine constitutional control in Romania' (EC 1997a: 15). A very recent statement by the European Commission repeated similar views, this time in the context of a Romanian constitutional crisis in the summer of 2012. As conveyed in a press release on an encounter between the head of the Commission José Manuel Baroso, and the Romanian prime minister Victor Ponta,

> President Barroso expressed his serious concerns about recent political events in Romania in relation to the *rule of law*, the *independence of the judiciary* and the *role of the Constitutional Court*. He underlined that the necessary checks and balances in a democratic system must be guaranteed. President Barroso made clear that *the Romanian Government must respect the full independence of the judiciary, restore the powers of the Constitutional Court and ensure that its decisions are observed*, appoint an Ombudsman enjoying cross-party support, ensure a new open and transparent procedure for appointing a General Prosecutor and Director of the Anti-Corruption Directorate and make integrity a political priority.
>
> (European Commission 2012a, 2012b; emphasis added)[5]

In January 2013, the European Commission repeated its views, and among other things stated that

> the place of the Constitution and the Constitutional Court has been restored *in line with the Commission's recommendations*. It is however essential that the President, the new government and parliament

> ensure the stability of the constitutional order, and all political parties should work to reduce the polarisation of the political system.
>
> (2013: 3; emphasis added)

In the light of these developments, it is probably not a coincidence that the 2003 comprehensive amendment of the Romanian constitution – in the light of EU accession – included an important 'upgrade' of the Romanian Constitutional Court, which until then had been subordinate to the Romanian Parliament. The parliamentary Commission for the Revision of the Constitution (*Comisia pentru elaborarea propunerii legislative privind revizuirea Constituției*) set up in 2003 indicated the highly significant European dimension to constitutional change as follows: '[T]he creation of the necessary constitutional frame for the integration of the country into Euro-Atlantic structures is not only the consequence of a historical evolution of Romanian society, but also a duty to ourselves, as to those that will come after us' (Romanian Commission 2003a: 2).

The external, European dimension also came clearly to the fore in the parliamentary debates on constitutional revision, such as the one held on 18 June 2003, in which the revision of the Constitution is portrayed (by prime minister Adrian Năstase) as a form of (external) modernization of the Romanian democratic state (Romanian Parliament 2003). As Năstase further argued,

> The revision of the Constitution and of legislation in general has become a practice nowadays in almost all democracies, which corresponds to the exigencies of the state of law. *The supremacy of constitutional norms* in the frame of the juridical system of a state calls for the necessity that it corresponds to historical-sociological evolution, singular in its capacity to consolidate the innovation and modernization of society.
>
> (Emphasis added)

The emphasis in the explanations and justification of constitutional amendment of the Commission on Constitutional Revision is on the Constitutional Court 'in the quality of a guarantor of the supremacy of the Constitution'. The emphasis on a court as final arbiter is 'essential to create a constitutional frame which ensures, on the level of modern necessity, judicial independence' (Romanian Commission 2003a: 3). The Commission concluded by arguing that 'the amendments on their whole will assure a better protection of the citizens in terms of the affirmation of rights and liberties in a constitutional and legal sense, [which in itself constitutes, pb] a fundamental principle for the Euro-Atlantic structures in which we need to integrate' (Romanian Commission 2003a: 4).

The legal-constitutional version of the Romanian Constitutional Court provided it with the power of ultimate interpretation of the Constitution as well as with powers of mediation and legal resolution with regard to conflicts between public institutions (Parau 2012: 663). The shift from democratic political control to judicial supremacy was largely abided to by the Romanian parliament, and in reality endorsed by almost the entire parliament (except for the *Partidul România Mare* (PRM) which was strongly against revising the constitution as such; cf. Blokker 2010a; Parau 2012).

Relating these tendencies to my discussion of the democracy-constitutionalism nexus, the democratic dimensions of the constitutional order were reduced both in a substantive (judicial supremacy) and a procedural sense (the revision process). As Parau argues, '[a]s in 1991, so in 2003, the Romanian people were involved only as an afterthought at the ratification stage, which hardly counts as popular input into the drafting process' (forthcoming, 2013c: 40). As she has argued also elsewhere, one reason for parliamentary consensus on the empowerment of the Constitutional Court was its hope that a third powerful actor would be able to act as a neutral arbiter in continuous political conflict and infighting (2012: 662–4). In reality, one of the main questions in the context of the constitutionalism–democracy nexus is whether a constitutional court can be considered a neutral, *super-partes* party without assuming political qualities in its own right[6] (cf. Blokker 2012b).

Turning to Slovakia, also the Slovak case shows some signs of externally triggered constitutional reform. Some of the emphasis, even if much less upfront than in the Romanian case, on constitutional reform into the direction of a legal-constitutional system with judicial supremacy can be detected in the Slovak reforms in the run-up to EU accession. In the Commission's opinion on Slovakia of 1997, it particularly expresses concern about the lack of independence of judges (EC 1997b). As Malová and Dolny also argue, the Commission expressed concerns about the stability of the democratic institutions and the lack of respect for Constitutional Court rulings (2008: 73; see also Broestl 2003: 147; Roharik 2003: 217). In its 1998 Regular Report, the Commission indeed particularly expressed concern for the 'disregard for the Constitutional Court rulings' (EC 1998: 13). It is, then, not surprising that the 2001 amendment of the Slovak constitution pointed to a strengthening and autonomization of the Constitutional Court's powers, including the increase of number of judges and the extension of their terms (Constitution Watch 2001; Lastic 2006; Malová and Láštic 2001: 25; Ucen 2002: 1078).[7] According to Broestl *et al.*, the amendments involve the

> strengthening of the position and legal powers of the Constitutional Court. The essence of this strengthening includes not only the expansion of the authorities of the Constitutional Court, but also the enforceability of its rulings and a higher level of protection of fundamental rights and freedoms.
>
> (2001: 169)

The amendment Law 90/2001 has been described as a 'significant amendment of the basic law of the country', not least because of the implications for the constitutional order itself (ibid.). Again, we see here a (modest) thrust towards a legal understanding of constitutionalism and constitutional democracy, and the endorsement of an idea of the latter that emphasizes the instrumental, in some ways negative dimension of constitutional democracy, and the stability of institutions, but in which little attention is paid to the wider, civic diffusion of norms and values of constitutionalism throughout political and civic society and the crucial role played by participation in such diffusion (cf. Malová and Dolny 2008; Rose-Ackerman 2005).

This brings us to a second dimension of substantive democracy in the context of EU accession. A further dilemma, which relates to the nature of the European integration process, regards that of an instrumental, technocratic approach to the law in which priority is given to the formal institutionalization of legal structures without due attention for immaterial, cultural aspects of the rule of law. As has been recently recalled by Jiri Přibáň, the 'return to Europe' of the ECE countries was significantly about the anchoring of the rule of law and democratic institutions, and EU membership and the run-up to accession (with its conditionality) importantly embedded this process in a wider European order grounded in the rule of law, democracy and human rights. But, as the same Přibáň (2009) argues, an important, structural tension has emerged between a technical and instrumental use of law by the EU, and an emphasis on what could be called output or instrumental legitimacy, on the one hand, and domestic democratization processes, substantive legitimacy and emphasis on the democratic and participatory potential of the law, on the other. In a similar vein, Puchalska has observed that 'the strong drive to join [for the accession countries, pb] might have led to practices designed to create compliance, at a superficial level at best, but without creating a supporting culture or entrenchment necessary for lasting and meaningful change'. One critical view on the locking in of the domestic processes of democratization in the larger EU process might then be that it 'could have a better chance if carried out in a responsive rather than a top-down fashion' (2011: 113; cf. Malová and Dolny 2008).

One example of this tension between instrumental and substantive rationality with regard to democratization – and between externally and internally driven democratization – becomes visible in the Romanian context. Bogdan Iancu has, for instance, discussed Romania's experience with judicial reform and lustration from this perspective. He argues that the European Commission – in monitoring the Romanian process of democratization, which was regarded problematic with regard to *inter alia* the independence of the judiciary and corruption – has been predominantly interested in an adherence of Romania to the criteria of political conditionality, which themselves are largely expressed in 'measurable constitutional problem areas of judicial reform and the fight against corruption' (2010: 30). This has, however, largely led to a disinterest in substantive and moral issues such as those that are tied up with lustration and transitional justice. In Iancu's view, '[t]he accession process has led to the aggravation of extant tensions, as the formalistic and directionless way in which the EU-driven constitutional and institutional reforms proceeded has perpetuated, entrenched, and legitimised the local 'instrumentalisation' of the rule of law' (ibid.: 31).

The relation between the EU constitutional order and the new constitutional democracies in ECE includes, then, in some of its dimensions potential perverse results with regard to substantive ideas of democracy. The process of EU accession has prioritized the top-down imposition of EU norms presented as self-evident and as 'beyond discussion' (Puchalska 2011: 108), thereby embedding the new democracies in the European order based on democracy and the rule of law, but at the same time 'depoliticising' democratic politics in these countries due to the limited involvement of national parliaments and the public, and providing room for the instrumentalization of constitutional dimensions. As Sajó has argued at the dawn of accession, a lack of popular participation might be problematic for processes of democratization and Europeanization in that

> [t]he lack of transparent popular representation may not be the ideal beginning for the people of the new member states about to set a foot on a common European path that is leading to a partially

> uncharted European decision making process without full representation (or with a new complex representative system based on partial representation).
>
> (2004: 202)

As Puchalska has also argued, 'the undemocratic application and enforcement of conditionality [might be] one of the possible causes of the damage inflicted on the democratic learning of ECE societies and governing elites' (Puchalska 2011: 109).

As many observers have argued, the process of Europeanization is ambiguous in that the EU has worked both as a stabilizing factor in the consolidation of constitutional democracies and as an undermining factor by hindering the maturation of democratic learning, capacities and behaviour. The European integration process signified a stabilization of national constitutional democracies, the rule of law and the protection of rights by means of the process of conditionality and the monitoring of harmonization of the legal orders in ECE (Sadurski 2004). But the EU equally complicated the exercise of new-won democratic capacities by insisting on swift and technocratic adoption of the EU *acquis* in the preparation to accession. This process was largely driven by executives and bureaucracies (for instance in the form of special institutions, such as was the case in the Czech Republic), largely sidelining parliamentary debate about significant legal changes (cf. Přibáň 2009: 354). Puchalska concludes that

> conditionality might have been more detrimental to democratic consolidation in the ECE countries than is acknowledged. The lack of clear standards, benchmarking and haphazard auditing by the Commission may have led to a mainly formal type of implementation, undermining the effectiveness of conditionality. The technocratic nature of the conditionality implementation contrasted with the basic democratic criteria of transparency, accountability and responsiveness.
>
> (2011: 116)

An additional requirement in the conditionality-driven process was the speedy incorporation of constitutional amendments 'necessary' for imminent accession, which has equally tended to compromise critical public debate on accession and the joining of a post-national order. As remarked by Albi, '[t]he latest EU enlargements . . . offered some evidence of nascent inroads by the EU into the national autonomy in determining the content of the constitutions' (2009: 121), such as in the example of constitutional provisions on judicial reform, as in the cases of Bulgaria, Slovakia and Romania. In the case of Romania, the constitution of which contains a particularly difficult amendment procedure, a revision bill was adopted after the instalment of a parliamentary committee in 2002, and led to the elaboration of the bill, a constitutional review of the bill in early 2003, and its discussion in parliament later that year. According to one observer, '[f]rom a qualitative and professional point of view, the debate on the proposals for revising the constitution were of a much higher level than that which can normally be observed in Romanian parliament' (Huiu 2003: 7). At the same time, the constitutionally obligatory referendum on constitutional revision made evident a lack of public interest and knowledge on the revision process and its implications. The referendum portrayed difficulties in attracting sufficient popular participation, which led to irregularities and undue governmental influence to raise participatory levels. Another observer argues that the low turn-out had to do with the 'nature of bureaucratic Europe-related constitutionalism', which consisted in a 'top-down and bureaucratic' drafting process as well as the presentation of the amendments to the wider public as unavoidable (Iancu 2010: 41–2).

A third, final, dimension of substantive democracy in the context of EU accession I want to discuss is the implicit promotion of a distinct model and idea of democracy, in many ways related to a fairly minimalist representation of representative, liberal democracy. The transition towards constitutional democratic regimes that commenced most visibly with the fall of communism in 1989 has been a process which has seen conflictive interpretations of constitutional democracy (see Blokker 2010a). At the same time, it cannot be denied that the key thrust in the constitutionalization of democracy in the region was towards a representative, liberal understanding of democracy. This predominant idea and model of democracy was equally visible in EU policy. As argued by Malová and Dolny, the 'EU directly promoted institutions stabilizing the horizontal division of powers, rule of law, human and minority rights protection, and corresponding behaviour of the elite, however the rapid and technocratic accession "logic" of the EU neglected the norms and rules of participatory and/or popular democracy' (2008: 67–8). In other words, the assessments of democratic progress and the establishment of the rule of law in the EC's reports focused on an institutional structure corresponding to a rather minimal, liberal-constitutional view of democracy, and 'reduced the understanding of political participation in CEEC mostly to free and fair elections', without paying attention to alternative, more civic and participatory forms or a 'strong democracy' (ibid.: 68, 76), which could have potentially strengthened attempts to promote such alternative views in local settings.[8]

Resentment against legal constitutionalism

EU accession involves a complexity of forms of national adaptation, implementation and reaction. Above, I have explored the influence of EU accession on national constitutional orders in terms of a legal-constitutionalist bias as well as regarding the endorsement of a (biased and limited) understanding of a democratic model and related institutional constellation. But, in particular in the post-accession period, EU accession has also invoked particularist reactions within distinct national arenas, which have criticized the idea of legal constitutionalism and judicial supremacy as well as external infringement on national constitutional orders. What might be understood as equally problematic in *both* cases – that of a legal-constitutional bias and of a resentment against such a bias – are the implications for democratic participation and an understanding of democracy as about civic self-government.

A dilemma that has then emerged in the post-accession period results from forms of domestic resentment against the top-down and hierarchical approach of the EU towards democratization and EU accession. This relates to the discussion about legal and democratic constitutionalism in that recently forms of backlash against legal constitutionalism and judicial supremacy can be observed in the region, in particular in the cases of Hungary and Romania. As observed above, such critique and political action against legal constitutionalism – even if sometimes articulated in terms of the protection of domestic democracy – do not, however, per se result in attempts to institutionalize more participatory and democratic forms of constitutionalism, quite the contrary. Below, I will discuss the Hungarian and Romanian cases in more detail, since they seem to pose the most radical challenge to legal constitutionalism in the last few years. Resentment against legal constitutionalism or legal resentment involves some, and sometimes, all of the following dimensions: the curtailing of the powers of the Constitutional Court; the imposition of a new constitution or related legislation without adequate pluralistic and public debate; a reference to a different idea of constitutionalism, based on constitutional tradition; a distinct, limited and exclusionary interpretation of rights; and the open defiance of EU institutions and the EU legal order.

Forms of resentment against legal constitutionalism have, however, not been limited to the two countries mentioned. Before discussing the cases of Hungary and Romania, it might be useful to briefly look at experiences in Poland. One instance of resistance against a EU 'template' could be found in the Polish stance in the mid-2000s towards the European Charter of Fundamental Rights and the government's decision[9] to ultimately opt out in 2007 with regard to rights in the 'sphere of morality'. The centre-right government that governed in 2005–7 pursued a strategy of opting out of the European Charter of Fundamental Rights, because of an alleged incompatibility with national democracy, and the 'sensitive issues' of public morality, that is the definition of the family, and human dignity in Polish law (Wyrozumska 2007). This 'resistance' of the Polish government could be interpreted as a failure of EU conditionality and the limited, or at least biased interpretation, of fundamental rights in the Polish context, as Puchalska observes.

The Polish resistance also points to a lack of civic-democratic involvement in fundamental choices in Polish democracy, at least in that particular instance. In this case, '[t]here was no public debate on the opt-out, not even in the Sejm [the Polish parliament, pb]' (Puchalska 2011: 118). Puchalska suggests that it might be the case that 'the undemocratic practices of EU conditionality perpetuated further the gulf between the governing and the governed, bolstered the elitism inherent in the political systems of the ECE countries and legitimised the old networks of 'clientelism' and patronage, to the detriment of democratic constitutionalism' (ibid.: 121).

But while in Poland the change of government in 2007 has relatively eased relations with the EU, other cases have emerged that openly defy a European constitutional order grounded in ideas of legal constitutionalism and judicial supremacy. The most radical example of political resentment against legal constitutionalism as well as European integration at large has emerged in post-2010 Hungary. This resentment is *inter alia* reflected in the rapid and largely non-participatory and majority-driven drafting of a new constitution by the current centre-right Fidesz government. In substance, the new Basic Law entails a shift away from the Hungarian attachment to a 'secular state based on a pluralist society', grounded in European traditions, as was evident in the constitutionalization process since 1989, and has led to the institutionalization of a new constitutional order that has its foundations in sovereigntist, 'historical and religious considerations' (Kovács and Tóth 2011: 198). What is significant about the new constitution is not least that 'in many respects it does not comply with standards of democratic constitutionalism and the basic principles set forth in article 2 of the Treaty on the European Union', as observed by a number of critical Hungarian legal scholars as well as by the Council of Europe's Venice Commission (Arato *et al.* 2011: 3; Halmai 2012).

The constitutional project of the Fidesz government involves clear dimensions of resentment against legal constitutionalism. The thrust of much of the process was against the democratic-constitutional order that has emerged since 1989, as the leaders 'sensed a fundamental (and in the short term irremediable) disillusionment with the liberal democratic system across all segments of the Hungarian political community and think they have a long-term solution that will appeal to the masses' (Szombati 2011: 2). The resentment against legal constitutionalism is based on an explicit reference to a different idea of constitutionalism, the unwritten 'historical constitution'. Scheppele (2004) already referred to such a sentiment in the early 2000s under the name of 'counter-constitutionalism'. The conservative thrust in the project could also be related to as a form of 'communitarian constitutionalism'. What is clear is that in the recent upsurge of communitarian constitutionalism the decisively legal-constitutionalist trajectory of the country has changed rather drastically. Whereas it cannot be denied that the country was characterized by a dualistic or tensional – civic-liberal and ethno-nationalist – political culture throughout the transformation years (cf. Blokker 2010a), the emergence of the latter in a full-blown constitutional project was hard to foresee. This is also because throughout the 1990s Hungarian democracy was often portrayed as an archetypal case of adherence to a human-rights-based legal constitutionalism in which ethno-national dimensions played a marginal role at best. In 2010, however, as argued by Jan-Werner Müller, a 'nationalist conservative revolution has triumphed in Budapest; its leaders are busy dismantling constitutionalism and the rule of law' (2011: 5). The so-called Basic Law (Alaptörvény) introduced by the centre-right Fidesz government in 2011 can be said to change the 'characteristics of Hungarian constitutionalism' from one grounded in the idea of a 'secular state based upon a pluralist society' to one having its foundations in 'historical and religious considerations' and placing emphasis on the 'family, nation, loyalty, faith and love'. The new Basic Law reinterprets the category 'We the People' in that in the 1989 Constitution the people referred to 'those citizens who reside in the country and who are the subjects of the legal rights and obligations', while in the Basic Law the reference is to 'one single Hungarian nation that belongs together' (Kovács and Tóth 2011: 198).

The Basic Law further emphasizes its nature of communitarian constitutionalism by means of an extensive National Avowal (Nemzeti hitvallás), a kind of preamble but better understood as a 'creed or confession of (political) faith used in a national context or performed by the nation itself' (Horkay Hörcher 2012: 42). The National Avowal refers, for instance, to a link between Christianity and Hungarian nationhood, the fundamental importance of the nation and the family, and the significance of the 'historical constitution'. One Hungarian observer confirms the communitarian constitutional dimension to the National Avowal and its reference to a collective identity and values:

> I do not think that the perceptible shift of emphasis from the defence of individual rights to a double focus on the defence of both individual rights and the socio-political values of the whole political community substantiated by the history of political thought and justified by the reflections on the often competing findings of recent re-conceptualisations of liberal democracies in communitarian, civic humanist and (neo- or civic-)Republican thought is misconceived or unacceptable. On the contrary, my understanding is that this is the result of a necessary development of democratic political theory initiated by recent Western experiences of political disinterest on the one side, and populist hyper-activism on the other side, both endangering the right workings of legitimate political institutions and of democratically elected agents in Western constitutional regimes. Given that the genre of the National Avowal by its very nature requires an identification with the 'first person plural' viewpoint, I take it as an effort by the constitution-makers to react adequately on these later developments of constitutional thought.
>
> (Horkay Hörcher 2012: 52)

At the same time, however, the same author warns against 'the dangers of a too strongly "nationalistic" constitutional programme', which concern – inter alia – the lack of participation by opposition and civil society in the constitutional drafting, a curtailment of the substance of judicial review of the Constitutional Court, the exclusionary definitions of membership of the political community, the curtailment of the freedom of expression, and retroactive legislation (see Kovács and Tóth 2011).

These dangers, however, are all too visible in the actual constitutional project. Some of the implications of the Fidesz constitutional programme are a drastic curtailment of the independence of the Hungarian constitutional court as well as of its powers of constitutional review. Already prior to the adoption and implementation of a new constitution, the Hungarian centre-right government used its ample majority to adopt a series of amendments (12 in total), some of which directly affected the status and role of the Hungarian Constitutional Court. The first amendment adopted regarded the powers of the Court in terms of review of financial legislation. As a reaction to the annulment by the Court of an Act on taxes, which *inter alia* operated retroactively, the government adopted a constitutional amendment that restricted the Court's review powers regarding financial issues. This was later inserted into the Basic Law.[10] The limits regarding the kind of legislation the Constitutional Court is allowed to review diminish the Court's capacity to perform a protective function regarding fundamental rights, given a *de facto* control to the current Fidesz majority (also because, ironically, the latter intends to arrange for socio-economic issues through entrenched or cardinal laws that need a two-thirds majority in parliament to be changed)[11] (Halmai 2011: 4). The Constitutional Court's functionality is further importantly reduced because of a radical restriction in terms of the actors that are able to initiate constitutional review (see below).

Other amendments involved changes in the nominaton of judges (*de facto* allowing the Fidesz government to nominate judges without consulting opposition or the judiciary), the extension of the judges' mandate as well as the number of judges (measures which might in this case not so much ensure the Court's independence, but rather protract political influence of the Fidesz party over time), and the chief judge is now nominated by the parliament (see Csink and Schanda 2012: 164–5; Kovacs and Toth 2011: 193–5). The overall attitude of the Orbán government was aptly conveyed in a speech delivered in Berlin in October 2012.[12] According to Orbán, the revision of the position of the Constitutional Court is reflecting the views of the Hungarian people. Hungarians respect the institution of the Constitutional Court 'but they are a bit ambivalent' toward it because, after all, this body can annul decisions of the representatives chosen by the people. 'The Hungarian way of thinking, the Hungarian stomach finds this more difficult to swallow than the people of Germany seem to.'

A particularly unfortunate change in the new Basic Law, regarding a generally weakly institutionalized democratic constitutionalism, is the decision to abolish the unique institution of *actio popularis*, which allowed individuals, as well as non-governmental organizations and advocacy groups, to petition the Constitutional Court directly.[13] This right has once been commented on by the former president of the Hungarian constitutional court as 'a substitute for direct democracy'.[14] The new Basic Law introduces a form of constitutional complaint, which can be used in specific individual cases of concrete breaches of the law.

It can be argued, however, that this 'extension of opportunities to submit constitutional complaints is no substitute whatsoever for the widely available right of private individuals and organisations to file petitions' (Arato *et al.* 2011: 28). Indeed, the *actio popularis* could be seen as a form of civic engagement with constitutional matters in that it is grounded in the idea of the initiator as a 'trustee of the public good' rather than an individual seeking to undo a past personal wrongdoing (Sadurski 2008: 6). Its abandonment appears just one of the indications of a radical move away from a democratic dimension in constitutionalism.

The constitutional politics of the Fidesz have not only had clear implications in terms of the substance of the constitutional order (and the role of the Constitutional Court in it), but have also shown many problematic aspects in the way the Basic Law has been adopted. A widespread critique has been that the Fidesz government has systematically ignored and marginalized oppositional forces as well as the wider public, and basically imposed a new constitution without wider public debate and without the necessary democratic legitimation that stems from a pluralistic involvement in constitution-making. The opposition parties were not involved in the drafting process (they actually boycotted the process because of insufficient inclusion, lack of public consultation and curtailment of the court) and did not support the draft that was elaborated by Fidesz. The draft was further not put to a referendum to obtain popular support either. The drafting process itself and the adoption of parliament in April 2011 was proceeding at a 'frenetic pace', as a member of the opposition party Lehet Más a Politika (LMP) has described it (Szombati 2011: 1). The frenetic pace and lack of inclusiveness were equally criticized by the Venice Commission (CoE 2011).

A related aspect of dubious and intransparent constitution-making has been the adoption of an 'omnibus constitutional addendum' in the form of the 'Act on Transitional Provisions to the Fundamental Law' in the last two weeks of 2011, that is, before the new Basic Law was entering into force (Halmai 2012: 5). The transitional nature of these provisions relates to the implementation of the constitution, but in reality these provisions went much beyond a mere provisional status in arranging for permanent changes. One indication of the lack of open democratic procedure is the fact that the provisions were passed in parliament on 30 December 2011, published on 31 December and entering into effect on 1 January 2012. In this, the 'primary purpose of this law – to give governmental institutions and citizens notice of how the constitution would be phased in – was lost' (Halmai and Scheppele 2012: 5).

A further ingredient to legal resentment is the repudiation of external influence, in this case in particular concerning the influence of the EU. In reply to the demands by the European Commission to adjust various aspects of the new Basic Law, Orbán replied in an interview that 'The whole matter is trivial. Hungary has to face up to objections against five to eight laws that have been passed' (*FAZ* 4 March 2012). On another occasion he has articulated slogans such as 'We do not need the unsolicited assistance of foreigners wanting to guide our hands', and further argued that 'Hungarians will not live as foreigners dictate, will not give up their independence or their freedom, therefore they will not give up their constitution either', and that '[f]reedom means that we decide about the laws governing our own life, we decide what is important and what isn't. From the Hungarian perspective, with a Hungarian mindset, following the rhythm of our Hungarian hearts. We will not be a colony' (*Guardian* 15 March, 2012). The language is clearly a Eurosceptical one, criticizing interference into national matters and underlining a traditional notion of political sovereignty, although Orbán contests 'that what is expressed in the Hungarian Constitution is being interpreted as something which belongs to the past' (*FAZ* 4 March, 2012). This anti-EU stance equally dovetails with Fidesz's insistence on the Hungarian traditional constitution as an alternative to European, liberal constitutionalism.

Also in the Romanian case, a (complex) conflict over legal constitutionalism, and the role of the Constitutional Court in particular, can be observed in recent years. Some observers have even indicated important similarities between the Hungarian and Romanian cases. Since the 'upgrading' of the Romanian Constitutional Court to a full-blown ultimate arbiter in constitutional matters, it can be argued that the Romanian system has become closer to a form of legal constitutionalism (see Blokker 2012; Iancu 2010). As seen in Chapter 3, the Constitutional Court gained competences in 2003, including the final say in constitutional matters, the constitutionality review of international treaties and other agreements and mediation in inter-institutional conflict. As a matter of fact, some scholars sustain that what could be seen as a Kelsenian model of constitutional court was already chosen by the constituent assembly in 1991 (Gilia 2012a: 73), to be only completed in 2003. The Court has however remained object of continuous critique. A conflictive attitude of political actors regarding its standing and (alleged) problems with a politicization of the Court has emerged on various occasions (Gilia 2012b; Perju 2010). In this regard, the standing of the Romanian Constitutional Court has remained problematic. For instance, Vlad Perju has argued that

> [a]fter two decades of the establishment of the Constitutional Court, it is not a successful institution. The Court has not become an example of deliberation and reflection regarding relations between citizens and the state . . . the Court does not have a formative role in the public sphere of society.
>
> (Perju 2010)

Concerns by political actors regarding the standing of the Court have, however, mostly not been informed by a democratic-constitutionalist mindset, criticizing the Court for undermining civic and parliamentary voice in a system dominated by Court activism. Rather, critique has more often than not been informed by a strategical desire to politically control the Court or to use the Court (and the Constitution) for particular, political purposes. In this context, it is not surprising that with the emergence of a stronger and more active Court in the 2000s, constitutional conflicts have become more frequent.

At least two moments of evident and deep constitutional crisis can be indicated. One important moment of crisis emerged in 2007, when a direct confrontation between President Traian Băsescu and the incumbent Liberal government led to the start of an impeachment procedure of the president, a procedure which in constitutional terms needs to be confirmed by a popular referendum. One of the salient constitutional dimensions to this crisis (apart from the head-on confrontation between political institutions) relates to the fact that according to the Romanian Constitution, impeachment can only follow from the identification of 'grave acts infringing upon Constitutional provisions' by the president (Art. 95(1)). In an advisory opinion, the Constitutional Court ruled that relevant acts by the president could not be qualified as 'grave', and also that the final responsibility was with the parliament (Advisory Decision 1, April 2007).[15] The parliament ignored the advisory opinion and followed the conclusions of a parliamentary investigation committee that stipulated that the president had violated the Constitution. And subsequently, it proceeded with the impeachment procedure (Tănăşescu 2008: 88–9). The political strategy of the centre-right government failed, however, as the popular referendum, held in the summer of 2007, reconfirmed popular support for Băsescu. The latter therefore stayed on as president.

The constitutional crisis of 2007 was repeated during the summer of 2012, when a renewed attempt to impeach President Băsescu was undertaken, this time by the social-democratic government of Victor Ponta. This time the political attitude towards the Court took more the form of an assault. As argued by a Romanian scholar, 'the year

2012 has been a year of constitutional battles for the Constitutional Court' (Gilia 2012b: 24). The apparent trigger to the crisis was a conflict over who should represent Romania at the meeting of EU leaders in Brussels on 27 June. But the Ponta government did not merely return to the impeachment procedure claiming the unconstitutionality of Băsescu's actions. The actions of Ponta and his socialist party went themselves into a clearly unconstitutional direction[16] by dismissing the speakers of both chambers of parliament (who were replaced by allies), as well as the Ombudsman, by restricting the powers of the Constitutional Court and threatening its judges with impeachment, and by issuing a decree (as well as a draft law) on the Law on Referendum in order to drastically increase the probability of a successful impeachment referendum. A further step taken was putting the control over the publication of the official gazette in the government's hands, thereby having effective sway over the public promulgation of laws (and therefore their implementation).[17]

The dramatic nature of the constitutional assault by the Ponta government has become clear from the reaction of the Constitutional Court, which has sent two very unusual complaint letters – in July and August 2012 – to the Council of Europe's Venice Commission as well as to European officials to ask for help against virulent attacks on its independence by the Ponta government. The Constitutional Court has clearly also showed some strength in resisting the attacks, by, first of all, issuing a negative decision on the amendment of the law on public referenda (against the government's intent to implement a simple majority), and second, in its decision on the invalidity of the referendum held on the impeachment of Băsescu. This referendum, held on 29 July, failed to reach the quorum of 50 per cent of the electorate, as upheld by the Constitutional Court in its earlier ruling. Therefore, the Constitutional Court ruled on 21 August that the referendum was void, which meant that Băsescu was re-installed. In this case, the Ponta government declared it would accept the court's decision.

A related episode regarding conflict over the role of the Constitutional Court in Romanian democracy relates to the expansion of the Court's powers during the 2000s. The original amendment package of 2003 included an attempt to enlarge the Court's powers towards the review of constitutionality of all resolutions adopted by the parliament and senate (beyond merely the constitutional review of the Standing Orders). Some Romanian scholars have judged such extension as exceeding the constitutional mandate (see Gilia 2012a). In fact, in 2003 the Court itself argued the following in its Decision on the constitutionality of the constitutional amendments (148/2003), regarding point j[18]:

> Also the legislative proposal to review, as foreseen in point j. that by means of an organic law the Constitutional Court can obtain also other attributions forms an activity which is forbidden by the existing constitutional regulation. The Court observes that it follows that this proposal is to be eliminated in order to *keep the political neutrality of this public authority* and to follow the direction indicated by the will of the original constituent power.
>
> (148/2003: 16, emphasis added; cf. Gilia 2012a, 2012b)

In 2010, however, a similar extension of the Constitutional Court's competences was provided through Law 177/2010, amending Law 47/1992 on the organization and operation of the Constitutional Court. This law provided the Court with the competence to judge on the constitutionality of the resolutions of the Plenary of the Chamber of Deputies, of the Senate and of the Plenary of the Joint Chambers of Parliament (Gilia 2012a: 74). This extension was, however, overturned again in 2012 by means of an Emergency Ordinance (38/2012), part of the constitutional assault by the Ponta government, and which returned the catalogue of competences of the Court to the state of affairs of prior to 2010. The Ponta government claimed that the extension of the Court's powers posed a threat to general parliamentary functioning. The Ordinance stated that the 'nature [of Law 177/2010, pb] is to create dysfunctionality in the activities of the Parliament'. According to a former Romanian Minister of Justice, Monica Macovei (2012), however, '[t]his [emergency ordinance, pb] clearly breached the constitution, which states (in Article 115/6) that "emergency ordinances cannot be adopted in the area of constitutional laws and cannot interfere with the regime of the fundamental institutions of the state"'. A similar observation was part of the objection that 63 parliamentarians referred to the Constitutional Court. The members of parliament further claimed that the absence of this type of constitutional review could lead to institutional imbalance and to a possible authoritarian turn (Gilia 2012a: 75–6). The Court reconfirmed in its opinion its competences in constitutional review and argued that such powers are strengthening the Court's standing as well as a democratic state governed by the rule of law (contrary to its statement in 2003).

These episodes of Romanian constitutional turmoil are related to resentment against legal constitutionalism, but in a different, more complex way than in the case of Hungary. While the Romanian Constitutional Court can be seen to have formally acquired the status of ultimate constitutional arbiter in 2003, this status clearly continues to be politically contested. Legal resentment has become most explicit in the constitutional crisis of the summer of 2012 described above, but unlike the Hungarian example, seem not (yet?[19]) part of a comprehensive constitutional project. Also the manifestations of Euroscepticism or denouncements of external interference are largely absent in the Romanian case. The Ponta government (re-elected with a large majority in December 2012) has repeatedly argued it will follow up on the recommendations made by the European Commission.[20]

Concluding remarks

As becomes clear from the discussion of Europeanization as well as domestic reactions in the form of legal resentment, the new democracies are far from 'settled' or 'consolidated' constitutional orders. While, on the one hand, legal constitutionalism is strengthened, or at least externally sustained, by forms of Europeanization, on the other, significant counter-trends have emerged that tend to significantly undermine some of the key tenets of legal constitutionalism (not least regarding the prominent role of courts and rigid, higher law constitutions). What is particularly worrisome from the perspective of this book are the repercussions for democratic or civic constitutionalism. The narrative in the book, with legal and civic constitutionalism as its main protagonists, is rendered more complex by the emergence of counter-constitititutional projects, in particular the Fidesz constitutional 'revolution' in Hungary, about which the last word has clearly not been said. The implications of the latter are not only detrimental for legal constitutionalism, but equally for democratic or civic constitutional forms, such as those related to local self-government, civic participation in the public sphere, or direct forms of civic political influence.

Notes

1 Some of what is discussed below appeared in an earlier version in Blokker (2012b).
2 In this, a certain simplicity and one-sided view on democratization cannot be denied, in that it is argued that while in general democracy has improved, there has also been a differentiated impact, not least due to differing initial circumstances. That is, while the countries that acceded in 2004 are now 'consolidated' democracies, the Bulgarian and Romanian democracies are still seen as 'semi-consolidated' (Spendzharova and Vachudova 2012: 40). This 'modernizationist' argument, so it seems to me, has certain difficulties with, for instance, accounting for current 'authoritarian' tendencies in the Hungarian case, often considered to be one of the democratic front-runners.
3 Although, admittedly, there is no consensus on which model this would be in practice (see Blokker 2010a; Haukenes and Freyberg-Inan 2012; Malová and Dolny 2008).

4 But also in other cases, such influence is visible, as for instance in the case of Poland. In the latter case, the 'Commission welcomed the strengthening of the powers of the Constitutional Tribunal by abolishing the power of the parliament to overturn the court's decisions by two-thirds majority' (Malová and Dolny 2008: 73).

5 As I will note below when discussing domestic resentment against legal constitutionalism, the issue of the mandate of the Constitutional Court is by no means clear-cut, and an external insistence on a restoration of Constitutional Court powers is not necessarily based on a more 'healthy' idea of a democratic-constitutional order (cf. Gilia 2012a, 2012b). I thank Cristina Parau for suggesting the complexity of the Romanian constitutional turmoil in 2012.

6 As I will describe more elaborately below, the Constitutional Court has become part of a number of far-going political conflicts during the 2000s, in which its authority has been questioned by political actors and recently, in 2012, curtailment of its powers attempted.

7 Relevant articles include 125(1) (constitutionality), 127(3) (infringements of rights), and 95(2) (referenda); see Malová and Lastic (2001).

8 Haukenes and Freyberg-Inan point to a different, more maximalist democratic model, that of Lijphart's 'consensus democracy'. This seems not fully in contradiction to what is stated here in that it *inter alia* confirms the remarks above on judicial supremacy and rigid constitutions (which they include in the consensus model, 2012: 6) as well as a certain 'bias' towards representative democracy and voter participation (cf. Lijphart 1991).

9 The government in the period 2005–7 consisted of a centre-right government of the Law and Justice party (PiS).

10 The relevant article is 37(4) of the new Basic Law (2012): As long as state debt exceeds half of the Gross Domestic Product, the Constitutional Court may, within its competence set out in Article 24(2)b–e), only review the Acts on the State Budget and its implementation, the central tax type, duties, pension and healthcare contributions, customs and the central conditions for local taxes for conformity with the Fundamental Law or annul the preceding Acts due to violation of the right to life and human dignity, the right to the protection of personal data, freedom of thought, conscience and religion, and with the rights related to Hungarian citizenship. The Constitutional Court shall have the unrestricted right to annul the related Acts for non-compliance with the Fundamental Law's procedural requirements for the drafting and publication of such legislation. English translation available at: www.kormany.hu/download/4/c3/30000/THE%20FUNDAMENTAL%20LAW%20OF%20HUNGARY.pdf.

11 The complexity (or strategic nature) of Fidesz's resentment lies in its preservation of the easy amendment rule on the one hand (relatively easy, although unlikely to be within the reach of future parliaments), and ample recourse to supermajority laws for non-constitutional issues, on the other, *de facto* increasing the entrenchment of a wide range of issues. As argued by Halmai, originally Fidesz was supposed to raise the barrier for constitutional amendment (in terms of a requirement of two-thirds majorities in two successive parliamentary sessions, separated by elections), as this was one of the reasons a new constitution was to be adopted. This tougher amendment rule was ultimately not adopted, but Fidesz 'chose to compensate for this failure by lifting a large number of ordinary policy issues

into the realm of law, thereby removing future parliaments to alter policy choices made by the present one' (Halmai 2011: 6). And as argued by Halmai and Scheppele, '[a]s a general trend, the old constitution used the supermajority requirement to ensure heightened protection for fundamental rights, but in the new Fundamental Law, the function of cardinal laws is to place rules about the structure of and personnel in governmental institutions beyond the reach of a (future) simple majority of Parliament' (2012: 6).

12 As cited in: http://hungarianspectrum.wordpress.com/ 2012/10/13/the-pitfalls-of-being-loquacious-viktor-orbans-interview-with-handesblatt/. For Orbán's speech, see: www.kas.de/wf/de/33.32367/.

13 This right was granted through article 32A (3): 'Everyone has the right to initiate proceedings of the Constitutional Court in the cases specified by law'. Among others, the abolishment of the death penalty in 1990 by the Constitutional Court was the result of *actio popularis*.

14 Cited in: Sadurski (2004: 22).

15

> Luând în dezbatere propunerea de suspendare a domnului Traian Băsescu din funcţia de Preşedinte al României, la data de 5 aprilie 2007, Curtea Constituţională a dat Avizul consultativ nr.1, potrivit căruia propunerea, se referă la acte şi fapte de încălcare a Constituţiei, săvârşite în exerciţiul mandatului care, însă, prin conţinutul şi consecinţele lor, *nu pot fi calificate drept grave*, de natură să determine suspendarea din funcţie a Preşedintelui României în sensul prevederilor art. 95 alin.(1) din Constituţie". *Rămâne ca Parlamentul să decidă*, pe baza datelor şi a informaţiilor care îi vor fi prezentate cu ocazia dezbaterilor, asupra existenţei şi gravităţii faptelor pentru care s-a propus suspendarea din funcţie a Preşedintelui României, în concordanţă cu dispoziţiile art.95 din Constituţie.
>
> (Emphasis added)

16 As mentioned, the Romanian constitutional scholar Ioan Stanomir (2012) has argued that the 'Romanian constitution has become an insignificant and irrelevant element' in Romanian politics, commenting on the Ponta governments' actions.

17 The actions of the Ponta government have been strongly criticized internationally, not least in the afore-mentioned progress report on Romania of the European Commission (European Commission 2012). The latter called on the Romanian government to return to serious reform in the name of the rule of law, as recent events have 'raised serious doubts about the commitment to the respect of the rule of law or the understanding of the meaning of the rule of law in a pluralist democratic system'. The Commission's report triggered a response by a large number of Romanian intellectuals and representatives of civil society that replied with a Letter to the EU, in which they argue that the Commission ignores the fundamental legal principle of "*audiatur et altera pars*" and thereby underestimates the unconstitutional and undue political behaviour of Băsescu. In addition, it fails to acknowledge the detrimental consequences of the crisis for Romanian parliament, which has turned into an "empty shell" (available at: www.stelian-tanase.ro/la-zi/scrisoare-catre-uniunea-europeana-bruxelles/). The response

was restated in the European Parliament on 12 September by the MEP Renate Weber, who accused in particular the Commissioner Reding for an exaggerated reaction not based on the facts, and ignoring the illegitimacy of Băsescu; see http://actmedia.eu/daily/heated-debates-among-mep-groups-over-the-political-situation-in-romania/42025.

18 The point j. originally read: 'j) îndeplineşte şi alte atribuţii prevăzute de legea organică a Curţii'.

19 As reported by the Romanian journal *Revista 22*, the large majority the Ponta government has won in the December 2012 elections has stimulated plans to revise the Romanian constitution (*Revista 22*, 5 February 2013, 'USL vrea referendumul pentru REVIZUIREA CONSTITUTIEI în septembrie. Ponta: Vrem ca Antonescu să fie PRESEDINTELE Comisiei de revizuire').

20 In its last report of February 2013, the Commission, however, argues that '[t]his assessment shows that Romania has implemented several, but not all, of the Commission's recommendations aiming at restoring rule of law and the independence of the judiciary' (European Commission 2013: 12).

7 Conclusions

New democracies in crisis?

The book has questioned the judicialization of democratic politics in the new democracies of Central and Eastern Europe. I have made an argument in favour of civic constitutionalism as a possible antidote against one-sided legal constitutionalism. And I have tried to show that while the new democracies have seen a strong turn towards what I have called legal constitutionalism since 1989, it is also possible to identify an – admittedly non-central and often latent – alternative tradition that explicitly values democratic participation and self-government. I have called this civic constitutionalism.

My problem with the predominance of legal constitutionalism in the new democracies of Central and Eastern Europe is that it has not only reinforced formal political institutions and the entrenchment of rights and the rule of law. There are indications that legal constitutionalism has also contributed to the exacerbation of a problematic state of democratic affairs and lack of entrenchment of constitutional democracy in its 'discomfort with democracy'. The legal constitutionalist idea of democratization, in terms of the institutionalization of a robust system grounded in the higher law of the constitution, entrenched rights and an independent constitutional guardianship, tends to ignore questions of political participation, public debate on fundamental values and rights, and the diffusion of a culture of constitutionalism throughout political and civil society.

In other words, the adoption of strong legal-constitutionalist institutions has had the possibly perverse effect of undermining some of the core dimensions of democracy, that is the development of democratic political culture, including a spirit of civic engagement, and a dynamic and critical interaction between the constitution, politics, and wider society. That these are not idle concerns is most clearly shown in the recent constitutional crises in Hungary and Romania. What strikes in these cases of democratic backlash is the lack of attachment to constitutional values and willingness to publicly deliberate on the fundamental values that hold together the political community amongst both politic elites and the wider public. The critique on legal constitutionalism is relevant here in that it points to the dangers of excluding political and civil society from partaking in the discussion and interpretation of constitutional values.

One of the book's main contributions is its attempt to link the largely theoretical debate on constitutionalism and democracy to the experiences and predicament of new democracies, in our case those in Central and Eastern Europe. I have shown that legal constitutionalism is indeed rather well entrenched – in formal-institutional terms – in these countries. And its emergence can be related both to internal forces and ideational traditions (not least the legalistic language of dissidents) and to a legal-constitutionalist bias of external actors, not least the EU. But this is not the whole story, so I have argued. In particular, when focusing on the variegated dissident tradition and dissident ideas of civic engagement and self-government, it is possible to identify constitutional forms that are less inspired by a legal-constitutionalist view, and which are closer to the participatory-democratic idea that I have related to civic constitutionalism. But the civic-constitutional tradition is relatively weak, and its record so far rather mixed. The comparative analysis of how the constitutional orders of the new democracies relate to constitutional revision, direct democracy and local self-government shows a general absence of the promotion of civic-democratic participation in constitutional revision, but also that most constitutions have reasonably well-entrenched dimensions of direct democracy and local self-government.

The story of the constitutional and democratic crises in some of the countries discussed, notably Hungary and Romania, is of a complex nature. But it is undeniable that the offensive against legal-constitutionalist structures – as undertaken by the Orbán and Ponta governments – has to do with a weakly entrenched constitutional culture amongst political forces as well as amongst the wider citizenry. As some Romanian scholars have observed in a report on the constitutional state of affairs in the country, the Romanian Constitution has a problematic relationship to its integrative function, and both citizens and politicians are not attached to the Constitution (Dima and Tănăsescu 2012). Bogdan Dima, one of the authors of the report, stated elsewhere: '[t]he conclusion was reached within the Commission that, at present, in Romania, there is no real feeling of constitutional patriotism and that the Constitution does not perform its integrative function in full' (2011: 157).

In Hungary, the new Basic Law has been adopted by a parliamentary super-majority, but without any structural interaction with the political opposition, and even less so with wider society in terms of public debate. But while the Fidesz party can be criticized for its authoritarian ways of imposing a new constitution, it can be equally argued that the opposition and wider society have been remarkably passive. As observed by one member of the opposition party Lehet Más a Politika (LMP),

> Besides a few heads of institutions ensuring checks-and-balances (e.g. two ombudsmen, the president of the Supreme Court), only a new formed citizens' movement and political parties in opposition have publicly voiced concerns. Moreover, turnout at the separate rallies organized by these different actors (the newly formed 'One Million for the Freedom of Press in Hungary' group, former prime minister Ferenc Gyurcsány, the Socialist party and LMP) has been shamefully low: approximately 2–500 people took part in each of the demonstrations held between 15 and 17 April [2011, pb]. This shows that the fragmented opposition has not managed to get a fundamental message across: that the *Constitution is not just a piece of paper unconnected to the social and political struggles of everyday life – its words matter*.
>
> (Szombati 2011: 4; emphasis added)

This absence of 'constitutional patriotism' and integration around the constitution is not a prominent issue in the theoretical debate, but should be more widely discussed, I believe. Returning to the thrust of the theoretical argument in the book, a constitutionalism more prone to sustained interaction between the constitution, on the one hand, and political and civil society, on the other, can stimulate more effectively a widespread attachment to constitutional ideas and values. But, what is more important, such a civic constitutionalism endorses a different idea of constitutions, not so much as enshrining the pre-commitments of democracy, but rather as facilitatory devices for a continuous societal debate on which fundamental rules and values are to guide the political community as such. These insights are admittedly more at the forefront in debates on popular and democratic constitutionalism (as shown in Chapter 2), but as yet have failed to register wide appreciation in the analysis of the new democracies in Central and Eastern Europe.[1]

The argument that the recent constitutional experience in the new democracies is tainted by a compromised relation of constitutions to the wider civic and political societies – for which they are supposed to provide the fundamental rules and values of interaction – does not mean that constitutions have not mattered. As I discussed in Chapter 3, one domain in which constitutions have been of great importance is that related to national sovereignty and the definition of statehood and citizenship. Here, it is clear that in all cases discussed, the constitutions have been expressions of new-found sovereign political communities. A certain attachment to modern sovereignty, as observed also by Albi (2005), however, also indicates 'obsolete' and problematic views regarding democratic politics. A statist view of sovereignty, related to distinct views on popular sovereignty, might reflect a distinct bias towards elitist views of democratic politics, with generally little concern for civic engagement, pluralism and multiple forms of democratic participation. I have argued that there is a relation between legal constitutionalism and a statist, centralized and top-down understanding of constitutional democracy here, in a shared emphasis on a centralized understanding of (constitutional) authority and a strong distinction between law, politics and society.

In terms of the entrenchment of constitutions as higher law and as embodiments of fundamental rights, it cannot be denied that the constitutions of the new democracies have played a crucial role in post-communist transformation. At the same time, though, the new constitutional orders suffer from 'participatory deficits'. As Richard Albert has argued, '[j]ust as there are constitutional structures that invite participation from citizens, there are constitutional design strategies that actually, though perhaps not intentionally, discourage popular participation' (2008: 25). One instance of this regards civic access to constitutional courts and constitutionality review. It seems unfortunate that in the new democracies few instruments are available for wider society to engage with fundamental rights and principles in terms of access to constitutional courts, if not by means of constitutional complaint. It is a case in point that the original, civic-participatory instrument of *actio popularis* that was available in the Hungarian Constitution has now been eliminated in the new Basic Law. The unique institution of *actio popularis* allowed individuals, as well as non-governmental organizations and advocacy groups, to petition the Constitutional Court directly.[2] The new Basic Law has introduced a form of constitutional complaint (as is more common throughout the region), which can be used in specific individual cases of concrete breaches of the law. But, as mentioned before, this 'extension of opportunities to submit constitutional complaints is no substitute whatsoever for the widely available right of private individuals and organisations to file petitions' (Arato *et al.* 2011: 28). It can be argued that the example of the *actio popularis* is one that favours a legal-constitutionalist vision, in that the constitutional project of *Fidesz* is an attempt at undoing a constitutional order based on this idea. But in my view, the instrument of *actio popularis* corresponds rather to a civic-constitutionalist view, in its emphasis on wide civic access to constitutionality review. Indeed, the *actio popularis* has once been commented on by the former president of the Hungarian Constitutional Court as 'a substitute for direct democracy' (Sadurski 2008: 22). In this, the *actio popularis* could be seen as a form of civic engagement with constitutional matters that is grounded in the idea of the initiator being a 'trustee of the public good', rather than an individual seeking to undo a past personal wrongdoing (ibid.: 6). If one accepts this civic-constitutionalist thrust of the *actio popularis* instrument, it means that it constituted an exception in the post-1989 Hungarian constitutional order, rather than a main characteristic of the latter's legal-constitutionalist nature. And the abolishment by the new Basic Law of this unique instrument (Schwartz 2000: 81) rather indicates a more general lack of civic-participatory instruments in both the pre- and post-2010 constitutional orders. And, in fact, while constitutional complaint is fairly widely available in the new democracies, institutions similar to the *actio popularis* are not.

Beyond civic access to constitutional courts, the constitutions of the new democracies are themselves in part non-conducive to civic participation as they all contain parts that are considered unamendable. For instance, the new Basic Law of Hungary invokes the 'inviolable and inalienable' nature of some fundamental rights (article I), the Slovak Constitution considers that fundamental rights are 'sanctioned, inalienable, imprescriptible and irreversible' (art. 12(1), while the Romanian Constitution, apart from prohibiting revision if it 'results in the suppression of the citizens' fundamental rights and freedoms', protects the 'national, independent, unitary and indivisible character of the Romanian State, the republican form of government, territorial integrity, independence of justice, political pluralism and the official language' (art. 152(2)). Again, I follow Albert's argument on 'supraconstitutionalism' in that 'unamendability clauses are supraconstitutional elements that frustrate the possibility of participatory democracy because they make certain constitutional guarantees unchangeable. Although they do so in the service of important principles of statehood and community, these supraconstitutional provisions are nonetheless counterconstitutional' (2008: 37). He goes on, '[u]namendability clauses undermine the prospect of instilling in citizens a sense of investment in and ownership of their state'. This is exactly one of the problems, I believe, that has emerged in the constitutional crises in Hungary and Romania, and is most likely also relevant in the other cases discussed.

Regarding the role of constitutional courts in the new democracies, it is hard to disagree with Sadurski's observation that 'all of the post-Communist countries of CEE have constitutional courts, and while the effectiveness of these tribunals varies, they have made a strong mark on the process of constitutional transition' (2008: 2). But it is equally true that too little attention has been paid to the dilemmas, tensions and perverse effects that may emerge in the institutionalization and practice of forms of legal constitutionalism, not least in terms of an enduring tension between constitutionalism as an ordering and stabilizing device and democracy as an uncertain and indeterminate process of verification of public views on the common good (see Blokker 2012b). It is undeniable that an emphasis on a higher law with entrenched rights and robust constitutional review has involved important 'corrections' of certain outgrowths of democratic politics and in this prevented forms of 'tyranny of the majority' or the endangering of the guarantee of universal rights. But it is equally true that new constitutionalism has been adopted at a price, not least with regard to the emergence of more widespread, publicly shared constitutional cultures as well as in terms of underexplored potentials of democratic constitutionalism and endorsement of civic engagement in the region. Democratic dilemmas that potentially emerge from strong, activist constitutional courts and robust constitutional review should be related to a broader and particular understanding of legal constitutionalism that tends to underplay aspects of democratic (formal and civic) politics and indeterminacy, and is overdetermined by notions of order, rationality, absolute truth and closure. As I have argued elsewhere (Blokker 2012b), this one-sidedness feeds into a potential 'democratic debilitation' in terms of – inter alia – a closure of constitutional interpretation, the displacement of majoritarian decision-making (also in cases that are not unambiguously warranted in terms of constitutionality), the distortion of policy-making and legislative irresponsibility.

In the book, I have not extensively engaged with a discussion of constitutional court activism and potentially perverse effects in terms of 'democratic debilitation', which 'occurs when the public and their democratically elected representatives cease to formulate and discuss constitutional norms, instead relying on the courts to address constitutional problems' (Tushnet 1995: 275). A fuller picture of these democratic problems than I could provide here would need to include a sustained analysis of the dynamics of interaction between politics, the constitutional courts and the wider public. The attempt here was rather to verify the importance of the legal constitutional tradition in the new democracies, as I discussed in Chapter 3, and to contrast this tradition with a different constitutional tradition, civic constitutionalism, as a potential 'anti-dote' to unbalanced constitutional democracy grounded in legalism (as discussed in Chapters 4 and 5).

My argument has been that it is possible to relate a different constitutional tradition, with a prominent emphasis on civic participation and self-rule, to important parts of the dissident discourses of the 1970s and 1980s. These discourses in themselves, as many scholars have attested, have played a significant role in the construction of constitutional democracies after 1989, and not only in terms of their legalistic dimension, but also regarding their civic, participatory dimensions and their emphasis on the importance of civil society. For instance, as Arato has argued, constitutional arrangements in the region have importantly contributed to the re-emergence of civic engagement and initiatives (2000: 71). But, as also observed above, while this civic-constitutional tradition is clearly available in the region and has informed parts of the constitutional architecture, it can at the same time be seen as often rather latent and not well entrenched. If a feature of the translation of radical, participatory democracy into constitutional structures is the constitutional allowance for civic constitutional assemblies and possibilities for citizens to deliberate on the fundamental rules of their political communities (as, for instance, is visible in some of the recent Latin American constitutions; see Colon-Rios 2012), in the new democracies of Central and Eastern Europe none of this has been included in the constitutions. In fact, the constitutional revision procedures barely allow for civic engagement, either upfront or in the form of confirmatory referenda.

In terms of the endorsement of instruments of direct democracy and local self-government, many of the constitutions discussed are clearly more robust in terms of their facilitatory role towards civic participation. Only the Czech Constitution does not explicitly allow for national referenda (but this has been object of considerable political debate throughout the 2000s) and in Hungary only recently the constitutional hurdles for civic participation have been increased (while an important instrument of direct democracy was abolished). Local and regional government are fairly well entrenched in the new democracies, except for a number of peculiarities. For instance, in the Hungarian Basic Law the right to self-government is no longer explicitly referred to, while in most countries the regional level of government has been introduced only at the end of the 1990s. In the case of the latter, the democratic importance of this level has only been increasing recently. In the case of Romania, the region has never been included in the constitution as a relevant territorial unit of government, while a 'democratic deficit' also exists as the regional level has been perceived of in purely administrative terms.

The conclusion has to be that while the civic-constitutional tradition is not robust, and cannot be identified as any kind of viable alternative to legal constitutionalism, some of the promises of civic constitutionalism have been realized in the new democracies. In this regard, the civic-constitutional dimension is equally part of the constitutional orders of the new democracies, even if it cannot be denied that in many of the new democracies it is now further under strain, not least in the cases of Hungary and, to a lesser extent, Romania. Thus, on a more pessimistic note, it is exactly in these cases that a more robust civic-constitutional dimension and related constitutional awareness of the political parties, citizens and social movements might have played the role of a crucial counterforce in the existing constitutional turmoil.

My final suggestion is, then, that one promising way out of the unbalanced constitutional projects of both legal constitutionalism and the current trends of legal resentment in Hungary and Romania lies in a re-invigorated civic constitutionalism. Admittedly, and as also observed above, there are only few signs of such constitutional ideas and practices in the new democracies. But let me conclude by pointing to a few examples of where some of the problems I have indicated have been the core concerns of civic societal actors (I will particularly refer to some interesting civic manifestations in Romania). The claims made by civil actors are not only in substance interesting contributions to a more civic and bottom-up understanding of constitutionalism, but evidently also in terms of practices that involve civic mobilization and public deliberation as constitutive elements in a democratically perceived constitutional order.

In the case of the Hungarian counter-constitutional 'revolution', many observers have pointed to the fact that opposition and resistance has been slow to develop and that civil movements have been fragmented and divided. An expert of Hungarian civil society, Jody Jensen, has, however, suggested that '[e]ven though Hungarian protests lack common and articulated goals, they do agree on a surprising number of fronts about the way democracy should work and what their role and the role of the government should be'. She goes on, '[o]ne basis for understanding . . . [is] the desire to have voice in democratic policy-making at all levels' (2012). Various civic movements have protested against the new Basic Law, the cardinal laws as well as the media law. One small but not insignificant Green movement, Lehet Más a Politika ('Politics can be different') (LMP), elected into parliament in 2010, has been consistently criticizing the Basic Law. LMP has on various occasions articulated concerns close to what I have called civic constitutionalism. In a statement on the draft Basic Law, issued by the European Green Party, it stated that LMP has 'major concerns about the contents of the draft of the new Constitution for the dismantling of the democratic checks and balances and weakening of civic participation', including the fact that '[t]he draft weakens the institutions of direct democracy. Constitutional questions cannot be voted on in national referendums, and local referendums are not included in the text' and '[t]he reform of the Constitution is criticised for the process not being transparent, for the inadequate consultation procedures and for the tight schedule' (LMP 2011). In general, LMP has favoured a 'democracy based on genuine participation and autonomy, which is transparent, accountable, and runs a state that fulfills its business efficiently' (LMP 2008).

Turning to the Romanian context, one important pro-democracy movement – Asociaţia Pro Democraţia (APD) – has consistently contributed to a form of 'grass roots' constitutionalism, by on various occasions making claims towards a more participatory understanding of constitutional democracy and attempting to raise civic awareness of constitutional matters (cf. Andreescu 2011: 33). In the wake of the presidential and constitutional crisis in 2007, for instance, APD started a public discussion on constitutional reform by means of various public debates in different Romanian cities. The APD's self-professed aim was to increase awareness of citizens around the issue of constitutional reform, not least with regard to the choice citizens need to make in the constitutionally arranged for referendum in case of amendment:

> Since the future reform will influence the consolidation of Romanian democracy for a prolonged period of time, it is necessary that the possible implications of the modifications are understood by the largest possible number of citizens. In contrast to the revision of 2003, which was made under pressure of an external imperative, the debate on a future change of the Constitution needs to take into account both the relations between institutions as well as relations between the state and society, and relations between various groups in society. At the same time, given the fact that every change of the Constitution is to be adopted by referendum, it is necessary to hold a public debate on the Constitutional revision to inform citizens on the issues they will vote on. What is more, the future modification of the Constitution offers a chance

> to hold an open debate which will help to enrich the political culture of the Romanian citizens, an essential aspect of the consolidation of democracy.
>
> (2008b: 6)

The same APD has been one of the driving forces in the organization of a Forum Constituţional, held in 2002, which consisted of an 'institutionalised structure of dialogue with civil society regarding the revision of the constitution' (Forum Constituţional 2002: 11), and was organized by the Romanian Parliament. The intention was to provide a public deliberative forum in parallel to the official Romanian Commission for the Revision of the Constitution.

An equally important civic initiative with regard to constitutional reform, already mentioned above, has emerged in the context of the 2007 and 2012 crises. A civic-driven initiative for the formation of a 'Commission for a New Constitution' was established in 2010 and hosted by the Horia Rusu Foundation (Dima 2011). The latter has organized a series of public debates in which important Romanian political and constitutional experts, including Daniel Barbu, Manuel Guţan and Elena Simina Tănăsescu, were involved. The attempt is to promote 'open participation to deliberation and critical argument' on pending constitutional revision. The thrust of the initiative was to counter the lack of public debate that had characterized political and juridical debate on revision in the past, not least by gathering opinions within civil society on wide-ranging constitutional reform (subsequently published in October 2012 in the form of an extensive report; see Dima and Tănăsescu 2012).

It seems appropriate to end this book with a reference to Hannah Arendt's idea of a 'lost treasure' or better 'the revolutionary tradition and its lost treasure'. My argument about the continuous strain between legal and civic constitutionalism, and between top-down, technocratic government and bottom-up, participatory government in the new democracies can be read as one in which the narrative of civil society of the 1980s largely – but not entirely – lost out against the 'machinery of government'. But, as Arendt argued in *On Revolution*, this machinery, result of the 'founders' 'political science', saved American democracy from despotism, but 'could not save the people from lethargy and inattention to public business, since the Constitution itself provided a public space only for the representatives of the people, and not for the people themselves' (1963: 238).

Notes

1 Two recent exceptions are Puchalska (2011) and Skapska (2011).
2 This right was granted through article 32A (3): 'Everyone has the right to initiate proceedings of the Constitutional Court in the cases specified by law'. Among others, the abolishment of the death penalty in 1990 by the Constitutional Court was the result of *actio popularis* (Sadurski 2008).

References

Main legal sources

Constitution of the Czech Republic of 1992, available at: www.usoud.cz/view/1419.
Constitution of Hungary, available at: www.servat.unibe.ch/icl/hu00000_.html.
Basic Law of Hungary of 2012, available at: www.kormany.hu/download/4/c3/30000/THE%20FUNDAMENTAL%20LAW%20OF%20HUNGARY.pdf.
Constitution of Poland of 1997, available at: www.sejm.gov.pl/prawo/konst/angielski/kon1.htm.
Constitution of Romania of 1991, available at: www.cdep.ro/pls/dic/site.page?id=256&idl=2.
Constitution of Romania of 2003, available at: www.cdep.ro/pls/dic/site.page?id=371.
Constitution of Slovakia of 1992, available at: www.concourt.sk/en/A_ustava/ustava_a.pdf.

Bibliography

Ackerman, B. (1991) *We the People*, Cambridge, MA: Belknap Press of Harvard University Press.

Adamova, K. (2010) 'Referendum in the Second Half of the 20th and at the Beginning of the 21st Centuries: its Potential and Limits', in M. Tomasek (ed.), *Czech Law: Between Europeanization and Globalization*, Prague: Karolinum Press: 48–53.

Albert, R. (2008) 'Counterconstitutionalism', *Dalhousie Law Journal*, 31(1): 1–54.

Albi, A. (2003) 'Postmodern Versus Retrospective Sovereignty? Two Different Discourses in the EU and the Candidate Countries?', in N. Walker (ed.), *Sovereignty in Transition*, Oxford and Portland, OR: Hart: 401–422.

Albi, A. (2005) *EU Enlargement and the Constitutions of Central and Eastern Europe*, Cambridge: Cambridge University Press.

Albi, A. (2009) 'National Constitutions in the Face of Europeanising and Globalising Governance: Falling behind Times?', in C. Closa (ed.), *The Reform Treaty and National Constitutions: towards further Europeanisation?*, 03/09 RECON, Oslo: ARENA: 119–42.

Anderson, G.W. (2012) 'Beyond "Constitutionalism beyond the State" ', *Journal of Law and Society*, 39(3): 359–83.

Andreescu, G. (2011) 'Înstrăinarea de valorile civice prin abuzul drepturilor constituţionale de marjă', in G. Andreescu, M. Bakk, L. Bojin and V. Constantin (eds), *Comentarii la Constituţia României*, Polirom: 31–88.

Arato, A. (2000) *Civil Society, Constitution, and Legitimacy*, Lanham, MD: Rowman & Littlefield.

Arato, A. (2009) 'Redeeming the Still Redeemable: Post Sovereign Constitution Making', *International Journal of Cultural, Politics, and Society*, 22(4): 427–43.

Arato, A. and Z. Miklosi (2005) 'Constitution Making and Transitional Politics in Hungary', in L. Miller and L. Aucoin (eds), *Framing the State in Times of Transition: Case Studies in Constitution Making*, Washington, DC: United States Institute of Peace: 350–90.

Arato, A., G. Halmai and J. Kis (2011) *Opinion on the Fundamental Law of Hungary*, June, available at: http://lapa.princeton.edu/hosteddocs/amicus-to-vc-english-final.pdf.

Arendt, H. (1963) *On Revolution*, London: Penguin Books.

Arjomand, S.A. (2003) 'Law, Political Reconstruction and Constitutional Politics', *International Sociology*, 18(1): 7–32.

Asociaţia Pro Democraţia (APD) (2008a) 'Reforma constitutionala in Romania – Teme, dezbateri si propuneri', available at: www.apd.ro/publicatie.php?id=58.

Asociaţia Pro Democraţia (APD) (2008b) 'Reforma constitutionala in Romania – Aspecte teoretice şi istorice legate de evoluţia constituţiilor', available at: www.apd.ro/publicatie.php?id=56.

Assembly of European Regions (AER) (2012) 'Hungary', available at: www.aer.eu/fileadmin/user_upload/MainIssues/Interinstitutional_Relations/HUNGARY_2012.pdf.

Bailey, S. and M. Elliott (2009) 'Taking Local Government Seriously: Democracy, Autonomy and the Constitution', *Cambridge Law Journal*, 68: 436–72.

Băisanu, S.A. (2011) 'Types of referendum in revised Constitution', in *Annals of 'Ştefan cel Mare'*, University of Suceava, Philosophy, Social and Human Disciplines Series, Vol. II: 77–84.

Baker, G. (1998) 'The Changing Idea of Civil Society: Models from the Polish Democratic Opposition', *Journal of Political Ideologies*, 3(2): 125–45.

Baker, G. (2002) *Civil Society and Democratic Theory: Alternative Voices*, London: Routledge.

Balázs, I. (1993) 'The Transformation of Hungarian Public Administration', *Public Administration*, 71: 75–88.

Balogh, Z. and B. Hajas (2012) 'Rights and Freedoms', in L. Csink, B. Schanda, and A Zs. Varga (eds), *The Basic Law of Hungary: A First Commentary*, Dublin: Clarus Press: 79–110.

Banciu, A. (2001) *Istoria constituţională a României: Deziderate naţionale şi realităţi sociale*, Bucharest: Editura Lumina Lex.

Battek, R. (1985) 'Spiritual Values, Independent Initiatives and Politics', in V. Havel *et al.* (ed. by J. Keane), *The Power of the Powerless*, London: Hutchinson: 97–109.

Baun, M. and D. Marek (2006) 'Regional Policy and Decentralization in the Czech Republic', *Regional and Federal Studies*, 16(4): 409–28.

Belko, M. and L. Kopecek (2003) 'Referendum in Theory and Practice: The History of the Slovak Referendums and Their Consequences', *Central European Political Studies Review*, 2–3/V, available at: www.cepsr.com/clanek.php?ID=165.

Bellamy, R. (2007) *Political Constitutionalism: a Republican Defence of the Constitutionality of Democracy*, Cambridge: Cambridge University Press.

Bellamy, R. and D. Castiglione (1997) 'Constitutionalism and Democracy – Political Theory and the American Constitution', *British Journal of Political Science*, 27: 595–618.

Bellamy, R. and D. Castiglione (2000) 'Democracy, Sovereignty and the Constitution of the European Union', in Z. Bankowski and A. Scott (eds), *The European Union and Its Order: The Legal Theory of European Union Integration*, Oxford: Basil Blackwell, 169–200.

Bence, G. and J. Kis (1980) 'On Being a Marxist: A Hungarian View', *The Socialist Register*, 17, 263–97.

Benda, V., M. Šimcčka, I.M. Jirous, J. Dienstbier, V. Havel, L. Hejdánek and J. Šimsa (1988) 'Parallel Polis or an Independent Society in Central and Eastern Europe: An Inquiry', *Social Research*, 55(1/2): 211–46.

Benzler, S. (1994) 'Transformation der Dauerzustand? Die Entwicklung der territorialen Selbstverwaltung in Polen', in U. Bullmann (ed.), *Die Politiek der dritten Ebene: Regionen im Europe der Union*, Baden-Baden: Nomos: 310–339.

Biernat, S. (2005) 'Demokratieprinzip im polnischen Verfassungssystem', in H. Bauer, P.M. Huber and K.-P. Sommermann (eds), *Demokratie in Europa*, Tübingen: Mohr Siebeck: 79–106.

Blokker, P. (2004) *Modernity and Its Varieties: A Historical Sociological Analysis of the Romanian Modern Experience*, unpublished PhD thesis, Florence: European University Institute.

Blokker, P. (2009) 'Democracy Through the Lens of 1989: Liberal Triumph or Radical Turn?', *International Journal of Politics, Culture, and Society*, 22(3): 273–290.

Blokker, P. (2010a) *Multiple Democracies in Europe: Political Culture in New Member States*, London: Routledge.

Blokker, P. (2010b) 'Democratic Ethics, Constitutional Dimensions, and Constitutionalisms', in A. Febbrajo and W. Sadurski (eds), *East-Central Europe After Transition: Towards a New Socio-legal Semantics*, Ashgate: 73–98.

Blokker, P. (2011a) 'Dissidence, Republicanism, and Democratic Change', in *East European Politics and Societies*, 25(2): 219–43.

Blokker, P. (2011b) 'Modern Constitutionalism and the Challenges of Complex Pluralism', in G. Delanty and S. Turner (eds), *The International Handbook of Contemporary Social and Political Theory*, London: Routledge: 406–16.

Blokker, P. (2012a) 'The Constitutional Premises of Subnational Self-Government in New Democracies', *Corvinus Journal of Sociology and Social Policy*, 3(1): 35–57.

Blokker, P. (2012b) 'Dilemmas of Democratization: from Legal Revolutions to Democratic Constitutionalism?', Special Issue in honour of the centennial anniversary of Raoul Wallenberg, *Nordic Journal of International Law*, 81(4): 437–70.

Blokker, P. (forthcoming, 2013) 'Constitutions and Democracy in Post-national Times: a Political-sociological Approach', special issue on 'Engaging the Cosmopolitan: Contemporary Approaches', *Irish Journal of Sociology*, 20(2).

Boltanski, L. (2009) *De La Critique: Précis de sociologie de l'émancipation*. Paris: Gallimard.

Bozoki, A. (2009) 'The Hungarian Democratic Opposition: Self-reflection, Identity, and Political Discourse', draft paper, on file with author.

Broestl, A. (2003) 'At the Crossroads on the Way to an Independent Slovak Judiciary', in J. Přibáň, P. Roberts and J. Young (eds), *Systems of Justice in Transition: Central European Experiences since 1989*, Aldershot: Ashgate: 141–62.

Broestl, A., J. Klučka and J. Mazák (2001) *Constitutional Court of the Slovak Republic (Organization, Process, Doctrine)*, Košice: Constitutional Court of the Slovak Republic.

Bryson, P.J. (2008) '"State administration" vs. Self-government in the Slovak and Czech Republics', *Communist and Post-Communist Studies*, 41: 339–58.

Calda, Milos (1999) 'Constitution-Making in Post-Communist Countries: A Case of the Czech Republic', paper presented at a panel of the Center for the Study of the Constitution at the American Political Science Association Convention, Atlanta, Georgia, 2/5 September.

Capkova, S. (2011) 'Slovakia: Local Government: Establishing Democracy at the Grassroots', in J. Loughlin, F. Hendriks and A. Lidstroem (eds), *The Oxford Handbook of Local and Regional Democracy in Europe*, Oxford: Oxford University Press: 552–75.

Carp, R. and I. Stanomir (2008) *Limitele Constituției. Despre guvernare, politică și cetățenie în România*, Bucharest: Editura C.H. Beck.

Carter, A. (1999) 'Václav Havel: Civil Society, Citizenship and Democracy', in A. Carter and G. Stokes (eds), *Liberal Democracy and Its Critics*, Cambridge: Polity Press: 58–76.

Cătănuș, A.M. (2011a) 'A Case of Dissent in Romania in the 1970s: Paul Goma and the Movement for Human Rights', *Totalitarianism Archives (Arhivele Totalitarismului)*, 34: 185–209.

Cătănuș, A.M. (2011b) 'Breaking the Barriers of Romanian Conformism: Dissent and Scientific Critique of Communism in Mathematician Mihai Botez's Thinking. A Case Study', *History of Communism in Europe*, 2: 345–68.

Cernicova, M. (2004) 'Reform of the Public Administration on the Local Level in Romania: Opening the System Towards the Citizens', in *Reforming Local Public Administration: Efforts and Perspectives in South-East European Countries*, Zagreb: Friedrich Ebert Stiftung.

Chambers, S. (1998) 'Contract or Conversation? Theoretical Lessons from the Canadian Constitutional Crisis', *Politics and Society*, 26: 143–72.

Charter 77 (1977) 'Charter 77 Declaration', in V. Havel *et al.*, *The Power of the Powerless*, edited by J. Keane, London: Hutchinson: 217–221.

Chiper, S. (2011) 'Unpacking Local Council Meetings: a Sociolinguistic Approach and Its Lessons for Participatory Democracy', *Argumentum: Journal the Seminar of Discursive Logic, Argumentati*, 9: 73–100.

Cholewinski, R. (1998) 'The Protection of Human Rights in the New Polish Constitution', *Fordham International Law Review*, 22(2): 236–91.

Cirtautas, A.M. (1997) *The Polish Solidarity Movement: Revolution, Democracy and Natural Rights*, London/New York: Routledge.

Closa, C. (2012) 'Constitutional Rigidity and Procedures for Ratifying Constitutional Reforms in EU Member States', in A. Benz and F. Kupling (ed.), *Changing Federal Constitutions: Lessons from International Comparison*, Leverkusen: Verlag Barbara Budrig: 281–311.

Cohen, J. and A. Arato (1992) *Civil Society and Political Theory*, Cambridge, MA/London: MIT Press.

Colon-Rios, J. (2009) 'The Second Dimension of Democracy: The People and their Constitution', *Baltic Journal of Law & Politics*, 2(2): 1–30.

Colon-Rios, J. (2011a) 'The Three Waves of the Constitutionalism-Democracy Debate in the United States: (And an Invitation to Return to the First)', Victoria University of Wellington Legal Research Papers, 1 VUWLRP 23/2011.

Colon-Rios, J. (2011b) 'The End of the Constitutionalism-Democracy Debate', Victoria University of Wellington Legal Research Papers, Paper No. 19/2011, Volume 1, Issue No. 4.

Colon-Rios, J. (2011c) 'Law, language and Latin American Constitutions', *Victoria University of Wellington Law Review*, 42: 367–86.

Colon-Rios, J. (2012) *Weak Constitutionalism: Constituent Power and the Question of Democratic Legitimacy*, London/New York: Routledge.

Colon-Rios, J. and A. Hutchinson (2011) 'Democracy and Constitutional Change', in *Theoria*, 58(127): 43–62.

Coman, P., E. Crai, M. Radulescu and G. Stanciulescu (2001) 'Local Government in Romania', in E. Kandeva (ed.), *Stabilization of Local Governments, Budapest: Local Government and Public Reform Initiative*, Budapest: Local Government and Public Service Reform Initiative/Open Society Institute: 351–418.

Constantinescu, M., A. Iorgovan, Ioan Muraru and E.S. Tănăsescu (2004) *Constituţia României revizuită. Comentarii şi explicaţii*, Bucharest: Editura All Beck.

Constitution Watch (2001) 'Slovakia', in *East European Constitutional Review*, 10(1).

Council of Europe (CoE) (2009) *Structure and Operation of Local and Regional Democracy: Romania. Situation in 2009*, Strasbourg: Council of Europe.

Council of Europe (CoE)/European Commission for Democracy through Law (Venice Commission) (2010) *Report on Constitutional Amendment: Adopted by the Venice Commission at its 81st Plenary Session (Venice, 11–12 December 2009)*, Strasbourg: Council of Europe.

Council of Europe (CoE)/European Commission for Democracy through Law (Venice Commission) (2011) *Opinion on the Constitution of Hungary*, Opinion no. 621, Strasbourg: Council of Europe.

Csink, L. and B. Schanda (2012) 'The Constitutional Court', in L. Csink, B. Schanda and A Zs. Varga (eds), *The Basic Law of Hungary: A First Commentary*, Dublin: Clarus Press: 161–70.

Czeszejko-Sochacki, Z. (1996) 'The Origins of Constitutional Review in Poland', *St. Louis–Warsaw Transatlantic Law Journal*, 15: 25–32.

Dagger, R. (2004) 'Communitarianism and Republicanism', in G.F. Gaus and C. Kukathas (eds), *Handbook of Political Theory*, London: Sage: 167–79.

De Graaf, L., D. Klimovsky, U. Pinteric and D. Camelia Iancu (2009) 'From Doorstep to City Hall and Back: Participatory Practices in Bucharest, Eindhoven, Kosice and Ljubljana', working paper, Tilburg University.

Dezsö, M. and A. Bragyova (2001) 'Hungary', in A. Auer and M. Buetzer (eds), *Direct Democracy: The Eastern and Central European Experience*, Aldershot: Ashgate: 63–93.

Dezsö, M. and A. Bragyova (2007) 'National Referendums in Hungary', in A. Jakab, P. Takacs, A.F. Tatham (eds), *The Transformation of the Hungarian Legal Order 1985–2005 – Transition to the Rule of Law and Accession to the European Union*, Alphen aan den Rijn: Kluwer Law International: 68–82.

Dienstbier, J. (1988) *Social Research*, 55(1/2): 229–33.

Dima, B. (2011) 'The Commission for a New Constitution: A Civil Society Perspective on the Process of Constitutional Revision', *Romanian Journal of Comparative Law*, 2: 151–72.

Dima, B. and E.S. Tănăsescu (eds) (2012) *Reforma Constituţională: Analiză şi Proiecţii – Raportul comisiei pentru o nouă Constituţie*, Bucharest: Universul Juridic.

Dobre, A.M. (2011) 'Romania: from Historical Regions to Local Decentralization via the Unitary State', in J. Loughlin, F. Hendriks and A. Lidstroem (eds), *The Oxford Handbook of Local and Regional Democracy in Europe*, Oxford: Oxford University Press: 685–714.

Dragoman, D. (2011) 'Regional Inequalities, Decentralisation and the Performance of Local Government in Post-Communist Romania', *Local Government Studies*, 37(6): 647–69.

Dragos, D.C. and B. Neamtu (2007) 'Reforming Local Public Administration in Romania: Trends and Obstacles', *International Review of Administrative Sciences*, 73(4): 629–48.

Drinoczi, T. (2007) 'Revisione e manutenzione costituzionale nell'ordinamento ungherese', in F. Palerno (ed.), *La Manutenzione Costituzionale*, Padova: CEDAM: 437–78.

Dryzek, J. and L. Holmes (2002) *Post-communist Democratization: Political Discourses across Thirteen Countries*, Cambridge/New York: Cambridge University Press.

Dworkin, R. (1995) 'Constitutionalism and Democracy', *European Journal of Philosophy*, 3(1): 2–11.

Dworkin, R. (1996) *Freedom's Law: the Moral Reading of the American Constitution*, Oxford: Oxford University Press.

European Commission (1997a) *Agenda 2000 – Commission Opinion on Romania's Application for Membership of the European Union*, Brussels: European Commission.

European Commission (1997b) *Agenda 2000 – Commission Opinion on Slovakia's Application for Membership of the European Union*, Brussels: European Commission.

European Commission (1998) *Regular Report from the Commission on Romania's Progress towards Accession*, Brussels: European Commission.

European Commission (2012a) 'Meeting between European Commission President, José Manuel Barroso, and Romanian Prime Minister, Victor Ponta', available at: http://europa.eu/rapid/press-release_MEMO-12-558_en.htm.

European Commission (2012b) *Report from the Commission to the European Parliament and the Council on Progress in Romania under the Cooperation and Verification Mechanism*, Brussels: European Commission.

European Commission (2013) *Report from the Commission to the European Parliament and the Council on Progress in Romania under the Cooperation and Verification Mechanism*, Brussels: European Commission.

Falk, Barbara (2003) *The Dilemmas of Dissidence in East-Central Europe: Citizen Intellectuals and Philosopher Kings*, Budapest/New York: Central European University Press.

Ferrara, A. (2011) *Democrazia e apertura*, Milan: Bruno Mondadori.

Forum Constituțional (2002) *Forumul Constituțional: Raport final*, available at: www.forumconstitutional.ro/raport_final.pdf.

Fowler, B. (2001) 'Debating Sub-state Reform on Hungary's "Road to Europe"', Working Paper 21/01, CREES.

Frankenberg, G. (1997) *Die Verfassung der Republik*, Frankfurt am Main: Suhrkamp.

Frankenberg, G. (2000) 'Tocqueville's question: the Role of a Constitution in the Process of Integration', *Ratio Juris*, 13(1): 1–30.

Frankenberg, G. (2003) *Autorität und Integration: Zur Grammatik von Recht und Verfassung*, Frankfurt am Main: Suhrkamp.

Frankenberg, G. (2006) 'Comparing Constitutions: Ideas, Ideals, and Ideology – Toward a Layered Narrative', *International Journal of Constitutional Law*, 4(3): 439–59.

Frey, Bruno S. (2004) 'Direct Democracy for a Living Constitution', Freiburg discussion papers on constitutional economics, No. 04/5, available at: http://hdl.handle.net/10419/4338.

Frishman, M. and S. Muller (2010) *The Dynamics of Constitutionalism in the Age of Globalization*, Hague: Academic Press.

Fung, A. and E. Olin Wright (2003) 'Thinking about Empowered Participatory Governance', in A. Fung and E. Olin Wright (eds), *Deepening Democracy: Institutional Innovations in Empowered Participatory Governance. The Real Utopias Project IV*, London/New York: Verso: 3–44.

Gâdiuţă F. (2012) 'The Romanian Constitutional Court's Relationship with the Ordinary Courts: What Are Some of the Causes of Its High Caseload?', *Review of Central and East European Law*, 37(1): 53–93.

Gado, G. (1988) 'Dissidents, Reformers Assess "Crisis" in University Journal', *JPRS Report*, 31 May: 10–13.

Garlicki, L. (2003) 'The Experience of the Polish Constitutional Court', in W. Sadurski (ed.), *Democratic Legitimacy and Constitutional Courts in Post-Communist Europe in a Comparative Perspective*, Dordrecht: Springer: 265–82.

Gawin, D. (2007) 'August 1980 in Light of the Republican Tradition', in *The Tischner Institute Journal of Philosophy*, 1(2007): 120–42, available at: www.tischner.org.pl/thinking_pliki/tischner_10_gawin.pdf.

Gawin, D. (2008) 'Civil Society Discourse in Poland in the 1970s and 1980s', Discussion Paper Nr. SP IV, Berlin WZB.

Gebethner, S. (2001) 'Poland', in A. Auer and M. Buetzer (eds), *Direct Democracy: The Eastern and Central European Experience*, Aldershot: Ashgate: 129–40.

Gilia, C. (2012a) 'Comments on Decision no. 727 of 9th July 2012 of the Constitutional Court of Romania', *Juridica. Acta Universitatis Danubius*, 8(3): 71–82.

Gilia, C. (2012b) 'Curtea Constitutionala sub imperativul reformei', *Sfera Politicii*, 6(172): 21–34.

Glinski, P. (2006) 'The Self-Governing Republic in the Third Republic', *Polish Sociological Review*, 1(153): 55–74.

Glodeanu, A. (2011) 'Referendumul în România – între utilitate şi utilizare', *Sfera Politicii*, 8(162): 94–101.

Goldoni, M. (2010) 'Il ritorno del costituzionalismo alla politica: il "Political" e il "Popular" Constitutionalism', *Quaderni costituzionali*, XXX(4): 733–55.

Goldoni, M. (2012) 'Two internal critiques of political constitutionalism', *International Journal of Constitutional Law*, 10(4): 926–49.

Goma, P. (1979) *Culoarea Curcubeului '77'*, Autura Autoruluim, available at: http://paulgoma.free.fr/paulgoma_pdf/pdf/LRP_Culoarea_si_Barbosul.pdf.

Grudzinska-Gross, I. (1997) 'Introduction: When Polish Constitutionalism Began', *East European Constitutional Review*, 6(2/3): 61–5.

Häberle, P. (1975) 'Die offene Gesellschaft der Verfassungsinterpreten. Ein Beitrag zur pluralistischen und "prozessualen" Verfassungsinterpretation', *Juristenzeitung*, 10: 297–305.

Hadjiisky, M. (2001) 'The Failure of the Participatory Democracy in the Czech Republic', *West European Politics*, 24(3): 43–64.

Halmai, G. (2003) 'The Hungarian Approach to Constitutional Review: The End of Activism? The First Decade of the Hungarian Constitutional Court', in W. Sadurski (ed.), *Democratic Legitimacy and Constitutional Courts in Post-Communist Europe in a Comparative Perspective*, Springer: 189–212.

Halmai, G. (2012) 'Towards an Illiberal Democracy. Hungary's New Constitution', *Eurozine*, available at: www.eurozine.com/pdf/2012-01-25-halmai-en.pdf.

Halmai, G. and K. Lane Scheppele (eds) (2012) *Opinion on Hungary's New Constitutional Order: Amicus Brief for the Venice Commission on the Transitional Provisions of the Fundamental Law and the Key Cardinal Laws*, available at: http://lapa.princeton.edu/hosteddocs/hungary/Amicus_Cardinal_Laws_final.pdf.

Hankiss, E. (1988) 'The "Second Society": Is There an Alternative Social Model Emerging in Contemporary Hungary?', *Social Research*, 55(1/2): 13–42.

Haraszti, M. (1983) 'Dissident Says Regime Crackdown Will Not Deter Samizdat', *East Europe Report*, No. 2168: 14–17.

Hart, V. (2003) 'Democratic Constitution Making', Special Report, United States Institute for Peace, available at: www.usip.org.

Haukenes, K. and A. Freyberg-Inan (2012) 'Enforcing consensus? The hidden bias in EU democracy promotion in Central and Eastern Europe', *Democratization*, iFirst: 1–29.

Havel, V. (1985) 'The Power of the Powerless', in V. Havel *et al.*, *The Power of the Powerless*, edited by J. Keane, London: Hutchinson: 23–96.

Havel, V. (1997) 'Address by Václav Havel, President of the Czech Republic, before the Members of Parliament', Prague, 9 December.

Hirschl, R. (2004) 'The New Constitutionalism and the Judicialization of Pure Politics Worldwide', *Fordham Law Review*, 75: 722–54.

Hirschman, A.O. (1991) *The Rhetoric of Reaction: Perversity, Futility, Jeopardy*, Cambridge, MA: Belknap Press of Harvard University Press.

Holc, J. (1995) 'The Language of Democracy and the Ethos of Solidarity', Loyolo College, available at: www.ucis.pitt.edu/nceeer/1995-808-22-Holc.pdf.

Holmes, S. and C. Sunstein (1995) 'The Politics of Constitutional Revision in Eastern Europe', in S. Levinson (ed.), *Responding to Imperfection: The Theory and Practice of Constitutional Amendment*, Princeton, NJ: Princeton University Press: 275–306.

Horkay Hörcher, F. (2012) 'The National Avowal', in L. Csink, B. Schanda and A.Z. Varga (eds), *The Basic Law of Hungary: A First Commentary*, Dublin: Clarus Press: 40–63.

Howard, D. (1995) 'Law and Political Culture', *Cardozo Law Review*, 17: 1391–429.

Huiu, I. (2003) 'Revizuirea Constitutiei: Radiografie Parlamentara', *Sfera Politicii*, 104: 5–8.

Iancu, B. (2009) 'Constitutionalism in Perpetual Transition: The Case of Romania' in B. Iancu (ed.), *The Law/Politics Distinction in Contemporary Law Adjudication*, Utrecht: Eleven Publishing: 187–211.

Iancu, B. (2010) 'Post-Accession Constitutionalism with a Human Face: Judicial Reform and Lustration in Romania', *European Constitutional Law Review*, 6: 28–58.

IDEA (International Institute for Democracy and Electoral Assistance) (2008) *Direct Democracy: The International IDEA Handbook*, Stockholm, available at: www.idea.int: 90.

Illner, M. (2010) 'The Czech Republic: Local Government in the Years After the Reform', in J. Loughlin, F. Hendriks and A. Lidstrom (eds), *The Oxford*

Handbook of Local and Regional Democracy in Europe, Oxford: Oxford University Press: 505–27.

Illner, M. (2011) 'The Czech Republic: Local Government in the Years after the Reform', in J. Loughlin, F. Hendriks and A. Lidstrom (eds), *The Oxford Handbook of Local and Regional Democracy in Europe*, Oxford: Oxford University Press: 505–27.

Ioncica, D. (ed.), (1998) *Geneza Constituției României: Lucrările Adunării Constituante*, Bucharest: Monitorul Oficial.

Isaac J. (2004) 'Rethinking the Legacy of Central European Dissidence', *Common Knowledge*, 10(1): 119–29.

Isaac, J. (1996) 'The Meaning of 1989', *Social Research*, 63(2): 291–344.

Jakab, A, (2012) 'On the Legitimacy of a New Constitution – Remarks on the Occasion of the New Hungarian Basic Law of 2011', available at: http://papers.ssrn.com/sol3/papers.cfm?abstract_id=2033624.

Jensen J. (2012) 'Hungary: the Vanguard of Europe's Rearguard?', *Open Democracy*, 10 October, available at: www.opendemocracy.net.

Jirous, I. (1988), *Social Research*, 55(1/2): 226–9.

Kis, J. (1989a) *Politics in Hungary: For a Democratic Alternative*, Boulder, CO: Social Science Monographs.

Kis, J. (1989b) 'Turning point in Hungary', Dissent, 235–41.

Kis, J. (1999) 'Das Erbe der Demokratischen Opposition', *Transit*, 18: 17–39.

Kis, J. (2008) *Politics as a Moral Problem*, Budapest: CEU Press.

Kis, J. (2011) 'Janos Kis on constitutional change and the current crisis in Hungary', speech at Central European University, 5 April, available at: www.ceu.hu/video/2011-04-05/ceus-janos-kis-on-constitutional-change-and-the-current-crisis-in-hungary.

Klich, A. (1996) 'Human Rights in Poland: The Role of the Constitutional Tribunal and the Commissioner for Citizens' Rights', *St. Louis–Warsaw Transatlantic Law Journal*, 1996: 33–64.

Kochenov, D. (2008) *EU Enlargement and the Failure of Conditionality*, Alphen aan de Rijn: Kluwer.

Konrad, G. (1984) *Antipolitics*, London: Quartet Books.

Kopecky, P. (2001) 'The Czech Republic: From the Burden of the Old Federal Constitution to the Constitutional Horse Trading among Political Parties', in J. Zielonka (ed.), *Democratic Consolidation in Eastern Europe. Vol. 1: Institutional Engineering*, Oxford: Oxford University Press: 319–46.

Kovács, K. and G.A. Tóth (2011) 'Hungary's Constitutional Transformation', *European Constitutional Law Review*, 7: 183–203.

Kramer, L. (2004) *The People Themselves: Popular Constitutionalism and Judicial Review*, Oxford: Oxford University Press.

Krisch, N. (2010) *Beyond Constitutionalism: the Pluralist Structure of Post-national Law*, Oxford: Oxford University Press.

Kurczewski, J. (1993) *The Resurrection of Rights in Poland*, Oxford: Clarendon Press.

Kurczewski, J. (2003) 'Parliament and the Political Class in the Constitutional Reconstruction of Poland', *International Sociology*, 18(1): 162–80.

Kurczewksi, J. and B. Sullivan (2002) 'The Bill of Rights and the Emerging Democracies', *Law and Contemporary Problems* 65(2): 252–94.

Kuron, J. (1981) 'Not to Lure the Wolves Out of the Woods: An Interview with Jacek Kuron', *Telos*, 47: 93–7.

Lastic, E. (2006) 'Get the Balance Right: Institutional Change in Slovakia during EU Accession and Membership', *Sociológia*, 38(6): 533–45.

Lastic, E. (2011) 'Slovakia – Restricted Direct Democracy in Local Politics', in T. Schiller (ed.), *Local Direct Democracy in Europe*, Wiesbaden: VS Verlag fuer Sozialwissenschaften: 237–44.

Lastic, E. (2012) 'If It Works, Fine, If Not, So What? Initiatives in Slovakia', in M. Setala and T. Schiller (eds), *Citizens' Initiatives in Europe: Procedures and Consequences of Agenda-Setting by Citizens*, Basingstoke: Palgrave Macmillan: 152–74.

Lehet Más a Politika (LMP) (2008) 'LMP: A New Political Force in Hungary', available at: http://english.lehetmas.hu/news/2/lmp-a-new-political-force-in-hungary/.

Lehet Más a Politika (LMP) (2011) 'Background: Green Worries about the Upcoming Hungarian Constitution Change', available at: http://europeangreens.eu/euroarchive/fileadmin/logos/pictures_news_and_events/Background-_Green_worries_about_the_upcoming_Hungarian_constitution_change.pdf.

Levinson, S. (1995) 'Introduction: Imperfection and Amendability', in S. Levinson (ed.), *Responding to Imperfection: The Theory and Practice of Constitutional Amendment*, Princeton, NJ: Princeton University Press: 3–12.

Lijphart, A. (1991) 'Constitutional Choices for New Democracies', *Journal of Democracy*, 2(1): 72–84.

Lindahl, H. (2011) 'Societal Constitutionalism as Political Constitutionalism: Reconsidering the Relation between Politics and Global Legal Orders', *Social and Legal Studies*, 20(2): 230–7.

Loughlin, J., F. Hendriks and A. Lidstrom (2011) *The Oxford Handbook of Local and Regional Democracy in Europe*, Oxford: Oxford University Press.

Loughlin, M. (1996) *Legality and Locality: The Role of Law in Central–Local Government Relations*, Oxford: Oxford University Press.

Loughlin, M. (2003) 'The Ten Tenets of Sovereignty', in N. Walker (ed.), *Sovereignty in Transition*, Oxford and Portland, OR: Hart: 55–86.

Loughlin, M. and N. Walker (2007) 'Introduction', in M. Loughlin and N. Walker (eds), *The Paradox of Constitutionalism: Constituent Power and Constitutional Form*, Oxford: Oxford University Press: 1–8.

Ludwikowski, R. (2000) 'Constitution Making in the Countries of Former Soviet Dominance: Current Development', *Georgia. Journal of International & Comparative Law*, 23: 155–267.

Lungu, I. (2002) 'Romanian Constitutional Nationalism', *Polish Sociological Review*, 4(140): 397–412.

Lutz, D.S. (1995) 'Toward a Theory of Constitutional Amendment', in S. Levinson (ed.), *Responding to Imperfection: The Theory and Practice of Constitutional Amendment*, Princeton, NJ: Princeton University Press: 237–74.

Macovei, M. (2012) 'The Romanian Coup d'Etat', in *European Voice*, 12 July.

Magen, A. and L. Morlino (eds) (2009) *International Actors, Democratization and the Rule of Law: Anchoring Democracy?* London/New York: Routledge.

Malová, D. (2001) 'Slovakia: From the Ambiguous Constitution to the Dominance of Informal Rules', in J. Zielonka (ed.) *Democratic Consolidation in Eastern Europe. Vol. 1: Institutional Engineering*, Oxford: Oxford University Press: 347–76.

Malová, D. and B. Dolny (2008) 'The Eastern Enlargement of the European Union: Challenges to Democracy?', *Human Affairs* 18(2): 67–80.

Malová, D. and E. Láštic (2001) 'The Gradual Amending of the Slovak Constitution: Combating the Ambiguous Rules in 1992–2001', *Central European Political Science Review*, 2(4): 103–28.

Mandel, M. (1997) 'A Brief History of the New Constitutionalism, or "How We Changed Everything so that Everything Would Remain the Same"', *Israel Law Review*, 32: 250–300.

Markovits, I. (2007) 'The Death of Socialist Law?', *Annual Review of Law and Social Science*, 3: 233–53.

Maxfield, E. (2012) 'Resistance to Change: Romania's Debate over Territorial Reforms', *Sfera Politicii*, 167(1): 12–20.

Michnik, A. (1985a) 'A New Evolutionism', in *Letters from Prison and Other Essays*, Berkeley, CA: University of California Press: 135–48.

Michnik, A. (1985b) *Letters from Prison*, Berkeley, CA: University of California Press.

Mill, J.S. (2004) *Considerations on Representative Government*, available at: www.gutenberg.org/files/5669/5669-h/5669-h.htm.

Molnar, G. (2000) 'Regionalism Civic', *Provincia*, I/2, 7. Available at: www.provincia.ro/pdf_roman/r000028.pdf.

Morlino, L. and W. Sadurski (2010) *Democratization and the European Union: Comparing central and Eastern European Post-communist Countries*, London/New York: Routledge.

Müller, J.W. (2011) 'The Hungarian Tragedy', *Dissent*, Spring: 5–10.

Mungiu-Pippidi, A. (1997) 'Interview with President of the Romanian Constitutional Court, Ion Muraru', *East European Constitutional Review*, Winter: 78–83.

Myant, M. (2003) 'Civil Society and Political Parties in the Czech Republic', in S. Smith (ed.), *Local Communities and Post-Communist Transformation. Czechoslovakia, the Czech Republic and Slovakia*, London: Routledge: 19–40.

Nedelsky, N. (2009) *Defining the Sovereign Community: The Czech and Slovak Republics*, Philadelphia, PA: University of Pennsylvania Press.

Olvera, A.J. (2013) 'The Concept of Civil Society and the Latin American Debate on Democratic Innovation', in E. Peruzzotti and Martín Plot (eds), *Critical Theory and Democracy: Civil Society, Dictatorship, and Constitutionalism in Andrew Arato's Democratic Theory*, London/New York: Routledge: 123–39.

Ost, D. (1990) *Solidarity and the Politics of Anti-Politics*, Philadelphia, PA: Temple University Press.

Ost, D. (2011) 'The Decline of Civil Society after "Post-Communism"', in U. Liebert and H.-J. Trenz (eds), *The New Politics of European Civil Society*, London/New York: Routledge: 163–77.

Paczolay, P. (1993) 'Constitutional Transition and Legal Continuity', *Connecticut Journal of International Law*, 8: 559–74.

Palermo, F. (2007) 'La "manutenzione costituzionale": alla ricerca di una funzione', in F. Palermo (ed.), *La Manutenzione Costituzionale*, Padova: CEDAM: 1–18.

Pallinger, Z.T. (2012) 'Citizens' Initiatives in Hungary: an Additional Opportunity for Power-Sharing in an Extremely Majoritarian System', in M. Setala and T. Schiller (eds), *Citizens' Initiatives in Europe: Procedures and Consequences of Agenda-Setting by Citizens*, Basingstoke: Palgrave Macmillan: 113–33.

Parau, C. (2012) 'The Drive for Judicial Supremacy in Central and Eastern Europe', in A. Seibert-Fohr (ed.), *Judicial Independence in Transition*, Heidelberg: Springer: 619–67.

Parau, C. (forthcoming, 2013a) 'Explaining Judiciary Governance in Central and Eastern Europe: External Incentives, Transnational Elites and Parliament Inaction', *Europe–Asia Studies*.

Parau, C. (forthcoming, 2013b) 'The Dormancy of Parliaments: The Invisible Cause of Judiciary Empowerment in Central and Eastern Europe', *Representation – The Journal of Representative Democracy*, Special Issue on 'Courts and Democracy' edited by Richard Bellamy and Cristina Parau.

Parau, C. (forthcoming, 2013c) 'Romania's Transnational Constitution: A Tradition of Elite Learning and Self-empowerment', in D. Galligan and M. Versteeg (eds), *The Social and Political Foundations of Constitutions*, Cambridge: Cambridge University Press.

Patocka, J. (1981) 'What Charter 77 Is and What It Is Not', in H.G. Skilling (ed.), *Charter 77 and Human Rights in Czechoslovakia*, London: George Allen & Unwin: 217–19.

Patyi, A. (2011) 'The Courts and the Judiciary', in L. Csink, B. Schanda and A.Z. Varga (eds), *The Basic Law of Hungary: A First Commentary*, Dublin: Clarus Press: 171–89.

Patyi, A. (2012) 'Local Government', in L. Csink, B. Schanda and A. Zs. Varga (eds), *The Basic Law of Hungary: A First Commentary*, Dublin: Clarus Press: 217–30.

Perju, V. (2010) 'A sosit timpul pentru reformarea Curtii Constitutionale? (Partea I)', available at: www.contributors.ro/idei-si-solutii/a-sosit-timpul-pentru-reformarea-curtii-constitutionale-partea-i/.

Peters, A. (2006) 'Compensatory Constitutionalism: The Function and Potential of Fundamental International Norms and Structures', *Leiden Journal of International Law*, 19: 579–610.

Petreşcu, C. and D. Petreşcu (2005) 'Resistance and Dissent under Communism – The Case of Romania', *Totalitarismus und Demokratie*, 2: 323–46.

Piasecki, A.K. (2011) 'Twenty Years of Polish Direct Democracy at the Local Level' in T. Schiller (ed.), *Local Direct Democracy in Europe*, Wiesbaden: VS Verlag: 126–37.

Pontuso, J.F. (2002) 'Transformation Politics: the Debate between Václav Havel and Václav Klaus on the Free Market and Civil Society', *Studies in East European Thought*, 54: 153–77.

Popławska, E. (1999) 'The Principle of Representative Government and Forms of Direct Democracy and Their Application in Polish Constitutional Law', in M. Wyrzykowski (ed.), *Constitutional Essays*, Warsaw: Institute of Public Affairs: 155–89.

Popławska, E. (2002) 'The New Constitutional Principle of Subsidiarity and "the Diminishing State" in Poland', *Journal of Constitutional law in Eastern and Central Europe*, 9(1): 51–95.

Post, R. and R. Siegel (2007) 'Roe Rage: Democratic Constitutionalism and Backlash', *Harvard Civil Rights–Civil Liberties Law Review*, 42: 373–434.

Post, R. and R. Siegel (2009) 'Democratic Constitutionalism', in J. Balkin and R. Siegel (eds), *The Constitution in 2020*, Oxford: Oxford University Press: 25–36.

Preda, C. (2002) 'La Nation dans la Constitution', in *Nation and National Ideology: Past, Present, and Prospects*, Bucharest: New Europe College: 390–445.

Preuss, U. (1995) 'Patterns of Constitutional Evolution and Change in Eastern Europe', in J.J. Hesse and N. Johnson (eds), *Constitutional Policy and Change in Europe*, Oxford: Oxford University Press: 95–128.

Preuss, U. (2010) 'Disconnecting Constitutions from Statehood: Is Global Constitutionalism a Viable Concept?', in P. Dobner and M. Loughlin (eds), *The Twilight of Constitutionalism?* Oxford University Press: 23–48.

Přibáň, J. (2002) *Dissidents of Law: on the 1989 Velvet Revolutions, Legitimations, Fictions of Legality, and Contemporary Version of the Social Contract*, Aldershot and Burlington, VT: Ashgate/Dartmouth.

Přibáň, J. (2005) 'Political Dissent, Human Rights, and Legal Transformations: Communist and Post-Communist Experiences', in *East European Politics and Societies*, 19(4): 553–72.

Přibáň, J. (2007) *Legal Symbolism: On Law, Time and European Identity*, Aldershot and Burlington, VT: Ashgate.

Přibáň, J. (2009) 'From "Which Rule of Law?" to "The Rule of Which Law?": Post-Communist Experiences of European Legal Integration', *Hague Journal on the Rule of Law*, 1(2): 337–58.

Přibáň, J. (2010) 'Legal Cultures in Transition: A Systems-Theory Approach', in A. Febbrajo and W. Sadurski (eds), *Central and Eastern Europe After Transition: Towards a New Socio-Legal Semantics*, Aldershot: Ashgate: 13–34.

Přibáň , J. (2012) 'Constitutionalism as Fear of the Political? A Comparative Analysis of Teubner's Constitutional Fragments and Thornhill's A Sociology of Constitutions', *Journal of Law and Society*, 39(3): 441–71.

Přibáň, J. and W. Sadurski (2006) 'The Role of Political Rights in the Democratization of Central and Eastern Europe', in W. Sadurski (ed.), *Political Rights under Stress in 21st Century Europe*, Oxford: Oxford University Press: 196–238.

Procházka, R. (2002) *Mission Accomplished: On Founding Constitutional Adjudication in Central Europe*, Budapest and New York: CEU Press.

Puchalska, B. (2011) *Limits to Democratic Constitutionalism in Central and Eastern Europe*, Aldershot: Ashgate.

Rawls, J. (1993) *Political Liberalism*, New York: Columbia University Press.

Regulska, J. (2009) 'Governance or Self-governance in Poland? Benefits and Threats 20 Years Later', *International Journal of Politics, Culture & Society*, 22(4): 537–56.

Renwick, A. (2006) 'Anti-Political or Just Anti-Communist? Varieties of Dissidence in East–Central Europe and Their Implications for the Development of Political Society', *East European Politics and Societies*, 20(2): 286–318.

Roberts, A. (2009) 'The Politics of Constitutional Amendment in Post-communist Europe', *Constitutional Political Econonomy*, 20: 99–117.

Roharik, P. (2003) 'The Judiciary and its Transition in Slovakia after 1989', in J. Přibáň, P. Roberts and J. Young (eds), *Systems of Justice in Transition: Central European Experiences Since 1989*, Aldershot: Ashgate: 213–29.

Romanian Commission for Revision of the Constitutiton (Comisia pentru elaborarea propunerii legislative privind revizuirea Constituţiei) (2003a) 'Expunere de motive', Bucharest: Romanian Parliament.

Romanian Commission for the Revision of the Constitution (Comisia pentru elaborarea propunerii legislative privind revizuirea Constituţiei) (2003b) *Raporta supra amendamentelor la Propunerea legislativă privind revizuirea Constituţiei*, Bucharest: Romanian Parliament.

Romanian Parliament (2003) 'Dezbateri generale asupra Propunerii legislative de revizuire a Constituţiei. Şedinţa Camerei Deputaţilor din 18 iunie 2003,' available at: www.cdep.ro/pls/steno/steno.stenograma?ids=5493&idm=2&idl=1.

Romsics, I. (2007) *From Dictatorship to Democracy: The Birth of the Third Hungarian Republic, 1988–2001*, Boulder, CO: Social Science Monographs: 367–71.

Rosanvallon, P. (2011) *Democratic Legitimacy. Impartiality, Reflexivity, Proximity*, Princeton, NJ: Princeton University Press (Kindle edition).

Rose-Ackerman S. (2005) *Building a Trustworthy State in Post-socialist Transition*, Palgrave Macmillan.

Rosenfeld, M. (1993) 'Modern Constitutionalism as Interplay Between Identity and Diversity', *Cardozo Law Review*, 14: 497–531.

Rytel-Warzocha, A. (2012) Popular Initiatives in Poland: Citizens' Empowerment or Keeping Up Appearances?', in M. Setala and T. Schiller (eds), *Citizens' Initiatives in Europe: Procedures and Consequences of Agenda-Setting by Citizens*, Palgrave Macmillan: 212–27.

Sadurski, W. (2008) *Rights Before Courts: A Study of Constitutional Courts in Postcommunist States of Central and Eastern Europe*, Dordrecht: Springer.

Sadurski, W. (2002) 'Constitutional Courts in the Process of Articulating Constitutional Rights in the Post-Communist States of Central and Eastern Europe: Part I: Social and Economic Rights', Working Paper LAW 02/14, Florence: European University Institute.

Sadurski, W. (2004) 'Accession's Democracy Dividend: the Impact of the EU Enlargement upon Democracy on the New Member States of Central and Eastern Europe', in *European Law Journal*, 10(4): 371–401.

Sadurski, W. (2005) 'Transitional Constitutionalism: Simplistic and Fancy Theories', in A. Czarnota, M. Krygier and W. Sadurski (eds), *Rethinking the Rule of Law after Communism*, London and New York: CEU Press: 9–24.

Sadurski, W. (2010) 'Constitutional Courts and Constitutional Culture in Central and Eastern European Countries', in A. Febbrajo and W. Sadurski (eds), *Central and Eastern Europe after Transition. Towards a New Socio-Legal Semantics*, Aldershot: Ashgate: 99–118.

Sadurski, W. (2012) *Constitutionalism and the Enlargement of Europe*, Oxford: Oxford University Press.

Sajó, A. (1995) 'Reading the Invisible Constitution: Judicial Review in Hungary', *Oxford Journal of Legal Studies*, 5(2): 253–67.

Sajó, A. (1996) 'How the Rule of Law Killed Hungarian Welfare Reform', *East European Constitutional Review*, 5: 31–41.

Sajó, A. (2004) 'The Impacts of EU Accession on Post-communist Constitutionalism', *Acta Juiridica Hungarica*, 45(3/4): 193–212.

Sajó, A. (2006) 'The Republic of Hungary', in C.A.J.M. Kortmann, J.W.A. Fleuren, W. Voermans and M. Kindlová (eds), *Constitutional Law of 10 EU Member States: the 2004 Enlargement*, Alphen aan de Rijn: Kluwer: IV: 3–55, IV: 15.

Scheppele, K.L. (1999) 'The New Hungarian Constitutional Court', in *E. Eur. Const. Rev.*, 8(4).

Scheppele, K.L. (2004) 'Counter-constitutions: Narrating the Nation in Post-Soviet Hungary', paper given at George Washington University, Washington, DC, 2 April.

Scheppele, K.L. (2005) 'Democracy by Judiciary. Or, Why Courts Can Be More Democratic than Parliaments', in A. Czarnota, M. Krygier, and W. Sadurski (eds), *Rethinking the Rule of Law after Communism*, London and New York: CEU Press: 25–60.

Scheppele, K.L. (2012) 'Romania Unravels the Rule of Law', in *New York Times*, blog Paul Krugman, 5 July, available at: http://krugman.blogs.nytimes.com/2012/07/05/guest-post-romania-unravels-the-rule-of-law/.

Schiller, T. (2011) 'Local Direct Democracy in Europe – a Comparative Overview', in T. Schiller (ed.), *Local Direct Democracy in Europe*, Wiesbaden: VS Verlag: 9–32.

Schmid, K. and V. Horsky (1995) *Das Ende der Tschechoslowakei 1992 in verfassungsrechtlicher Sicht. Einführung zu den Verfassungstexten von Zdeněk Jičínský und Vladimír Mikule*, Berlin: Verlag.

Schwartz, H. (2000) *The Struggle for Constitutional Justice in Post-Communist Europe*, Chicago: University of Chicago Press.

Skapska, G. (2011) *From 'Civil Society' to 'Europe': A Sociological Study on Constitutionalism after Communism*, Leiden: Brill.

Skinner, Q. (1990) 'The Republican Ideal of Political Liberty', in G. Bock, Q. Skinner and M. Viroli (eds), *Machiavelli and Republicanism*, Cambridge and New York: Cambridge University Press: 294–309.

Skinner, Q. and M. Van Gelderen (2002) *Republicanism and Constitutionalism in Early Modern Europe*, Cambridge: Cambridge University Press.

Slosarcik, I. (2001) 'The Reform of the Constitutional Systems of Czechoslovakia and the Czech Republic in 1990–2000', *European Public Law*, 7(4): 529–47.

Smismans, S. (2007) 'New Governance – The Solution for Active European Citizenship, or the End of Citizenship?', *Columbia Journal of European Law*, 13: 595–622.

Smith, M. (2011) 'The Uneasy Balance between Participation and Representation: Local Direct Democracy in the Czech Republic', in T. Schiller (ed.), *Local Direct Democracy in Europe*, Wiesbaden: VS Verlag: 33–53.

Smith, S. (2003) 'Transformation as Modernisation: Sociological Readings of Post-communist Lifeworlds', in S. Smith (ed.), *Local Communities and Post-Communist Transformation. Czechoslovakia, the Czech Republic and Slovakia*, London: Routledge: 1–18.

Solidarity (1981) 'The Self-governing Republic', available at: www.bolshevik.org/Pamphlets/Solidarnosc/solidarnosc_appendix.html.

Solyom, I. (1994) 'The Hungarian Constitutional Court and Social Change', *Yale Journal of International Law*, 19: 223–37.

Solyom, L. (2003) 'The Role of Constitutional Courts in the Transition to Democracy: with Special Reference to Hungary', *International Sociology*, 18: 133–61.

Soós, G. and L. Kakai (2010) 'Hungary: Remarkable Successes and Costly Failures: An Evaluation of Subnational Democracy', in J. Loughlin, F. Hendriks and A. Lidstrom (eds), *The Oxford Handbook of Local and Regional Democracy in Europe*, Oxford: Oxford University Press: 528–51.

Soós, G. (2010) 'Hungary', in M.J. Goldsmith and E.C. Page (eds), *Changing Government Relations in Europe: From Localism to Intergovernmentalism*, London: Routledge: 108–26.

Spendzharova, A. and M. Vachudova (2012) 'Catching Up? Consolidating Liberal Democracy in Bulgaria and Romania after EU Accession', *West European Politics*, 35(1): 39–58.

Stănescu, M. (2004) 'Despre dizidenţă în România comunistă (1977–1989)', *Sfera Politicii*, 106: 39–47.

Stanomir, I. (2012) 'Constituţia României a devenit un element insignifiant', EVZ.ro, 11 July, available at: www.evz.ro/detalii/stiri/ioan-stanomir-constitutia-romaniei-a-devenit-un-element-insignifiant-991426.html.

Stone Sweet, A. (2008) 'Constitutions and Judicial Power', D. Caramani (ed.) *Comparative Politics*, Oxford: Oxford University Press: 217–39.

Stone Sweet, A. (2009) 'Constitutionalism, Legal Pluralism and International Regimes', *Indiana Journal of Global Legal Studies*, 16(2): 621–45.

Swianiewicz, P. (2001) 'Sympathetic Disengagement: Public Perception of Local Governments in Poland', in P. Swianiewicz (ed.), *Public Perception of Local*

Governments, Budapest: Local Government and Public Reform Initiative: 208–211.

Swianiewicz, P. (2011) 'Poland: Europeanization of Subnational Governments', in J. Loughlin, F. Hendriks and A. Lidstrom (eds), *The Oxford Handbook of Local and Regional Democracy in Europe*, Oxford: Oxford University Press: 480–504.

Szmyt, A. (1999) 'Representation – Elections – Democracy', in P. Szarnecki, A. Szmyt and Z. Witkowski (eds), *The Principles of Basic Institutions of the System of Government in Poland*, Warsaw: Sejm Publishing Office: 119–34.

Szombati, K. (2011) 'The Betrayed Republic. Hungary's New Constitution and the "System of National Cooperation"', Prague: Heinrich Böll Stiftung, available at: www.cz.boell.org/web/52-972.html.

Sztompka, P. (2004) 'From East Europeans to Europeans: Shifting Collective Identities and Symbolic Boundaries in the New Europe', *European Review*, 12: 481–96.

Tănăsoiu C. (2008) 'Intellectuals and Post-Communist Politics in Romania: an Analysis of Public Discourse, 1990–2000', *East European Politics and Societies*, 2(1): 80–113.

Tănăsoiu, C. (2011) 'Revisiting Dissent Under Communism: the Unbearable Lightness of Solitude', *History of Communism in Europe*, 2: 323–44.

Teubner, G. (1997) 'Global Bukowina: Legal Pluralism in the World Society', in G. Teubner (ed.), *Global Law Without a State*, Aldershot and Brookfield, VT: Dartmouth: 3–28.

Teubner, G. (2012) *Constitutional Fragments. Societal Constitutionalism and Globalization*, Oxford: Oxford University Press.

Thornhill, C. (2011) *A Sociology of Constitutions*, Cambridge: Cambridge University Press.

Thornhill, C. (forthcoming) 'A Sociology of Constituent Power: The Political Code of Transnational Societal Constitutions', draft, on file with the author.

Tierney, S. (2004) *Constitutional Law and National Pluralism*, Oxford: Oxford University Press.

Tierney, S. (2012) *Constitutional Referendums: The Theory and Practice of Republican Deliberation*, Oxford: Oxford University Press.

Tischner, J. (2009) 'The Ethics of Solidarity', *The Tischner Institute Journal of Philosophy*, 1(2007): 37–51, available at: www.tischner.org.pl/thinking_pliki/tischner_3_ethics.pdf.

Tismăneanu, V. (2009) 'The Revolutions of 1989: Causes, Meanings, Consequences', in *Contemporary European History*, 18(3): 271–88.

Tomoszek, M. (2010) 'Proportionality in the Judicial Review of Constitutional Amendments', paper presented at the VIIIth World Congress 'Constitutions and Principles', International Association of Constitutional Law, Mexico City, December.

Tucker, A. (1999) 'The Politics of Conviction: The Rise and Fall of Czech Intellectual-Politicians', in A. Bozoki (ed.), *Intellectuals and Politics in Central Europe*, CEU Press: 185–206.

Tucker, A. *et al.* (2000) 'From Republican Virtue to Technology of Political Power: Three Episodes of Czech Nonpolitical Politics', *Political Science Quarterly*, 115(3): 421–55.

Tully, J. (1995) *Strange Multiplicity: Constitutionalism in an Age of Diversity*, Cambridge and New York: Cambridge University Press.

Tully, J. (2007) 'A New Kind of Europe? Democratic Integration in the European Union', *Critical Review of International Social and Political Philosophy*, 10(1): 71–86.

Tully, J. (2008a) *Public Philosophy in a New Key*, Cambridge: Cambridge University Press.

Tully, J. (2008b) 'Modern Constitutional Democracy and Imperialism', *Osgoode Hall Law Journal*, 46: 461–93.

Tully, J. (2012) 'Middle East Legal and Governmental Pluralism: A View of the Field from the Demos', *Middle East Law and Governance*, 4: 1–39.

Tushnet, M. (1995) 'Policy Distortion and Democratic Debilitation: Comparative Illumination of the Countermajoritarian Difficulty', *Michigan Law Review*, 94(2): 245–301.

Tushnet, M. (1999) *Taking the Constitution Away from the Courts*, Princeton, NJ: Princeton University Press.

Ucen, P. (2002) 'Slovakia', *European Journal of Political Research*, 41: 1075–83.

Uhl, P. (1985) 'The Alternative Community as Revolutionary Avant-Garde', in V. Havel *et al. The Power of the Powerless*, edited by J. Keane, London: Hutchinson: 188–97.

Valea, D. (2010) 'The Constitutional Court – An Innovation in the Romanian Constitutional System', *Curentul Juridic*, 40: 54–62.

Valea, D. (2011) 'The Control of Constitutionality of the Initiatives for Revision of the Romanian Constitution', *Curentul Juridic, The Juridical Current*, 47: 91–102.

Waldron, J. (1999) *Law and Disagreement*, Oxford: Clarendon Press; New York: Oxford University Press.

Waldron, J. (2006) 'The Core of the Case Against Judicial Review', *Yale Law Journal*, 115: 1346–406.

Walker, N. (2002) 'The Idea of Constitutional Pluralism', *Modern Law Review*, 65(3): 317–59.

Walker, N. (2009) 'Beyond the Holistic Constitution', University of Edinburgh School of Law, Working Paper No. 2009/16.

Weber, R. (2001) 'Constitutionalism as a Vehicle for Democratic Consolidation in Romania', in R. Elgie and J. Zielonka (ed.), *Democratic Consolidation in Eastern Europe Volume 2: Constitutions and Constitution-Building: A Comparative Perspective*, Oxford: Oxford University Press: 212–43.

Weber, R. (2002) 'The Romanian Constitutional Court: In Search of its Own Identity', in W. Sadurski (ed.), *Constitutional Justice, East and West: Democratic Legitimacy and Constitutional Courts in Post-Communist Europe in A Comparative Perspective*, The Hague, Kluwer International: 283–308.

Weiler, J.H.H. (2003) *Un'Europa cristiana: Un saggio esplorativo*, Milano: BUR Saggi.

Wesolowski, W. and A. Gawkowska (2001) 'Solidarity in Theory and Practice', in H. Tam (ed.), *Progressive Politics in the Global Age*, Oxford: Blackwell.

Wiener, A. (2008) *The Invisible Constitution of Politics: Contested Norms and International Encounters*, Cambridge: Cambridge University Press.

Williams, K. (2011) 'When a Constitutional Amendment Violates the "Substantive Core": The Czech Constitutional Court's September 2009 Early Elections Decision', *Review of Central and East European Law*, 36: 33–51.

Wolin, S. (2008) *Democracy Incorporated: Managed Democracy and the Specter of Inverted Totalitarianism*, Princeton, NJ: Princeton University Press.

Wydra, H. (2007) *Communism and the Emergence of Democracy*, Cambridge and New York: Cambridge University Press.

Wyrozumska, A. (2007) 'The Charter of Fundamental Rights of the European Union in the Reform Treaty and the Polish Objections', *Polish Quarterly of International Affairs*, 4: 11–40.

Wyrzykowski, M. (1999) 'The Limits of Rights and Freedoms – The Limits of Power', in M. Wyrzykowski (ed.), *Constitutional Essays*, Warsaw: Institute of Public Affairs, 257–72.

Wyrzykowski, M. (2000) *Constitutional Essays*, Warsaw: Institute of Public Affairs.

Zielonka, J. (1989) *Political Ideas in Contemporary Poland*, Aldershot and Brookfield, VT: Avebury.

Żółkoś, M. (2004) 'Human Rights and Polish Dissident Traditions: the Civic Republican Perspective', Studies in Social and Political Thought, 10, University of Sussex, available at: www.sussex.ac.uk/Units/SPT/journal/archive/issue_10.html: 57–78.

Index